FORTUNE'S WARRIORS

JAMES R. DAVIS

FORTUNE'S WARRIORS

PRIVATE ARMIES AND THE NEW WORLD ORDER

Douglas & McIntyre

VANCOUVER · TORONTO

Douglas & McIntyre
2323 Quebec Street, Suite 201
Vancouver, British Columbia
Canada v5t 4s7

National Library of Canada Cataloguing in
Publication Data
Davis, James R., 1962–
     Fortune's Warriors
     Includes index

     ISBN 1-55054-744-5 (cloth)
     ISBN 1-55054-888-3 (pbk)

     1. Mercenary Troops. I. Title
UB321.D38 2000   355.3′54   C00-910866-1

Editing by Brian Scrivener
Typeset at Cardigan Industries
Cover design by Peter Cocking
Cover photograph: AP photo / Canapress
Printed and bound in Canada by Friesens
Printed on acid-free paper ∞

We gratefully acknowledge the financial
support of the Canada Council for the Arts,
the British Columbia Ministry of Tourism,
Small Business and Culture, and the
Government of Canada through the Book
Publishing Industry Development Program
(BPIDP) for our publishing activities.

This book is dedicated to the men of the former
free company Executive Outcomes, who went where no one
else would go, to do a job no one else would do, to end (for a time)
two senseless African wars, and who did it with élan. *"May their souls
never lie with those cold and timid souls who will never know
either the joys of victory or the agonies of defeat."*

Contents

Acknowledgements

IN COMPLETING THIS MANUSCRIPT, I have to express my thanks to some of the many people who helped me put it together. The first thank you must go to Scott McIntyre for encouraging me to write again. I had thought that my first book would be my last. Of course, the rest of Scott's team equally deserve credit: thanks to Barbara for starting and Brian for finishing, Terri for organizing, Kelly for promoting, and Dorothy for remembering. I also have to thank some close friends for their support throughout the thick and very thin, including Warren, Ken, Harris, Mike, and Jeff (wherever you are pal!). Finally, I wish to express my complete admiration for Team Davis because without them, none of this would be possible.

–JIM DAVIS

Prologue

THE BOOK YOU ARE ABOUT TO READ is definitely one of political, philosophical, and moral concern. It is an examination, from a first-hand perspective, of one of the most controversial issues in the world today: the privatization of international security.

We are at the moment witnessing the beginning of a transformation in global politics as they pertain to conflict resolution. It is a shift from the traditional national army and its role in "politics by other means" to a much more sophisticated and complex system relying on transnational corporations, private incorporated armies, military consultants "for hire," and the subcontracting of national security.

At the most glamorous, we are talking about mercenaries and soldiers of fortune. But these are just the more colorful permutations. Behind them lies a whole spectrum of modern variants that exist in the shadows of international relations. Some of these offer services sold freelance. Others are the routine tools of both First and Third World nations.

Is it shocking to know that in the past twenty-five years the United States, Britain, France, Russia, and Canada have each employed mercenaries to achieve their foreign policy goals? Is it of exceptional note that the United Nations is a regular employer of these shadowy figures? Can the fact that the longest running mercenary contract in history is being paid for by the Roman Catholic Church be considered controversial?

I believe the answer to the above questions is yes.

The following book is an investigation of these issues. It is probably a story that many great powers in the world would rather be left unwritten. However, left in the shadows and unregulated, these forces pose a distinct threat to global stability and the international rule of law.

Before proceeding, the reader should realize that I am a member of this community. I am a former soldier who, upon leaving his national army, became involved in the world of private armies and international private security. Much of my research is first hand. As a participant I have access to many sources that would otherwise be unavailable to the scholars and bureaucrats who occasionally offer comments on this topic.

Throughout my travels and research, I have sat down with my peers in the industry and discussed the issue of the privatization of security. From mercenary to foreign aid volunteer, I have found among them a great desire to bring this shadowy world out into the daylight and address the issues of regulation, international control, and the setting of clear parameters for the industry. We all agree that the trend towards privatization and the transfer of power to non-state-controlled agencies is likely to continue. In fact, it is my belief that it is an unstoppable process.

Due to the poor reputation of the industry in general and the occasional witch hunts that pursue its members, many of my sources will have to remain anonymous. Others will be fictitious characters based on real people. This is unfortunately a reality of the modern security industry. Hang the word mercenary on an individual, a government or a corporation and it brings with it condemnation and, occasionally, much worse.

You will find that the book is centered on a cast of characters and several nations. In particular, Sierra Leone and Angola are the two countries where the issue of the privatization of international security has clearly been played out over the last decade. Both are virtual case studies in the failure of traditional security institutions and the emergence of private sector resources that have filled the void.

The subject matter is controversial and thought provoking. Please remember that my argumentation is partisan in nature. As an author involved in the business he hopes to discuss, my opinions are colored by my personal experience and convictions. However, mine is also an insider's view of an industry that rarely emerges from the shadows – one that for the good of the world at large and the other members of this profession needs to be examined openly, honestly, and without the moral protestations often attached to the subject matter.

Therefore, accept my welcome into the world of the corporate soldier.

I

INTO THE SHADOWS

IT WAS EARLY IN MARCH 1997, and I was walking through an impressive shopping mall located in downtown Vancouver, Canada. It was midday and the mall was busy with the office crowd rushing about on lunch-hour errands. I was accompanying my client, a Mr. Rakesh Saxena, who had just wrapped up a long lunch-hour meeting at the hotel restaurant. Walking with us on this day was Bob L., one of Saxena's many lawyers. As we wove through the daytime crowds, I kept station at my client's right shoulder and let my eyes wander over the people as they passed. As Saxena's bodyguard and security advisor, that was what I was paid for.

As we descended an escalator on our way to the car park, Saxena turned to me and said, "Jim, I want to go after a mining project in Sierra Leone. We'll need a big security force, five hundred men, vehicles, helicopters … everything."

I tried to keep the surprise out of my expression and concentrate on getting the details. It was difficult, however, as my pulse rate must have doubled with these words.

"You'll want to set up a new company to handle the project," he continued, "Bob here will go over the details with you," motioning to the young and eager lawyer at his left shoulder.

I looked at Bob and he smiled somewhat grimly. Apparently this was as disconcerting to him as it was to me, but probably for many different reasons. As a corporate lawyer in Vancouver Bob had probably heard a few strange requests before, but this was obviously something new.

Setting up a shell company to handle an aggressive mining security contract in West Africa is more the stuff of novels than of real life.

Certainly I had a rather surreal feeling about Saxena's sudden request. It was just too large an issue to deal with in so short a moment. Yet, it wouldn't do to let my personal confusion impinge upon my professional calm. As my mind raced over Saxena's request, outwardly I tried to maintain a cool demeanor.

"Okay," I acknowledged. "Bob, I'll give you a call later."

At that, our little group split up, with Bob heading off to do whatever lawyers do when asked to set up shell companies for high-risk, quasi-mercenary offshore operations. If I were he, I would have been heading to the nearest bar to have a good, stiff drink. Unfortunately, I was still accompanying Saxena and I would have to put off any contemplative lubrication until later.

Around us, the people of Vancouver went on about their daily tasks – shopping, browsing, and sipping gourmet coffees – entirely unaware that a major international mercenary contract with far-reaching consequences for several nations had just begun within their midst. In the days ahead a major war would result from our conversation, governments would be toppled, and prestigious international figures would face condemnation and criticism around the globe.

As I watched these faces about me on the way to our car, I could not help but begin to feel that familiar sense of alienation from the world around me. The people I saw, each of them, had no idea who I was, what I did or what I was about to do. Nor would they understand if they did know. I had felt this way many times before. When I came home from Africa three years earlier, it was the same. So, too, after Croatia, Bosnia, and other places. That underlying feeling that, somehow, I didn't belong here. That I really wanted to get back there, back where I could do the job I do best: soldiering.

In 1996, I left the Canadian Armed Forces after over a decade of service. I had been an infanteer with the Royal Canadian Regiment stationed in Canada and Germany. My specialty was in reconnaissance and intelligence, spending my time sneaking about behind or within "enemy" lines during military exercises. Later, I joined the Canadian

Airborne Regiment and became a paratrooper with Number 3 Commando. During my career, I had seen operational service in the former Yugoslavia in 1992 and in central Africa in 1994. I had worked alongside the British SAS, U.S. Special Operations forces, the French Foreign Legion, the Gurkhas, and a host of others, including even Russian airborne troops. By the age of thirty-five, however, I had had enough of regular service and resigned from the Forces. I knew there must be more to life than Canada's army and so set out to find a new life and career in the civilian world. Unlike many of my military contemporaries, I firmly believed that service life had given me a valuable set of tools that had a commercial value in the private sector.

Although many doubted the wisdom of my decision, I firmly believed that I was making the right choice.

Three months after retiring, I received a phone call from a distinguished former member of the SAS. He was living in Canada and had set up his own security company to cater to high-end security projects for governments and corporations. Alan Bell had served for twenty-two years in the British Forces, including the Royal Marine Commandos and the 22nd Special Air Service Regiment. His resume read like a history of the armed conflicts that the United Kingdom had been involved in since the 1970s. Bell had been handling personal security for Margaret Thatcher during a trip to Canada when he realized that there was a market for top caliber security professionals in the Canadian private sector. After leaving the British Army, he created Bell & Associates, Canada's premier security consulting firm.

Initially, I never met Bell face to face. I was told that he maintained contacts in the Canadian Forces and had heard that I might be available for work. Given my number by someone I probably knew but have never discovered who it was, he made me an offer that intrigued me. After some initial pleasantries, Bell got down to business.

"Jim, how would you feel about a close protection project?"

After thinking about it for a moment, I replied, "Well, I did some VIP security in the Forces in Yugo and Africa, so I think I could handle it. Where is the job?"

"Vancouver," replied Bell. "It will be a two-month contract and the pay is $5,500 a month plus all expenses." Actually, it would work out to nearly $7,000 a month with the per diem worked in. It didn't take me long to do the math. We were talking about roughly one-third of my annual military salary for just two months' work.

"You will be working with another consultant," Bell continued. "It's a woman, if that makes any difference. She'll be in charge."

"I don't have problem with that," I replied. "What are the details?"

"Well, we'll get back to you on the details. I can tell you that the job will start at the end of January. I will give you a call in a couple of days with specifics."

With the end of the phone call, my pulse was definitely racing. A small shiver went through me. There I was, a soldier with no clear idea where he was going, and out of the blue an offer lands in my lap. A lucrative offer at that. The gods were definitely smiling on me. Bell got back to me with the details several days later and by the end of the third week in January a ticket had arrived for Vancouver. I also had $2,500 deposited to my bank account by Bell as an advance on my pay.

"Rather trusting," I thought.

On the appointed day, I arrived at the airport completely over-dressed in a suit and trenchcoat and carrying a briefcase. Having no idea who the client was or what his pastimes were, I had to pack for every eventuality. Maybe he liked to go jogging in the morning and I would have to run with him. Maybe he liked to sail, ski or hike? I had called Donna, the team leader, to ask for details, but she told me she wouldn't discuss the client over the phone. So, I packed as many clothes as I could to account for any eventuality and wore what couldn't fit in the case.

Donna was to meet me when I arrived at the airport in Vancouver. Trouble was, I had no idea what she looked like. I collected my bags from the carousel and stood, sweating profusely in my overcoat, examining the faces in the crowd.

What was I looking for? All Bell had said was that Donna was a deco-rated veteran of British special forces and was very fit and experienced. My gaze went to every woman in the room. Which one was she?

I knew the numbers of women who ever made it into British special forces were minimal. Mostly, they were recruited by a secret agency within the Ministry of Defense to help male soldiers blend into urban environments during undercover work. Each had to pass an exceptionally cruel and often bizarre selection course. Whoever I was looking for would be an unusual woman.

Suddenly, there she was. I knew it was she, but how I knew would be hard to explain. As one soldier to another, there is something in the way a person carries himself that gives it away. A certain casual confidence. It is also in the eyes. As everyone knows, the eyes are windows to the soul, and a soldier's eyes usually have witnessed some intense events.

Donna was dressed casually in jeans and a loose white shirt. On her feet were hiking boots, and she walked with a casual confidence. Roughly five foot eight with light brown hair and a solid build, she somehow both stood out from the crowd but also blended in perfectly. A perfect undercover operator.

Smiling warmly, Donna approached me as if she knew me and stuck out her hand.

"Jim, glad to meet you. Let's go," she said in a soft English accent and immediately turned to walk towards the car park. Grabbing my gear, I fell in beside her. Reaching the plain white rental car, I threw my bags in the back and climbed in beside her.

We made small talk for a few moments. Then, in what has become a regular greeting ritual in the security community, we both began to find out if there was anyone we both knew in the industry or the military. It is a way of confirming who you are. I had trained with the SAS and Donna knew many members of that regiment after years of working alongside them. She brought up some names. Some I knew; others I didn't. I made sure I didn't lie because it was quite clear that I was being vetted.

Was I who I said I was, and could I be trusted? If we could identify someone we both knew, then we could check each other out. Since that first time, this ritual has been repeated wherever I have traveled and worked. It is your passport into the community.

I have learned that there is very real problem in the industry with "wanna-be's" and Walter Mitty's. Because records on who has served in military special forces are not made available to the public, all sorts of characters claim to have pasts which they have made up. Just recently, I met an American who was recruiting people for a project in the Middle East. When I asked him his background, he claimed to be an ex-Green Beret whose record included being inserted by submarine into Afghanistan back in the 1980s! For those unfamiliar with geography, that was quite a claim, since that nation is hundreds of miles from the nearest ocean.

Alan Bell tells a story (quite frequently, I might add) of a character who showed up in his offices looking for a job.

"This guy sat down and began to tell me how he had been in the SAS," Bell explains. "I played dumb and asked him what the SAS was? This guy had read all the right books because he went on to explain who they were and what they did. Then he told me that he had been in a certain troop in a certain squadron through a certain number of years."

"I listened quietly and then told him that he was just the guy we were looking for with a record like that … except for one issue: his observation skills. The guy felt a little put out about someone declaring an ex-SAS vet had poor observation skills, until I pointed to the wall behind me where my SAS plaque was hanging from the same troop in the same squadron during the same years he'd claimed to be with it. There were even pictures of me and the sixteen guys in our troop."

Somehow, Donna had finally reached a conclusion about me, or at least figured she had enough information to check me out. She then pulled out a briefing pad and began to fill me in.

The client was a Mr. Rakesh Saxena, an Indian-born financier and entrepreneur. Saxena was being sought for extradition by the government of Thailand over accusations of a role in the collapse in the Bank of Bangkok. The threat of kidnapping or murder to prevent Saxena from testifying was real enough to encourage him to seek protection. Saxena had turned to Bell & Associates to meet these needs.

Donna and I were to provide "bodyguard" services to Saxena. However, that term is no longer popular among serious practitioners of protection services. Bodyguards are thought of as big, obvious bruisers who work by physical intimidation. In truth, these types rarely are successful. They lack training for the most part and are rarely sophisticated enough for serious clients.

The professional bodyguard (BG), Close Protection Specialist (CPS) or Personal Protection Officer (PPO) is more often very "gray" and works by blending in with the background. Carrying briefcases and dressed in expensive suits, they are most often thought of as business men or women and dismissed as being unimportant. Sometimes their presence is overt, but they are becoming increasingly invisible. CPS's appear to be executive assistants or business consultants or to have some other common role in the corporate world. They have offices on executive floors and have desks filled with reports, forms, and correspondence. Even co-workers often do not realize that in reality they are security personnel.

During my military career, I had done some close protection work. In Sarajevo in 1992, I was employed as a detachment commander in what was called the "Intervention Force." Basically a twenty-one-man reconnaissance team, we escorted VIPs around the city, rescued hostages, and handled whatever other special tasks were required. In Africa, I had commanded a close protection team that escorted two senior United Nations officials to a meeting on the Zaire-Rwanda border during the Hutu-Tutsi wars.

Donna drove me around Vancouver, taking me to various venues that the client frequented, and explained the routine at each location. Then we headed over to the corporate offices on Hastings Street to meet the client.

Our meeting was brief. Saxena turned out to be a very short, affable man who, despite his wealth, was dressed casually in an open-necked shirt and sports jacket. In his mid-forties, he had the look of a slightly harried and overworked but competent businessman. Born in India and raised around the world, he spoke five languages and had a bright look in his eye.

"Jim, pleased to meet you," Saxena said as he stuck out his hand. My first impression was that, although Saxena stood only slightly over five feet, he was not intimidated in the slightest by my six-foot, two-inch frame. We chatted briefly, but I could tell he was anxious to get back to work. Donna, aware of his moods, quickly intervened and whisked

me out of his offices. I was then introduced to Lance M., whose tour
of duty was coming to an end and whom I would be replacing. Lance
was a serving reserve Canadian Forces officer on the weekends and a
long-time consultant of Alan Bell's during the week. Lance and I only
had a moment for introductions and a few minutes of small talk, however, before Donna pulled me out of the company offices to continue
the tour.

Back in the car, we headed north out of Vancouver across the mag-
nificent Lions Gate Bridge. As I took in the spectacular view of the Vancouver skyline, Donna continued to brief me. The story as it unfolded
was both intriguing and a little frightening.

Saxena was an international financier. He was a man who with a
phone call could move millions of dollars – rarely his own money,
though. After a life filled with moving amongst the world's rich and
powerful, his contacts spread from Moscow to Tokyo to Washington.
On the strength of his recommendation, his network would financially
back a new project or withdraw from an existing one.

Before fleeing to Canada, Saxena had been retained as a financial consultant to the Bank of Bangkok in Thailand. According to the information we had, Saxena, in his official role of advisor, had recommended to
the bank that it invest large unsecured loans to clients around the world.
Usually, the recipients of these loans were some of Saxena's many business contacts. Eventually, most of the loans were defaulted on, and the
subsequent financial debt brought down the bank.

The game gets more interesting at this point. Saxena, being only an
advisor to the bank, had no signing authority for these loans. His role
was strictly to advise. When the collapse came, many fingers pointed
at Saxena. While this was certainly enough reason to worry, the real
threat apparently was coming from the darker side of Thai politics.
According to information we had received, a very powerful Thai military general had an agenda that included getting Saxena arrested on
other accusations. This general, while a serving officer, controlled a
vast business empire that had come up against Saxena's business interests. It appeared to Saxena that the general would use the present situation to eliminate a business competitor.

Saxena's only choice was to get out. He would leave the country, but, in an act of good faith, he left his wife and children behind. Saxena chose Canada probably on the advice of one of his lawyers, owing to our lax judicial system. With the right legal team, Saxena could fight extradition for years. Outside the general's grasp, Saxena could defend his name and his role in the collapse of the Bank of Bangkok from the safety of Canada.

However, a team of Thai police arrived in Vancouver in 1996 to arrest Saxena and extradite him to Bangkok. Accompanied by Canadian officials, Saxena had become desperate. In what was either a very stupid or extremely cunning move (I have never concluded which) Saxena arrived at a meeting with a suitcase full of money. Arrested on charges of attempting to bribe government officials, Saxena would be held in Canada under house arrest until these charges could be dealt with. This maneuver on Saxena's part effectively ended the threat of extradition to Bangkok in the near future.

Fearing that the general might be inclined to try a more deadly and significantly less legal alternative, Saxena had looked about for a Canadian company to provide him with bodyguards. Not just big bruisers, but a team of highly skilled close protection professionals. Alan Bell had won the contract.

When we arrived at Saxena's residence, my optimism didn't increase any. Our client lived in a beautiful Art Deco home on the Pacific coast in the village of Lions Bay. My immediate concern was that anyone coming after Saxena could land by sea, conduct an attack or kidnapping, and be gone into international waters before Canadian law enforcement could respond.

I looked at Donna as we pulled into the driveway. I could tell she knew what I was thinking. With a shrug that explained much, she walked me around the house. She showed me the alarm system, the clouded-glass windows, and the rather effective blind systems. From the outside, no one could see anyone moving in the house. Motion sensors surrounding the house would provide early warning of any approach. Inside, the well-appointed basement floor belonged to the security team. Donna showed me my room and I dropped my gear.

Finally getting to shed some layers, I was quite relieved. Donna then led me up to the kitchen where, over tea, we spent several hours going over security measures, passwords, routines, and Saxena's idiosyncrasies.

Saxena drank quite a bit. He was a very lonely man and his security team spent much of its time just sitting with him watching hockey, for which he had a passion, or just talking. Saxena loved to tell stories of the places he had been and the experiences he had had. I would discover that he was also a very generous man. Nearly every night, he would buy over a hundred dollars' worth of Indian food and present it to his CP team. With relish he would watch us eat and take great pleasure in our obvious enjoyment of the curried delicacies. I had never eaten Indian food before, but I found I quite enjoyed the menu. Donna, trying to watch her slim figure, would only pick at these delicacies. Therefore, it fell to me to consume the lion's share. C'est la vie.

Donna and I knew that we were not considered his equals. The Indian system is a very class-oriented culture and, while Saxena was very cosmopolitan, he definitely held on to some of that attitude. We were trusted advisors and occasional confidants, but not equals.

During the day, I would drive Saxena in to the office, making sure we avoided the heavy traffic and never departing at the same time. Once in the office, I would sit down at my desk and get to work surfing the Internet and reading the media reports coming out of Thailand.

Almost from day one on the job I became a security consultant for Saxena. On the drive in, he would ask me what I thought of Angola or Colombia or Madagascar. He would say that he was interested in a project in a certain region and wanted to know more about the politics and risks there. I would spend the next few days researching these places and produce a report. As a former intelligence-trained soldier, I found this work straightforward and enjoyable. It also filled the hours at the office, which could often stretch well into the night.

Saxena was most interested in the large number of Canadian companies earning large revenues mining diamonds and gold in Africa. Here, he thought, was a way to make some tidy profits. Donna and I logged many hours researching Angola, Zaire, Algeria, and other African states. The country that most caught Saxena's eye was Sierra Leone. This country had rich mineral deposits including diamonds, gold, bauxite, and rutile. At the time Sierra Leone had an elected government with a tenuous grip on the nation and a huge foreign debt to service.

The country was an ideal opportunity for Saxena. It had all the elements necessary: unstable government, large foreign debt, and inviting natural resources. Having insufficient funds in the treasury to develop these projects itself, the government would welcome foreign investment capital. Saxena had the capital to invest and, with the current conditions in country, he could probably wring a good agreement from the local government.

So began my education and involvement into the world of international security. In late February 1997 I began to study Sierra Leone. Everything was in my domain: history, politics, security issues, and the identification of the power brokers. Over the coming weeks, I quickly became somewhat of an expert on Sierra Leone. I presented my report to Saxena and left it at that. Several days later, our client dropped the bomb on me in that Vancouver mall.

Later on the same day, I discussed the project with Alan Bell by phone at his offices in Toronto. At this point I had still never met Bell and felt a little uncomfortable taking on such an important project. For his part, Alan Bell was an opportunistic pessimist when it came to potential business. He instructed me to run with it and see how it developed.

Over the next few weeks, I began to put together a package on the situation in Sierra Leone. My motto has always been, "Fail to plan, plan to fail," and therefore I began a truly thorough investigation into the region. Again, I examined the recent history of the country, its present financial state, government infrastructure, and virtually every other bit of information I could glean.

The country was just emerging from a brutal six-year civil war. Libyan- and Liberian-backed terrorists had been fighting a bitter struggle with the government over control of the diamond-mining areas, and the fighting had been targeting civilians in a horrific fashion. South African mercenaries had entered the fray on the government's side and in less than six months had won the war, all but eliminating the terrorists. The mercenaries then supervised a democratic election which brought a former United Nations bureaucrat into office. Then, bowing to international pressure and owing to a lack of pay, the mercenary company, Executive Outcomes (EO), pulled out.

This was the situation in Sierra Leone I found myself looking at as I sat in my office in downtown Vancouver. EO was leaving, and the rebels seemed to have been driven from the country. Peace seemed to have taken hold, and, with a new government in power, everyone was looking forward with hope to a promising future.

Saxena had located a prospective business partner in Sierra Leone, a Mr. Samir Patel. Patel's company, Jupitor Export-Import Inc., held the mineral rights to a giant bauxite deposit in western Sierra Leone. Although Saxena had been hoping for a diamond concession, after running the numbers on the bauxite mine, he determined it to be a potentially very profitable venture in its own right.

Over the next few weeks, Saxena began to put together the pieces necessary to get the mine up and running. One critical element in the plan would be security. This would be my department, so I drafted a proposal to provide all the necessary security. This was not to prove an easy task.

The first obstacle to arrive in my path was Saxena's new partner. On March 11, I spoke with Patel on the phone from Conakry, Guinea, about the situation in Sierra Leone. Patel was insistent that everything was quiet and the war was well over. Although I didn't express concern during our talk, I had my suspicions that all was not as tranquil as Patel was portraying. I had been hearing reports of increasingly violent attacks around the country launched by well-armed rebels who struck swiftly and then melted into the jungle.

It was obvious that, with EO gone, the new government was having trouble rounding up all the terrorist stragglers. Without the professional leadership of the South Africans, local military forces were proving inadequate to secure the entire country. The few terrorists left had reverted to what is known as a "level-one" guerrilla struggle. In this type of warfare, small groups of guerilla fighters conduct only pinpoint attacks and avoid decisive engagements with security forces.

All the signs indicated that they would continue to resist surrender and would pose a real threat to any business venture in Sierra Leone.

Later that day, I faxed Patel a list of sixteen questions covering a variety of topics concerning security in the area, local facilities, logistic capabilities, and medical resources. My intent was to gain as much first-hand information as I could. Two days later I received a fax back from Patel. In it, he described a country that was a model of peace and rebuilding.

"The feeling portrayed by your questionnaire is the opposite that is [sic] reality on the ground here in Sierra Leone. ... The elected government is in control.... There is at present no threat whatsoever to our company or its personnel...."

The letter went on to say that all was quiet and the government was actively seeking foreign investment to aid in rebuilding the country. My concerns were unfounded, and there was really no need for Saxena and his partners to make a large investment in security. What the letter failed to note was that on February 19 a strong rebel force had managed to cut the Bo-Freetown highway for two days. On March 7 rebel forces ambushed an army patrol and killed fourteen soldiers. Reports continued to surface about a rebel stronghold that survived in the Kangari Hills, and skirmishes between rebels and pro-government militias were occurring frequently in the east.

Naturally, Patel quickly refuted my reports to Saxena. There were two conclusions that I drew immediately from these protests: either Patel knew about the attacks and wanted to make sure that Saxena and his money wouldn't be scared off; or, as is more likely the case, he had no professional experience in the security field and wasn't skilled enough to draw the proper conclusions. Either way, a struggle developed for Saxena's opinion on the security situation in Sierra Leone.

In the end, Patel underestimated Saxena's knowledge of life in Africa. Saxena accepted all of my reports, studied them thoroughly, and then used them as bargaining tools when and where they were needed as contract negotiations developed. In this way, Patel must have often found himself caught off-guard by Saxena's intimate knowledge of local activity and would have been at a loss to guess how much his future business partner actually knew.

In the end, an agreement was reached. Saxena and his Canadian partners would create a new mining company by buying out an existing shell corporation that was already listed on the Vancouver Stock Exchange. The First Impressions Singles Network, a dating service, was purchased and its name was changed to Global Mineralfields Inc. The bauxite mine would be re-opened as soon as possible. However, neither Saxena nor his Canadian investors had seen the mine they were buying. It was decided that a reconnaissance to inspect the facilities would be a requisite part of the due diligence process.

In early May, a group flew from Vancouver to Freetown, the capital of Sierra Leone, to investigate the new acquisition. This group consisted of Saxena's Canadian partners, Les Hammond, Peter Pilling, and Mervan Fiessal, and a geologist, Ron Lyle. On the security side, Alan Bell and I were to go along to conduct a security assessment. However, as the departure date drew near, we were told that only one security consultant would go. Bell told me he would go and I would be involved in any follow up.

By this time, my two months were up anyway, so I headed back to my home near Winnipeg, Canada. Despite being somewhat out of the picture, I continued to follow what was going on. In the end, I was quite glad I had not gone along.

All went well at first, and the group met with Sierra Leone's President Ahmad Tejan Kabbah to discuss the matter of bauxite mining in the western Port Loko region. President Kabbah and his government seemed well disposed to the project, and no real obstacles to the plan were identified. One small problem did arise when the group insisted Bell find them all weapons for a trip up to the mine area in Port Loko. Bell refused, explaining that if they ran into the terrorists and were armed, they would all be killed. There was no hope of holding off a rebel ambush with four businessmen and one ex-soldier. Instead, Bell hired a local security company to provide a couple of armed guards. In the event of trouble, the guards would probably take the brunt of the rebels' wrath, leaving the businessmen to be roughed up and robbed. Although Hammond didn't like it, the group went ahead unarmed.

After looking over the area, Bell was impressed with the sheer size of the mine concession. It covered several hundred square kilometers. To guard it all would take an immense security force. The initial plan was to select about six hundred former Sierra Leonean soldiers and run them through a two-week selection program. With luck, we would finish with about three hundred good candidates. These would then be put through an intensive training program to prepare them for duties as an armed security force. Weapons and equipment would be purchased from Executive Outcomes, who had left a good quantity of materiel in the country after its withdrawal.

Alan envisioned deploying a ten-man training team to get the security force up and running, and then a long-term commitment of several managers. A new company he had created in Vancouver would run the project. Globe Risk Holdings Incorporated would become the new mining security arm of Bell's security company. As for my new role, I was to be offered a position as an instructor. I was elated. Less than a year after departing the Forces, I would be a key player in a new international security company.

Unfortunately, just when everything appeared to be going great, someone pulled the rug out from under us. On May 24, Bell flew out of Freetown to begin arrangements for the new security company. The remainder of the party under Les Hammond had decided to stay a few extra days to tie up the due diligence process. On the following day, a disgruntled Sierra Leonean officer led a military coup to overthrow the Kabbah government.

On arriving in London on the morning of the May 25, Bell heard the news of the coup and was immediately on the phone to Saxena. His partners were now in grave danger. Saxena asked Bell if he could arrange a rescue attempt. Immediately, Bell began making phone calls and set about arranging for the evacuation of the stranded party.

On May 26, he flew back to Conakry, where he chartered a small airplane. A message was sent to Hammond, who was hiding with his party and thirteen hundred other foreigners at the Hotel Mammy Yoko in Freetown. He was instructed to go each day at 3 PM to a field just outside of the city and wait for rescue. Alan and his pilot made three trips out to the field at the appointed hour each day to meet the trapped group. The first two days, no one showed, and they had to return to Conakry. Finally, on the third day, Hammond and his team made it to the rendezvous, and they were rescued.

Although he would be glad to have his partners return unscathed, it would obviously be a bittersweet homecoming for Saxena. Just when the project had looked so promising, an illiterate, malcontent army officer had smashed the whole effort. Of course, the maiden contract of the fledgling Globe Risk Holdings Inc. was also lost in the tumult of another African civil war.

Sitting at home in Canada, I drew little comfort from the knowledge that my predictions of continued hostilities had been borne out. While Bell had been in Sierra Leone, I had traveled to Petawawa, Ontario, to recruit a training team for the project. As the home of the former Canadian Airborne Regiment, it was the best place to find a few good quality personnel for the project. Unfortunately, after raising the hopes of a few of my former comrades-in-arms that a good job awaited them on Civvy Street, I was unable to produce.

After discussing the situation with Bell, we decided to just wait and see what happened. It was possible that the coup would be short lived and that the project would continue as planned when the situation was resolved.

Over the next several months the new junta proceeded systematically to destroy Sierra Leone. "President" Johnny Paul Koroma represented his government to the world while dressed in a t-shirt, baseball cap, and sunglasses. Revolutionary United Front (RUF) forces, allegedly the "people's army," went on a rampage that destroyed the nation's infrastructure, including the torching of several government buildings. Newspaper editors were arrested and their presses shut down. Human rights abuses, atrocities, and starvation stalked the people. Many citizens of Sierra Leone fled across the nation's borders into refugee camps in Guinea.

Back in Canada, we just sat and waited. There was nothing we could do to influence the outcome, and I began to move on to other projects while the Sierra Leone contract languished. Other events would, however, soon draw us back into the conflict.

Saxena decided that a new opportunity had presented itself with the current coup in Sierra Leone. The international community had continued to refuse to recognize the rebel government of Koroma and his RUF allies. This gave his junta no political influence outside of their borders. The United Nations, and in particular the United States and Britain, continued to call for the reinstatement of the elected Kabbah government but without any real force behind their convictions. With President Kabbah waiting patiently in Guinea for any opportunity to regain control of his country, the stage was set for Saxena to intervene.

The elements favoring Saxena were clear. No international body wanted the junta to remain in power. At the same time, no international body seemed ready to commit any effort to ousting the rebels from Freetown. With lucrative diamond, gold, rutile, and bauxite concessions to offer as a reward, there was clearly an opportunity for private enterprises to intervene in the affair. Saxena made the decision to investigate the possibility that a privately hired military force could recapture the country. In exchange for funding such an enterprise, Saxena hoped to receive a controlling interest in the mineral resources of Sierra Leone.

With this idea in mind, the first call he placed was to Alan Bell in Toronto. When Saxena explained what he had in mind, Bell was immediately suspicious. Saxena wanted us to put together a team of mercenaries who, supported by loyal Sierra Leonean militia, would invade Sierra Leone and destroy the rebels.

This new enterprise would be strictly a mercenary venture and would hold significant ramifications for anyone involved. Bell would later comment: "Once you take that first mercenary job, you cannot take it back. You're pretty much committed for the long term. Once you become a mercenary, you will always be a mercenary."

However, Bell had to balance this new request against losing the entire bauxite mine security contract if he refused. There was also another consideration as well. The close protection contract Bell had with Saxena was becoming a problem. Saxena was under considerable stress with the loss of his bauxite project, and his extradition hearings were weighing heavily on him. His demands on his security team were becoming unreasonable, and there were more headaches than Bell was prepared to accept. The troubled Saxena was already considering canceling the close protection contract, so turning down the mercenary project would not sit well with him.

When I was contacted about this new development, I have to admit that I was surprised. The original bauxite project that I had set up was strictly a security job. We would have employed only Sierra Leoneans and a few ex-patriate managers. Such an arrangement, in my mind, could not very well be considered a mercenary contract. However, this new development would clearly be a mercenary venture.

After some thought, I tentatively agreed to take part in the operation if it went ahead. I had many reservations about the prospect, but I was willing to consider it. There were several reasons why. For many months now, I had been following every twist and turn of the events in Sierra Leone. Although I had never been there, I felt like I almost knew the place as well as Canada. I truly felt sorry for the average Sierra Leonean who was caught up in this continuing horror. Now, I was being offered an opportunity to use my professional skills to bring an end to the rebel stranglehold on the country. It would be a chance to help liberate a people to whom I had become quite attached. During my time as a United Nations peacekeeper, I often had to turn away as human tragedies occurred because my orders did not allow me to intervene. Now, here was an opportunity to actually make a difference.

Such an opportunity certainly had merit. However, I had to consider seriously the larger question: Was I prepared to become a mercenary? I had been offered mercenary work before and had always turned it down. Not from any moral objection I had to this line of work, but because the scales of money versus survival always tipped, for me, in favor of living. In this case, however, I was willing to consider it. I decided that, if the venture went ahead, I would deal with the ramifications of becoming a mercenary afterwards.

Fortunately, the difficult decisions belonged to Bell. Our position in Sierra Leone was a house of cards that could come down if he made the wrong choice.

"I never actually considered taking the mercenary contract," Bell later explained. "However, Saxena was a client and I thought we should advise him as best we could. I offered to do a feasibility study for him on the present situation, the ramifications for his business interests there, and possibly suggest some courses of action."

The proposal Bell put together for Saxena came with a price tag of CDN$24,000. Saxena's response was immediate and not particularly pleasant. He balked at Bell's suggested cost for the study. He believed that this was excessive, as we already had a security contract with him. Up until this point, the security advisory services had been provided as part of the existing duties of the CP team at no extra charge. However, this new project could prove to be extremely complex in terms of conduct, political support, logistics, and overall organization, not to mention risk to the consultants doing the study. Bell felt that, before we invested any large effort, a retainer up front would be necessary.

Saxena was unwilling to commit the extra funds to the feasibility study. In the row that followed, Bell decided that Saxena was becoming too difficult to deal with. The two parties decided to cancel the feasibility study and also terminate the close protection contract. A rule that had been clearly explained to me when I joined Bell's firm was that we never broke the law. Saxena's ambitions were not technically illegal in the strictest sense of the word, but the idea of hiring mercenaries to replace one African government with another could not necessarily be thought of as a respectable activity.

Globe Risk could easily have carried out such an operation. We had the experience, the personnel, and the means. What we lacked was the desire to become a mercenary company. Certainly, this would be a challenging project, but once it was over, that would be the end of the company and possibly our professional reputations, as far as the more legitimate security industry was concerned. Was there another mercenary contract waiting after the Sierra Leone job? If not, where would we go as a firm and as individuals?

The original contract for Sierra Leone was strictly a security operation. The guards would be locals; we would take no active role in any armed conflict beyond protecting mine employees and their equipment. Yes, the guards would be armed, but they would not be soldiers. Our role would be one of management only. On the whole, it would have been a security guard contract much like any other. It was entirely possible that many more such contracts would become available around the world if the one with Global Mineralfields in Sierra Leone did not work out. Therefore, Bell decided to walk away forever from mercenary work and focus on the legitimate side of the international security industry.

Globe Risk has now conducted projects in Africa, South America, Asia, and southern Europe. In none of these areas did company personnel carry weapons or train others to carry weapons. The new tools of the trade are laptop computers, cell phones, and briefcases. The company's marketable product is its consultants' experience in international security, their ability to gather intelligence and collate it into useful information, and their capacity to work safely in areas of high risk. Nowhere in the firm's corporate profile does it specify that its people will patrol jungles with machine guns or topple unpopular dictators.

Yet, Globe Risk has never fully escaped an association in many people's minds with the mercenary trade. The fact that the mercenary world has now emerged from the shadows to become incorporated, registered, and openly advertised makes our predicament even more difficult.

The question I began to ask myself after the Sierra Leone venture fell through was, where does the line lie between mercenary and security contractor? What are the actual laws concerning such activity? How much of an emerging trend is this involvement in international security by private companies? Where in the market does Globe Risk place itself? Most importantly, how could we distance ourselves from the mercenary world?

2

THE SHADOW PROFESSION

WHILE I WAS STILL a serving soldier, I knew that there existed a private-sector world of security. I had friends who had retired and become security guards. Phil Aprile, a comrade-in-arms from 3 Commando who served with me in Rwanda, retired and became a private investigator. Yet, like many people, I considered the word "security" to refer to night watchmen, minimum-wage mall-security guards, home alarm systems, and access control systems. International security was the domain of politicians and global alliances such as the United Nations, NORAD, NATO, and the Warsaw Pact. Or was it?

I also knew a little about mercenaries. In the former Yugoslavia I had met quite a few. Some were Australian, others British or European, and there was even a smattering of Canadians. Like most people, I considered them to be less than professionals and more than likely criminals on the lam.

I had read a few of the military history books concerning mercenaries such as "Mad" Mike Hoare's account of the famous 5 Commando in the 1960s Congo. I also knew a little about the British mercenary disaster in 1970s Angola.

In the weeks before my release, I met with a retired Canadian general who had been working in Africa and wanted to know if I wanted a job with Executive Outcomes. Although I had heard of the South African mercenary company, I knew nothing about them. I never took the offer seriously.

However, after my experience with Saxena and Sierra Leone, I was thrust into the world of private international security. The problem for me was figuring out where I fit in. Where was Bell's company, Globe Risk, in all of this? What was a mercenary, and what exactly was an "international security consultant"?

The biggest question to be answered in my mind was what do you call a retired soldier who travels to the world's hot spots and deals with security issues? To my thinking, we couldn't really call ourselves professional soldiers; there was just too much of a confusing connotation to that. Security professional? The problem with that term was that it could refer to a run-of-the-mill security guard. I was certainly more highly trained than a mall guard. I was a professional. But a professional what?

But first, what do I mean when I say professional? Essentially, the dividing line between professionals and other groups of workers is a matter of education. The university-qualified careerist is generally considered a professional. The longer the degree program, the more prestigious the profession. Therefore, the traditional professions are synonymous with the types of degrees available through university education programs. Law degrees, economics degrees, medical and scientific degrees – these are the foundations for the well-earned title of "professional."

For those who wind up in the workforce out of a public education or college background, there are diverse employment opportunities. Some may lead to professional status, but more often they fall into the category of occupations rather than professions.

For the world of international private sector security, this issue – the distinction between who should be considered a professional and who should not – is key. In the traditional way of thinking, military service is both a means and an end. It may be a career, but it begins and ends within the confines of national military service. For the career soldier, his or her life may well be spent in his or her country's army until the age of retirement. Then, perhaps with a small pension, the retired soldier finds some new line of work to live out his or her days.

The American military has institutionalized this process with the G.I. Bill. In return for a period on military service, American soldiers can look forward to thousands of dollars in education grants upon their retirement. They can then go on to a university degree and a professional career. In Israel, the mandatory retirement age for all ranks in the Israeli Defense Forces has been forty-five years of age for many years now. Consequently, the majority of retired military officers, still in their prime, move into senior management positions with corporations or turn to politics. Many of Israel's prime ministers have been retired military officers.

Whether officer or enlisted man, however, one's profession of soldiering ends with the departure from military service. By this standard, there is no modern frame of reference for the retired soldier who continues to work in the military or international security field as a "professional." It is this fact more than any other that causes so much soul-searching and confusion around the world when the larger question of mercenaries, professional soldiers, security experts, and their brethren are considered.

Until the latter half of the twentieth century, military service was not a particularly intellectual career. For the common soldier, the skills he required to conduct his business could be acquired with only a few months of training. For the ambitious officer, the situation was somewhat different, and he would normally require some university training, or at least the breeding and money required to purchase a commission and promotion. In the latter half of the twentieth century, however, the situation changed dramatically.

With the advent of the Cold War, soldiering became far more complex than at any time in history. In the West, military forces of the various nations were severely outnumbered by their counterparts in the East. In terms of both manpower and amount of equipment, the Soviet and Chinese blocs had an immense advantage over the West. To counterbalance this disparity, the West turned to technology and professionalism for an advantage. Every western soldier needed to have a diverse skill set, understand tactical strategy, and be able to realize political necessities.

For the average military serviceman, carrying a rifle soon became only a minor part of his or her career skill set. Now everyone needed a basic understanding of communications, intelligence, navigation, mechanical repair, weapons systems, and combat engineering. Additionally, the average junior NCO was trained not only in platoon-level tactics, but also in the deployment of unit and command level assets. A corporal in a western army could usually direct artillery fire, vector fighter aircraft onto targets, blow up bridges, and make tactical choices based on overall strategy.

This new level of skills required of western armies forced many to adopt a "professional" military structure. There was simply too much knowledge and experience required of latter-twentieth-century soldiers to operate efficiently in any other fashion. Consequently, over a twenty-year career, the average professional western soldier would study the equivalent of several university degrees' worth of material and become proficient in many areas of study.

This trend can most clearly be seen in the huge investment made by the West in "special forces." Having already committed a great deal of resources toward the creation of an average soldier, many nations selected their best and brightest individuals to receive even more specialized training. This produced junior officers and NCOs who could operate on a strategic level as well as a tactical one. By inserting very small numbers of these specialists into regions in conflict, results all out of proportion to their numbers could be achieved. On several occasions, three or four of these individuals sent to an area of conflict have decided the course of that nation's history.

To accomplish these feats, special forces only rarely rely on firepower. Instead, they devise strategies that more directly interfere with their opponent's ability to wage war or perpetuate conflicts. A perfect example of this capability was demonstrated in The Gambia in 1981.

Many people in the world were witness to the pomp and pageantry of the Royal Wedding between the late Lady Diana Spencer and His Royal Highness, the Prince of Wales. One of those who managed an invitation to the church to hear the vows in person was the president of The Gambia, Sir Dawda Jawara. While the president was in London, however, five hundred Libyan-backed terrorists were making an attempt to seize control of his country. The communist rebels quickly seized the presidential palace, the radio station, and one of the president's wives and her children.

The British Foreign Office, aghast at the implication of losing a good ally in West Africa to the communists, sent three SAS men to the area to see if they could put things right. A force of Senegalese paratroopers had managed to land and seize the airport outside the capital city of Banjul, but they had made no headway in exploiting their bridgehead. In response, the rebel leader, Kukli Samba Sanyang, announced over the state radio that he was prepared to slaughter the president's family if the Senegalese did not withdraw.

Into this situation flew the three SAS men, one of whom was the regiment's second-in-command, Major Ian Crooke. With the permission of President Jawara to take whatever actions they deemed necessary, the three men left the airport and sneaked through the rebel lines into the city. Here they found the British ambassador hiding under a desk in his embassy and managed to find out what was happening with the hostages.

Next, Crooke led his two men on a successful mission to rescue the president's family from under the noses of their rebel guards and return to the embassy with them. Leaving the president's family safe within the British compound, the three men then returned to the airport, sneaking through the rebel lines once again. Here they took command of the Senegalese paratroopers and led them in an attack on the surrounding rebel positions. The rebels broke and continued to fall back until, four days later, the attempted coup was over and the rebels were arrested. The SAS men then quietly slipped away and no notice of their involvement was made public for many years.

The fact that three special forces men, operating without direction, could resolve a crisis of this magnitude is a perfect illustration of their skills. That the coup was defeated without resort to costly military interventions or dangerous political jousting between East and West blocs makes their contribution even more important.

During the 1991 Gulf War, special forces operated inside Iraq on various missions. The most important of these were the locating and destruction of mobile SCUD missile launchers. By firing these weapons at Israel, the Iraqis had come close to destroying the American-led coalition against Saddam Hussein. The Coalition Forces' response to this crisis was to deploy small teams of special forces to find the mobile SCUD launchers and target them for aircraft strikes. In this fashion, roughly one hundred special forces soldiers from Britain and the United States prevented the entire coalition army from falling apart for political reasons.

The investment in training these individuals really does make them professionals in the truest sense of the word. Their education, their qualifications and their valuable contribution to complex political and military concerns places them on par with any other more widely accepted professions.

Consequently, on leaving their respective national armies, most special forces soldiers become a highly-sought-after commodity in the international marketplace. Their services are often in demand by governments, industry, and even the United Nations. Normally these people retire in their mid-thirties or early forties and, finding their skills a marketable product, there is little incentive for them to embark on a wholly new, non-security-related career. Often, several retired soldiers will join forces to form security service companies that provide everything from alarm systems and bodyguarding right up to full mercenary services.

The progenitor for the modern international security company was Watchguard Ltd., formed in the early 1970s by the legendary Colonel David Stirling. The six-foot, four-inch Stirling had been a bright young commando officer in North Africa in World War II when he dreamed up the idea of the Special Air Service. The unit he created went on to become the role model for special forces for generations to come. After the war, Stirling became involved in helping the British government conduct officially "deniable" missions around the world.

He also began to accept contracts, always with the full knowledge of the British Foreign Office, from foreign governments which needed his expertise. To service this business, he set up Watchguard. Bringing together a team of retired special forces officers and men, he marketed his knowledge of international security to friendly nations.

One of the primary services Watchguard offered was a counter-coup-d'état program for unstable Third World governments. Stirling would deploy teams to train professional-quality presidential body-guard units to provide a first-line defense. Then his men would set up secret safe houses around the country to which the head-of-state could escape in the event of a coup attempt. These facilities would be equipped with food and water, clothing, and communications equip-ment to maintain contact with the outside world and continue to influ-ence events within the country.

This second line of defense was backed up by pre-positioned assets and resources outside the country to maintain the government in the event it had to exist in exile for any amount of time.

This was the beginning of the modern international private security industry. Since that time, hundreds of other firms have followed in Watchguard's wake. Most have been dismal failures. Many pursued mostly mercenary work and became embarrassments to their home governments. A few shifted with the years into high-technology intel-ligence services.

For instance, an American company named Airscan maintained a contract through the 1990s to provide high-tech patrol aircraft to pro-tect oil rigs off the coast of Angola. Retired Brigadier General Joe Stringham won the contract from Chevron to ensure that Angolan criminals, terrorists, and looters never made it from shore out to the mighty rigs and endangered any crew.

Airscan's aircraft were high-flying twin-prop planes outfitted with infrared cameras, side-scan radar, and electronic interception equip-ment. Operating day and night, the firm's patrols ensured no nasty surprises could take the platforms unaware.

In Colombia, the war on the drug cartels is a never-ending night-mare. For most lawyers, judges, police or military officers who are honest enough to refuse the ever-present bribes, a bullet is the most likely future. Into this mess entered a retired U.S. Marine major, Gil Macklin.

One of the few bright spots in the war on drugs in Colombia in recent years has been a special police unit known as the Copels. Macklin was hired by the Colombian government to recruit a unit of young men each of whom had suffered some personal tragedy at the hands of the cartels. He then put this group through an intense training program in small-unit tactics and weapons skills. The Copels he built up were a highly trained and motivated unit with the courage to take on the powerful bosses of the cocaine industry.

This unit went on to systematically take down entire cartels, starting at the bottom and working up to the top. Despite horrific casualties within its ranks, it was this unit that finally netted Pablo Escobar of the notorious Medillin cartel.

While he never led them in action, Macklin was never far away. The combination of his military skill in marine special forces techniques and a belief in the morality of his work led this American to make a major contribution to putting the cartels existing at that time out of business.

While these latter two examples involve retired soldiers operating in the private sector around the world, neither involves men fighting for foreign countries. In other words, they are not mercenaries but are instead examples of the shadow profession of international private security. They are using their exceptional military "education" as a business commodity. The market for these services has been growing since the Cold War and has really taken off in the last ten years.

According to the Bonn Institute, the international security industry was worth close to US$60 billion annually in 1998 and is expected to be worth $200 billion in another ten years. At the forefront of this industry are the shadow professionals.

The difficulty is the fact that the international security industry can consist of everything from large-scale mercenary companies down to one-man consulting firms who work for the United Nations. It is just too wide a market to lump everyone under one heading. It is also too controversial. As we discovered in Sierra Leone, the line between mercenaries and security providers can be very fine. What is needed is some clarity and organization on the subject. For the purposes of this book, it is essential.

Where everyone in the world is familiar with the popular notion of mercenaries and what they are all about, very few have ever given

much thought to this shadowy group in the middle between mercenarism and the common mall-guard type of domestic security. Here
we can find the former soldiers who take on the projects that require
a high degree of professional skills and experience but fall well short
of mercenary work.

To give this middle ground a title, I will refer to it as the "International Security Industry." This group occupies the area of the industry between the mercenary trade and the common domestic security
industry.

To begin, it is best to divide the private security industry into recognizable segments. The most obvious division will be between the
"security" and "military" sectors. Some firms, such as Britain's Control
Risks, operate only in the security industry serving corporate and government clients. They take no direct role in either conducting military-
style activities or supporting military forces.

On the military side, there are two divisions: those that provide military combat functions and those that provide military-style security
services. Firms such as Watchguard of the 1970s or Executive Outcomes of the 1990s provided military advice and skills up to and including mercenary combat. Other firms, such as London-based Defense
Systems Limited (DSL) or Military Professional Resources Incorporated (MPRI) out of Virginia, U.S.A., operate primarily in the military
sphere providing various skills and services up to, but not including,
mercenary combat.

Having divided the industry into separate military combat, military
security, and non-military security realms, we can begin to bring some
order to the situation. What follows below is an explanation of the
three categories that I will use throughout this book: *Security Services,
Military Security Services,* and *Military Combat Services.*

The first category is *Security Services.*

These are firms that provide non-military advice and services to
non-military clients. Included in this group would be investigation
services, crisis management planners, risk assessment analysts, and
corporate intelligence services. It would also include training services,
bodyguards, equipment suppliers, and technology providers.

KPMG Investigations and Security Inc. is a prime example. KPMG is one of the world's largest and most successful business accounting and auditing companies. It regularly conducts projects for governments and Fortune 500 companies on a worldwide basis. Its security-consulting arm, KPMG Investigations and Security Inc., works very clearly in the area of international security services. In 1999, for example, this group was working closely with the government of Bahrain to help control that country's nearly one-billion-dollar money-laundering rackets.

Control Risks, a company we will look at more closely in subsequent chapters, also works exclusively in this area. In 1999, Control Risks conducted a security audit of the Canadian ambassador's residence and offices in Bogotá, Colombia. It also provides security consultants for clients whenever a kidnapping of a corporate employee occurs anywhere in the world. Like most of these firms, Control Risks was founded by a retiring group of military officers.

The second category is *Military Security Services.*

Military security services supply personnel, equipment, training, arms, and expertise in military skills to various clients. The condition is that their personnel never cross the line into active involvement in either combat or combat support, thus becoming mercenaries.

In this case, "military security" refers to any and all functions normally attributed to military formations other than combat duties. This could include weapons and tactics training, intelligence training, counter-terrorist training, military technology training, military logistic or transport services, field medical skills, armed guard services, and even military research-and-development advice.

Military security services can be provided to foreign governments, militaries or police forces, as well as to non-governmental agencies or the private sector. A security company hired by a mining company to provide "professional" armed ex-soldiers as security guards would fit into this category. If the company did not import professional guards but instead hired local non-professional guards, then it would fall under the first category, security services.

One area in which military security services are becoming increasingly visible is in the international disaster-relief assistance and humanitarian-aid industries. Military veterans are the world's leading experts on solving complex logistical issues. When aid organizations move into war zones around the world, their people need to be transported, fed, and housed. Food aid and supplies need to be delivered in bulk to remote zones. Private military expertise is often retained to provide advice, support, personnel, and equipment to get the job done efficiently. These groups also realize that security is critical and are increasingly resorting to hiring military security service consultancies to organize protection for them.

Defense Systems Limited of London is a prime example of this latter group. It has supported humanitarian aid organizations with military logistics skills in the Balkans for several years now. It also trains foreign counter-terrorist units and provides highly trained ex-military guards for foreign embassies in hostile nations.

Other similar firms would be MPRI (U.S.A.), Teleservices (Angola), Saladin (U.K.), Levdan (Israel), Vinnell Corporation (U.S.A.), and Gray Security (South Africa).

Another element in this group would be an operation like Black Bear Consulting, run by retired Brigadier General Ian Douglas of Nepean, Canada. Douglas is one of the United Nations' chief military consultants for peacekeeping operations. During the 1990s, whenever the U.N. was examining a new operation, Douglas was one of the contractors who would fly out to the region, make a military assessment, and provide the Security Council with deployment options. Douglas has conducted these services in Sierra Leone, Angola, Uganda, Rwanda, Zaire (Democratic Republic of Congo), and many other global trouble spots.

The final, and most controversial, category, is *Military Combat Services*. These companies, usually referred to as Private Military Companies or "PMCS," would include any company that provided military skills, equipment, manpower, training or other services that also included combat or combat support functions. These are the modern mercenary companies.

One factor that often clouds this issue is that PMCS will regularly provide services that would fall under the Military Security Services

heading or the more traditional Security Services category in addition
to the occasional Military Combat Services. Not all PMC activity has
a combat or combat support function. For instance, Executive Outcomes provided mercenaries in Africa for nine years but also provided
consultants to resolve kidnappings in Asia. This latter activity would
normally be handled by a security consultancy such as Control Risks.
Similarly, Watchguard provided non-combat advice to foreign governments in counter-coup d'état preparedness, but it also hired mercenaries to fight in foreign wars.

The deciding criterion here is the combat issue. If a company
includes combat functions in its repertoire, regardless of whether it
provides any other service common to the international security industry, it would fall into the Military Combat Service category.

Crossing the line separating the rest of the industry from military
combat services is much like losing your virginity. Either you are a
mercenary company or you are not. Once you take that step, there is
no going back. As Alan Bell said to me in 1997: "Once you take that
first mercenary job, you cannot take it back."

Examples in this last category would be Executive Outcomes, Sandline International, and Keeni-Meeny Services (KMS).

So these are the three categories into which I divide the international security industry. The division is logical and, in my experience,
accurate. Please note that this organization applies only to the international market. On the domestic side, in whatever country, the security industry is organized much differently. Here we would find guard
companies, alarm companies, investigation services, computer firewall
firms, and Internet security providers. The list would be very diverse.
However, this book is not concerned with the domestic industry and
that topic is for others to discuss.

So what, then, is the advantage in breaking down the international
community into such simple but accurate groups? The first is the
means to the ultimate end: regulation. If any type of consensus is ever
to be reached on the industry and how it can either contribute to global
security or be prevented from interfering, regulation is the key. Before
any draft legislation could ever be presented to the United Nations,

however, the industry will need to be broken down into its component parts or we risk throwing the baby out with the bath water.

The second value in such a categorization is in the interests of the companies themselves. Most legitimate security companies would welcome the idea of being able to point to a set of criteria and say, "Here we are!" Globe Risk could certainly have used such criteria when the company was first set up. Firms like Defense Systems Limited, which is always singled out in media articles as one of the modern "mercenary" companies, could clearly say that they do not belong to that group. Based on the criteria set out above, DSL is instead a military security services company.

The final feature of this system is in the clear drawing of a line in the sand. If a military security services company, or a security services firm for that matter, crosses the line and conducts military combat operations, however limited the scale, then it can clearly be labeled as a PMC. There would be no jumping back and forth. For the good of the international private security industry, there can be no confusion in this regard.

Within the PMC industry, however, few companies will submit willingly to the label of "mercenaries." The moral connotation that accompanies that word simply carries too much baggage. Executive Outcomes, despite years of fielding some of Africa's best combat troops and winning two wars for its clients, refused to accept the mercenary title.

One reason that EO could get away with such a claim is the lack of a definition of what exactly constitutes a mercenary under international law. The United Nations, the Organization of African Unity, the Organization of Security and Cooperation in Europe, and numerous other international bodies have been struggling with that issue for years now.

So that raises our next question: Who is a mercenary?

3

DEFINING THE MERCENARY

"Mercenary: ... one that serves merely for wages; esp: a soldier hired into foreign service."
  – Merriam-Webster Dictionary

BEFORE ANY SERIOUS EXAMINATION of who or what exactly constitutes a mercenary can begin, the incredibly thorny issue of defining the term must first be addressed. It is this problem that is at the root of all of the controversy surrounding the military security professional. The blanket term "mercenary" has come to refer to a wide assortment of characters and groups and brings credit to none of them. Carrying the title mercenary can place one into the lowest depths of moral depravity that an individual can sink to.

The primary problem with the word is that it suffers no clear definition.

Throughout the ages, the term has carried many different meanings and connotations. Now, in the twenty-first century, there are no less than five different categories of individuals and groups that could be classed as mercenaries. Some of these groups are "legitimate" entities that serve the United Nations and NATO. Others are often the foreign policy tools of major western governments. Some have never risen above the level of brutal thugs who prey upon the innocent. Consequently, creating a single definition that will exonerate some groups while still targeting the more "rogue" elements is not a simple challenge.

To make matters worse, over the past few decades the term has been regularly applied to an increasingly diverse collection of characters who may or may not have any connection with the profession of arms or warfare. Terrorists, drug smugglers, and wandering groups of fanatical religious extremists are routinely placed within the mercenary community by international institutions and the popular media. When such groups are included in the same profession as the "legitimate" mercenaries, it obscures any effort to make a distinction between the two. The consequent confusion impairs attempts to impose a ban on the activities of the less savory elements.

The issue of the corporatization of international security adds an additional obstacle. In a traditional sense, wars are open conflicts waged between two or more groups. However, the predominant trend in the latter twentieth century was the small-scale ethnic, religious or ideological contest. These types of wars are usually long, drawn-out guerilla conflicts marked by savagery and extensive propaganda. Officially referred to as "Low Intensity Conflicts" (LICs), they present political quagmires for the major powers. When the regional parties involved in such struggles needed assistance, they often found little more than moral support resulted from their official requests for aid from international organizations. Inevitably, then, these combatants would turn to the private sector to provide arms, advice, training, and logistical support.

To service this market, a wide array of modern, quasi-mercenary companies has popped up over the years. Completely illegal arms dealers and terrorist organizations run some. Others are officially sanctioned, publicly traded corporations that provide military support to their clients.

The result is a complex, confusing, emotionally and politically charged issue that official bodies wince at, minor powers fear, and various lobby groups seize as a platform.

Since the middle of the last century, attempts have been made to deal with the mercenary question by both creating a definition and enshrining it in international law. The ultimate intent has always been to stop the use, support, and training of mercenaries. As of the time of writing, none of these efforts has yet succeeded because the very word mercenary is partisan in nature. Although no group gladly suffers association with the title, the use of professional soldiers is viewed as an accepted practice by some and a despised attack on international civil rights by others. Depending on which side of the moral argument you fall will probably affect your overall opinion.

One real element of the challenge is the record of the professional soldier. Historically, mercenaries have been a cornerstone of the world's military development. Such a statement will no doubt leave a foul taste in the mouth of a few military historians; however, it is largely irrefutable. The only gray area involved is the changing nature over the centuries as to who may qualify as a mercenary. The history of warfare is full of mercenary involvement. If one accepts that any individual or group that joins a foreign army to fight its wars for pay and/or adventure is a mercenary, then our martial heritage is rife with such men.

Karl Maria von Clausewitz, one of history's most famous military philosophers, was a Prussian officer who served for two years as a mercenary in the Russian army. For the past century, the writings of Clausewitz have functioned as a standard textbook for every respectable military academy around the world. Another famous military philosopher and soldier, Antoine Henri Jomini, was a Swiss officer who served in the French and Russian armies. Prince Eugen of Savoy-Caringon was a Frenchman by birth who joined the Hapsburg Emperor's army as a mercenary and rose to the rank of field marshal. He became one of the most influential figures on the battlefields of Europe in his time. One of his regular allies was John Churchill, the first Duke of Marlborough. A hero of British military history, the duke traveled to France as a young man to serve as a mercenary under the French Marshal Henri Turenne and learn the arts of war. Later, he returned to England to command the armies of England against his former employers.

During the late Middle Ages and Renaissance periods, it was an accepted practice to seek service in foreign armies. In fact, for royalty or the upper class of the European nations it was a predominant trend. King James II of England sent his son, the Duke of Berwick, to France to serve as a mercenary officer and study warfare. Later, after his Protestant enemies deposed the king, the duke followed James to Ireland to win a Catholic victory there. When the attempt ended in failure, Berwick joined the nearly 10,000 Irish patriots who accepted exile rather than laying down their arms. Most of these men, Berwick included, became known as the "Wild Geese" and were some of the eighteenth century's most famous mercenaries. Berwick led a battalion of these Irish fighters to France where he eventually rose to become a French field marshal.

The famous Scotsman John Graham, the Earl of Claverhouse, was sent to France as a mercenary for King Louis xvi before being recalled to join the fight for a Scotland free from English rule. Named as second-in-command of the Scottish armies by the now exiled James ii and awarded the title Viscount of Dundee, Graham went on to lead the last successful Scottish claymore (sword) charge against government soldiers armed with muskets in 1688. For his bravery and courage he has been remembered in history as "Bonnie Dundee."

Emperor Leopold ii of Austria sent his son Charles to apprentice under the Duke of Saxe-Teschen. This royal progeny went on to command the Army of the Rhine and delivered Napoleon his first defeat at Aspern-Esserling in 1809.

As the above examples demonstrate, the idea of serving in a foreign army was not unusual in European history. It was expected that all males of noble breeding be well versed in the arts of war. When no conflict was available to a nation's youth, they were often sent off to find service in foreign wars and learn their military skills. This was an essential ingredient in maintaining the power balance of Europe. Having experienced soldiers to command a nation's armies when a threat appeared was a form of insurance against disaster.

In his rather bitter treatise *The Prince,* Niccolo Machiavelli wrote of this issue:

> ... a prince should therefore have no other aim or thought, nor take up any other thing for his study, but war and its organization and discipline, for that is the only art necessary for one who commands.... it not only maintains those that are born princes, but often enables men of private fortune to attain that rank.

Historically, there has been almost an official policy towards not only sending off young men to become mercenaries, but also hiring mercenaries when and where they were needed. During the American War of Independence, American hero George Washington hired German mercenaries to train and lead his armies into battle. The men they trained went on to fight German mercenaries hired by the British Crown to put down the rebellion.

One of the clearest examples of the key role mercenaries played in military history was in the battle of Waterloo in 1815. In 1812, over fifty percent of Napoleon's 700,000-strong Grande Armée was made up of foreign mercenaries. Even Napoleon's Imperial Guard employed battalion-sized mercenary units of Tartars and Mamelukes. Also within the French ranks were the last remnants of the Wild Geese, whose battalions had served the French for over a century.

On the English side, there were similar numbers. Britain's forces had become badly overstretched by the early 1800s with large contingents deployed in the Far East, North America, and Spain. The manpower required to fill up the British regiments forced the English to hire vast numbers of foreign soldiers. Hessian mercenaries made up a major portion of the British armies in Canada. The Nepalese Gurkhas were recruited into the Honourable East India Company to help this British interest secure its hold on Asia.

By 1815 and the Battle of Waterloo, Wellington's army of 60,000 included 40,000 hired foreigners. Chief among these was the King's German Legion, a British mercenary unit that was led by a mixture of English and foreign officers and employed mostly hired German soldiers. Formed in 1803 of Hanoverian exiles, it soon began to admit Poles, Hungarians, Danes, and Russians. It was the first of the modern "foreign legions."

The Legion was of brigade strength and included light infantry, cavalry, and artillery. Under Wellington, it proved itself to be among the best the British had to offer during the Peninsular wars. The Legion's 1st Hussars were Wellington's preferred cavalry unit during that conflict and the Jaeger (hunter) light infantry had few peers within the British infantry line regiments.

The King's German Legion followed Wellington to France to meet the resurgent Napoleon in 1815. They were to distinguish themselves at Waterloo with one of the most heroic exploits of any mercenary unit in history. The stand made by the Legion's 2nd Light battalion at the La Haye Sainte farm was a remarkable action that exemplified the soldierly characteristics of honor, courage, and loyalty. Three hundred and seventy-six mercenaries held that tiny farm against repeated assaults by an entire corps of French infantry. Eventually out of ammunition, they fought with fists and bayonets. By the end of the day, only forty-two survived.

With the loss of La Haye Sainte in the early afternoon, the advantage fell to the French, who immediately brought up their guns to fire on the British line. The battle of Waterloo might have been lost by the English but for the entrance of another great mercenary, Gebhard von Blucher.

Born in Rostock in Northern Germany, Blucher joined the Swedish army at the age of fourteen. He was admitted to a cavalry regiment and fought the Prussians during the Seven Years War. After being taken prisoner by his Prussian enemies, he changed sides and joined the Prussian 8th Hussars. He was sent to fight the French and eventually rose to the rank of field marshal in the Prussian army.

At the beginning of the 1815 war with Napoleon, Blucher was hired out of retirement to lead a Prussian army of 84,000 men from Belgium against Napoleon's return. He first met the French at Ligny, about sixteen miles southeast of Waterloo.

On the afternoon of June 16, Blucher's Prussians had drawn themselves up on the exposed forward slope of a hill overlooking the Ligny brook. Facing them was Marshal Ney and about one-third of Napoleon's army. This force consisted of about 64,000 infantry and 12,500 cavalry.

When the battle commenced, the French artillery decimated the exposed Prussians. The ensuing battle was bloody and horrible. Despite the Prussian superiority in numbers, the combination of artillery and the ensuing fires in the fields staggered the Prussian lines.

After several hours of bitter combat, victory went to the French. By the end of the day, 16,000 Prussians lay dead and another 8,000 had fled the field. The French losses were about 12,000 all told, but they had won the day.

Field Marshal Blucher had been badly hurt leading a last desperate cavalry charge. Knocked from his horse, he had landed unconscious in the mud. The field marshal was found and rescued by his aide-de-camp and carried from the field. His army was left in disarray. As night fell, the Prussians retreated from the field.

Napoleon, on hearing of the victory, was flushed with his first success. He now assumed the old mercenary would take his battered army and withdraw to lick his wounds. He did not count on Blucher's determined fighting spirit.

Blucher had been taken to a small cottage in the village of Mellem and was tended by his aide. Eventually, his second-in-command, Field Marshal Wilhelm Gneisenau, discovered his whereabouts. When Blucher regained consciousness, they called their chief officers together and the two old mercenaries debated the next move.

Gneisenau, a Saxon mercenary who had fought for the Austrians, the British in North America, and finally the Prussians, counseled that they should retreat from the area and abandon the fight. Their force had suffered a tremendous defeat and was obviously not ready to meet the French again any time soon. Blucher disagreed. He had promised Wellington that his force would stand by the British and he was determined not to break that vow. Eventually, Gneisenau acquiesced and agreed that they would go to Wellington's aid.

The Prussian commanders spent the rest of June 17 reorganizing their force and taking stock. Blucher sent a message to Wellington that they had been beaten at Ligny, but were now going to conduct a flanking march to the village of Wavre. Wellington would later write that Blucher's decision was "the decisive moment of the century!"

Wavre was a small village laying eight miles east of Waterloo. As Napoleon's forces advanced north towards Waterloo along the main road, the Prussians were doing the same thing to the east. Blucher was making a dangerous and bold march parallel to the French, hoping to remain undetected.

The next day, Blucher and his Prussians reached Wavre, swung left, and headed west towards Waterloo and the French flank. As Napoleon was concentrating on smashing the now isolated British lines at

Waterloo, he was surprised to see the advance guard of Blucher's army approaching in the distance on his right flank. This certainly would have given him pause. He had told his generals that it would be at least two more days before the Prussians could be ready to fight again.

To ensure the Prussians stayed out of the upcoming battle with Wellington, Napoleon had sent one of his generals, the Marquis de Grouchy, and 33,000 men in pursuit of the retreating Prussians on the previous day. His orders to Grouchy had been indecisive, though, and Grouchy had failed to make any significant contact with Blucher's army. Napoleon compounded the problem of the threat to his flank by announcing to his men that the force approaching was Grouchy's, not Blucher's.

When his soldiers, who were already wavering in the face of Wellington's stubborn defense, discovered this deceit, it nearly broke their resolve. When the famous Imperial Guard was committed and was repulsed, it was too much. The French attack collapsed.

By the end of the day, the French army was routed. The British and the remainder of the King's German Legion had stood fast on the ridge. Hougemount held on the right flank, and the Prussians drove in from the east. The stand made by Baring's mercenaries at La Haye Sainte had held the French advance long enough for the Prussians to arrive. Their courage and fighting spirit played a decisive role in defeating Napoleon's dreams of a new French empire.

Although history commonly remembers Wellington as the victorious commander of Waterloo, it must be considered a slight against Field Marshal Blucher and his Prussians that appropriate credit is rarely given them. This noble and determined German mercenary must receive equal due for the defeat of the French. Without his risky flanking maneuver against Napoleon, Wellington might very well have lost the day. Certainly, mercenaries were the decisive force on that battlefield in June 1815.

Until the 1860s, the British government also sanctioned one of the largest mercenary armies ever to exist. The military wing of the Honourable East India Company was a private organization that normally had more men-under-arms than the entire British military combined

– all paid for out of company profits. The Company even ran its own officer school in England, entirely separate from the regular army academies.

Certainly this widespread use of mercenary services made the British an enthusiastic employer of professional soldiers. In 1756, Lord Egmont addressed the issue before British Parliament:

> ... I shall never be for carrying out a war on the continent of Europe by a large body of national troops, because we can always get foreign troops to hire. This should be the adopted method in any war....

In 1854, Albert the Prince Consort suggested that the British government create a foreign legion along the lines of the recently created French Foreign Legion for service in the Crimean War. He was no doubt recollecting the loyal service rendered by the King's German Legion forty years earlier during the wars in Spain and France.

The conclusion that one can draw from these few examples is that the mercenary was an integral element of warfare on the historical battlefield. The profession of arms was one that crossed borders quite freely in ages past.

As a consequence, until the most recent decades there has never been a great impetus to regulate, or even define, the mercenary. His profession was simply an accepted extension of domestic and international policy. Countries at peace encouraged their young men to serve as mercenaries in foreign conflicts and thereby gain valuable combat experience against the day when those skills might be needed at home. Nations conducting wars would eagerly hire large numbers of foreigners to prevent great tumult in their domestic economies during times of conflict. When the wars of the 1700s and 1800s were fought with armies in excess of several hundred thousand men, few nations could afford to pull such numbers away from their home industries. In their place, foreign volunteers filled out the European ranks.

For some states, entire economies were based on the export of mercenary soldiers or even entire units. The Swiss cantons' sole export for centuries was fine mercenary troops. The various German principalities existed by hiring out their regiments and earning a bounty for each man. This readily available supply of well-trained and experienced professional soldiers was an essential ingredient in the wars carried out in Europe and abroad. It was a practice that benefited all sides equitably.

During the twentieth century, the situation did not change appreciably until the 1970s. Prior to that, foreign volunteers were an accepted norm. During World War I, Americans anxious to get involved joined either the Canadian or the French army. In the United Kingdom, nearly two hundred thousand Gurkhas were enlisted between the allied Indian army and the British Forces to serve in the trenches of France. The contest in Spain between the fascists and the royalists in the mid-1930s was largely fought with foreign help on both sides.

During World War II, the British armies were again flushed out with all manner of foreign volunteers. Entire units of foreign troops operated within the structure of the British army. The Polish Parachute Brigade is a prime example. Nominally referred to as the "Polish army in exile," these men were commanded, housed, trained, equipped, and paid for by the British government. There was also the West African Division made up of volunteers from numerous African nations – some British colonies, others not. This group was dispatched to fight the Japanese in Burma.

Among other foreign units in British service was No. 10 Inter-Allied Commando made up of volunteers from around Europe. This group even included X Troop, a small unit consisting of Germans who had fled to the western Allies. There was also a French squadron formed within the British SAS consisting of French and Belgian volunteers.

One of the most amazing organizations in the British order of battle was Popski's Private Army. Commanded by Vladimir Peniakoff, a Russian raised in Belgium and schooled in England, the group was recruited in Egypt to fight the Germans, initially targeting hit-and-run sorties against the German forces in the deserts of Northern Africa. Nicknamed "Popski" by British signalers, Peniakoff was given his own unit in 1942 by the British 8th Army and a virtually free hand in running it. Dubbed by the popular press "Popski's Private Army," it recruited all manner of characters and was more reminiscent of a modern-day pirate company than a regular military unit. The accomplishments of the PPA are legend, including being the first true Allied soldiers to reach Rome during the Italian campaign.

The Free French Forces during the war included the famous Foreign Legion, but other foreign units were also hired. Several regiments of North Africans were engaged to supplement the ranks of the homeless French army. One of these groups, the fearsome Goumiers, were turned loose during May of 1944 on the German forces behind the Gustav line in Italy who had held up the combined strength of the British and American armies for over six months. The knife-wielding Goumiers not only broke the German defenses, they penetrated so far that the German commander was forced to begin his withdrawal.

The Americans similarly hired foreign volunteers. Kachin mercenaries in Burma were hired to act as scouts and raiders in the South Pacific. The United States also engaged groups of Chittagonian Muslims to fight a guerrilla war with the Japanese in the jungles of Southeast Asia. The American government quietly looked the other way when a retired American air force officer, General Claire Lee Chennault, led a group of hastily decommissioned pilots to China to help Chiang Kai-shek defeat the communists and the Japanese. Chennault created the Flying Tigers, one of the more famous mercenary groups of the last century. After the war, Chennault went on to form CAT (Civil Air Transport), a group of mercenary pilots who flew transport aircraft into war zones to help supply their clients' war efforts. CAT supplied the French Foreign Legion at Dien Bien Phu in French Indochina and eventually evolved into the CIA-supported Air America that supplied covert operations in Vietnam.

Even the Germans created foreign units during World War II. With competition for manpower very stiff between the Wehrmacht and the Waffen SS branches of the German forces, it was a struggle for each group to meet its recruitment needs. The Wehrmacht usually won these contests, forcing the Waffen SS to look elsewhere. By the end of the war, the fighting arm of the SS became a virtual foreign legion. There were Dutch units, Norwegian units, Romanian units, and many other Europeans. When the Ukraine was "liberated," the Ukrainians' hatred for the Russians motivated nearly thirty thousand volunteers to sign up with the Waffen ss to fight their former masters.

During the 1960s, the Americans hired mercenaries from China, Laos, Korea, the Philippines, and Cambodia to fight in Vietnam. They hired mercenaries to help anti-Castro Cubans make a disastrous attack on Cuba at the Bay of Pigs. In Africa, millions of U.S. dollars went to hiring mercenaries in Angola and the Congo. In one well-known instance, the famous scene of the last American helicopter hovering over the U.S. embassy in Saigon in the final moments of the Americans' ignominious retreat from South Vietnam was not a military helicopter. It was owned and flown by mercenaries from Air America risking their lives to rescue the last Americans remaining in the communist-overrun country.

The British government of the 1960s used mercenaries to help the Royal Yemeni army defeat Egyptian-backed communists in that country's civil war in 1963–64. They also began a long-standing tradition of allowing their retired officers (and even a few serving officers) to head off and lead mercenary units, initially in Oman and Brunei. The British government would regularly consult with their known mercenaries when contracts were undertaken to ensure that the operations ran parallel with British foreign policy objectives.

As a direct consequence of this historical record, until the late 1960s there had never been any motivation internationally for defining the mercenary or even limiting his activities. The use of foreign volunteers and professionals was an accepted, if not overly emphasized, practice. The western world had relied on these services in ages past and felt no compunction about continuing in the same fashion.

The first direct clash between the mercenary profession and the world-at-large came as a direct result of Cold War politics. At the beginning of 1960, political pressure in the United Nations and on the streets of the European capitals forced the various powers to reconsider their colonial policies. In England, France, Belgium, Portugal, and Holland, maintaining direct control over their far-flung empires was difficult to justify in the face of international socialist opposition and indigenous independence movements. Very quickly, the European powers began almost tripping over each other to cast away their colonial possessions.

As noble and inevitable a gesture as this was, its execution was poorly conceived. The Europeans had maintained order in their possessions by holding political power closely and backing it up with experienced military forces. When these states were cast adrift without a well-instituted power transfer or a security apparatus sufficient to prevent civil upheaval, the result was usually violent. Sometimes within days of independence being declared civil wars erupted for control of the new state.

Another problem lay in the tribal nature of Africa. The national borders within the continent were, for the most part, drawn up in the courts and parliaments of Europe and did not reflect ethnic or cultural realities. Each nation included several major tribal groups that were often suspicious of and uncomfortable with each other. These issues had been subdued under colonial rule, but in the absence of such a controlling regime, ancient rivalries resurfaced. Because loyalty was tribal and not national, power in the post-colonial governments often reflected tribal lines as opposed to open democracy. The majority of African leaders surrounded themselves with their own tribal members and consequently inspired other tribal groups to resent the governing power. In almost every African conflict since 1960, factions have been divided along tribal lines.

In one of the first of these civil uprisings, the newly liberated Belgian Congo fractured along regional and tribal lines. With the departing Belgians handing power over to the leftist Patrice Lumumba, the resource-rich province of Katanga announced its intention to secede. Immediately, the Baluba tribe within Katanga revolted against the newly declared Katangan government. To defeat the Balubas and back up his secessionist policy, the Katangan president, Moise Tshombe, hired roughly five hundred white mercenaries. These professional soldiers began training a new Katangan army and then led them against the Baluba.

However, the Congolese government under Lumumba was loath to let the richest of its provinces slip away so easily. Lumumba began protesting loudly before the United Nations that such an action would cripple his new country economically. As a civil war erupted in the

Congo over this secession attempt, the United Nations chose to attempt its first peacekeeping mission. The U.N. sent a force of twenty thousand troops to force the Katangan province to give up its quest for independence. After three years of often bitter fighting between the mercenaries and the peacekeeping forces, Tshombe relented and went into exile.

During the entire affair, many speeches were made in the United Nations decrying Tshombe's use of mercenaries. It seemed somehow unfair that a black African politician would consider using professional soldiers from former colonial powers to fight his battles. Perhaps it was felt that white European mercenaries were more than a match for the Congolese armed forces and this move tipped the balance of the conflict in an uneven fashion. How could the fledgling "Armée Natio-nel Congolese" (ANC) defeat such forces?

In a peculiar twist common to Africa, within a week of the peace-keepers departing the Congo, Patrice Lumumba was jailed and exe-cuted for treason by his own cabinet and Moise Tshombe was invited back from exile to take control of the entire country. The reason his leadership was requested was to deal with a new armed revolt that was sweeping westwards from the Sudanese and Ugandan borders and threatening to overrun the entire nation.

The Simbas were a large collection of terrorists who considered themselves invincible under the influence of a combination of witch-craft and large doses of narcotic drugs. They were murdering, tortur-ing, and destroying everything in their path, and the ineffectual Con-golese army was unable to stop them. Once again, the newly installed Tshombe turned to mercenaries to defend his nation. Mercenaries under the redoubtable Colonel Mike Hoare and a Belgian colonel by the name of Vanderwalle managed to defeat the revolt and save the Congo in less than two years.

However, the issue was never that simple. The Congo was the first strategic card in Africa to be played in the game of Cold War politics. Over the next twenty-five years, the African continent would play a key role in the contest between the Warsaw Pact and the NATO allies. Because representative democracy was imposed by former colonial powers, the majority of new African nations were easily drawn into the communist sphere of influence. In a situation where national power and economic wealth were held by a privileged few, the average African was easily swayed by the socialist argument. "People's revolutions" sprang up everywhere on the continent.

Naturally, the Soviets and their allies saw Africa as a key element in weakening the western alliance. Despite decolonization, many European nations depended on importing raw materials from Africa and marketing exports to their former colonies. If the Eastern Bloc could secure most of Africa, it would have a serious influence on western economies. It would also give the Soviets a firm platform on NATO's southern flank.

In response to this threat, NATO constructed a giant base in the central jungles of the Congo. The Kamina base was a completely modern facility designed to house up to thirty thousand NATO troops. Complete with airfield, barracks, and storage facilities, it was designed to give the West a major staging area in Central Africa.

In this fashion, the Congo became a strategic goal for both the West and the East. The Simbas quickly accepted a contingent of Chinese military advisors. The movement's leaders were hard-core communists and welcomed the support. The West was determined to prevent a communist state from being formed in central Africa, and the CIA pumped equipment and money into Tshombe's war effort. The Soviets, despite a hatred of the Chinese, were equally determined to bring the Congo under their sway, or at the very least frustrate the West's plans. They began a program of support for the Simbas through local proxies in East Africa.

When the Simba revolt was defeated in 1965 by combined mercenary and ANC efforts, the Eastern Bloc was not pleased. Had it not been for the western mercenaries, the Congo would likely have fallen to a communist movement and provided the Russians with a strategic asset in Africa which would have included the completed and valuable Kamina base. As masters of propaganda, the communists then began a concerted effort to remove the mercenary card from the West's strategic hand.

The Simbas were portrayed in the United Nations by socialist voices as a legitimate liberation movement. Their defeat by the mercenary-backed Congolese government was vociferously condemned. On December 20, 1968 the U.N. General Assembly heard a motion that declared:

> ... the practice of using mercenaries against movements for national liberation and independence is punishable as a criminal act and that the mercenaries themselves are outlaws and calls upon the Governments of all countries to enact legislation declaring the recruitment, financing and training of mercenaries in their territory to be a punishable offence.

This was to be one of the first modern calls for the complete banishment of the mercenary globally, but specifically in Africa. The reasoning was various, but to the Africans it generally centered on the concept of residual anti-colonialism. When the Organization of African Unity (OAU) formed in 1963, it was intent on resisting attempts by former colonial masters to interfere in the affairs of independent African nations. Of course, the unwritten issue was prevention of western influence, because these were the former colonial powers. Rarely was any criticism directed at the massive military and political aid delivered by the Eastern Bloc.

In the eyes of the OAU, the difference between the two antagonists was mainly due to the propensity of the West to either condone or tacitly support mercenary operations. The idea that European or white South African professional soldiers could be used to defeat fledgling black armies was not consistent with an image of African self-sufficiency. Regardless of whether the mercenaries were supporting a repressive regime or helping to liberate an enlightened African state, these operations were a clear symbol of foreign domination and interference in postcolonial Africa.

It was this sentiment that spurred the first motions in Africa and subsequently the United Nations to eliminate what was propagandized as the "plague" of mercenarisim. In 1972, the OAU presented the "Convention for the Elimination of Mercenaries in Africa." The general thrust of the document was summed up in the preamble:

> Considering the grave threat which the activities of mercenaries rep-
> resent to the independence, sovereignty, territorial integrity and har-
> monious development of Member States of OAU ... decided to take
> all measures to eradicate from the African continent the scourge
> that the mercenary system represents.

Within the body of the document, the OAU offered one of the first
attempts to define the mercenary in international law:

> Under the present Convention a 'mercenary' is classified as anyone
> who, not a national of the state against which his actions are directed,
> is employed, enrolls or links himself willingly to a person, group or
> organization whose aim is:
> A to overthrow by force of arms or by any other means the govern-
>   ment of that member state of the Organization of African Unity;
> B to undermine the independence, territorial integrity or normal
>   working of the institutions of the said State;
> C to block by any means the activities of any liberation movement
>   recognized by the Organization of African Unity.

The language of the OAU document was clearly defensive in nature.
From an African standpoint, such a mutual defense pact was clearly a
policy aimed at reducing outside interference in OAU affairs and limiting the West's ability to topple any left-leaning African governments.

However, the document fell well short of the mark when defining
who can be considered a mercenary. There was no mention of payment for services, a hallmark of any mercenary venture. No mention
was made of whether an individual's actions must include combat
functions to fall under the definition. In the case of a civil war within a
non-member state, the OAU seems to withhold judgment as to who is
a mercenary based on whose side the OAU chooses to support. Should
the OAU choose not to support a government trying to suppress an
armed rebellion, any involvement of allies in any fashion can be considered mercenary in nature.

It was also a thinly disguised attempt to control the "Colons." The
term refers to Europeans who for generations had lived in the colonies and who had chosen to stay after independence. These people

often supported political parties or movements that favored close ties with the former colonial power. They were also almost uniformly anti-communist as well. When a communist-backed civil war broke out in their home states, they inevitably took up arms to help the pro-western governments defeat them. Therefore, the OAU had to find a way to authorize condemnation of such "European" meddling in left-ist liberation movements. Hence the last clause about interfering with any national liberation movement supported by the OAU.

The definition was first put to the test in the disaster that was the independence of Angola in 1975. On the very day the Portuguese handed over power to the Angolan people, open war broke out for control of the government. The socialist MPLA won the first battle and quickly gained control of the capitol in Luanda, but they were hotly contested by the FNLA in the north and UNITA in the south. All sides in the conflict immediately sought out foreign military expertise, regard-less of the OAU ban on such action.

The dominant MPLA quickly brought in four hundred Russian mili-tary advisors, several hundred East German intelligence experts, and a twelve-thousand-strong brigade of Cuban troops. Soviet armor and weapons were delivered, and training of the new Angolan people's army began as the MPLA hurried to consolidate its hold on power. Over the course of the next five years, the Russians would spend the equivalent of four billion dollars propping up the MPLA – this despite a secret KGB report that MPLA leader Agostino Neto was psychologically unstable.

In the south, UNITA turned to the South Africans for help. Even though UNITA was a black African movement, the South African govern-ment was willing to lend support regardless of its domestic apartheid policies. The South Africans were more concerned about a communist stronghold forming on their northern borders than about having black-African allies. The South African Defense Forces (SADF) launched an offensive in late 1975 that crossed 1,000 kilometers of Angola and came within 100 kilometers of reaching Luanda. Only the massive quanti-ties of Russian armor in MPLA hands and the support of the hardened Cuban combat troops managed to stop the South Africans.

The United States, watching its communist enemies throwing at least a division worth of foreign troops and supplies into the region, could not sit by and do nothing. However, its options were limited. It couldn't back the South Africans because of the American anti-apartheid stance. It couldn't send in its own troops and risk another defeat and embarrassment such as they had recently endured in Vietnam. Instead, the Americans picked the unknown third choice, the FNLA under Holden Roberto. In return for a promise to set up a pro-western government, the Americans supplied financing, military equipment, and CIA operatives for the war effort. They also arranged for anti-Castro mercenary pilots to supply an air force. The only condition was that Roberto could not recruit his mercenaries in America.

Instead, Roberto used the CIA money to hire a group of British mercenaries. Unfortunately, he knew little of the mercenary market and, instead of professionals, his agents recruited a large body of released criminals, misfits, and mentally disturbed men with little or no military experience. The man he put in charge of all FNLA military forces had only reached the rank of private before being dishonorably discharged from the British army. In a terrible parody of a keystone cops serial, these "mercenaries" quickly set upon one another and spent little or no time fighting the MPLA or the Cubans.

While fighting a holding action in the south against UNITA and the South Africans, the MPLA and Cuban forces quickly destroyed the FNLA and their incompetent mercenary troops. Many of the mercenaries were killed and several were taken prisoner. In a show trial broadcast around the world, thirteen American (yes, some turned up anyway) and British mercenaries were tried and convicted of murder and mercenarism as defined by the OAU conventions. Four were executed and the remaining nine were sentenced to long prison terms.

To support their convictions of the western mercenaries, an "International Commission of Inquiry into Mercenaries" was established in Luanda, Angola in June 1976. The MPLA government selected a group of left-leaning lawyers and politicians and directed them to create a legal framework in which the convictions could be justified under international law. The principal mission of the commission was to select the criteria defining a mercenary.

The result was a document which listed four separate conditions against which a potential suspect had to be measured. To find an individual "guilty" of mercenarism, he had to meet all of the criteria in each of the four categories. These were:

- He fights in a foreign country;
- He does not fight as a soldier of his own country;
- He fights for personal profit, whether or not he has some ideological motivation; and
- The purpose for which he fights is to interfere with a people's right to self-determination.

The committee, set up and run by the People's Republic of Angola, produced its report just in time to witness the executions of four mercenaries and, in doing so, justify the court's decision and the penalties imposed. The entire affair was a well-orchestrated, expertly executed plan to strengthen the MPLA position, discredit the West's interference and, with luck, end mercenary activity in the region.

This was one of the first tests of international law with respect to mercenaries. It was also an example of the conflict between Cold War powers, intent on defeating each other's designs on a de-colonized Africa. Had the U.S.-backed FNLA won, the Cuban, Russian, and East German forces would have been held up in the West as having tried to force communism on a new democratic state. With a communist MPLA victory, the FNLA's western mercenaries were targeted with having attempted to interfere in Angola's internal affairs. Using the OAU's theme, the mercenaries were chiefly condemned for their actions to "interfere with a people's right to self-determination."

The definition produced by the Angolan government's commission conveniently exonerated the extensive Russian, East German, and Cuban military involvement while condemning their opponent's choice of foreign support. The bias was so apparent that the definition was never widely accepted by the international community, especially in the West.

In response to the Angolan report, the British government organized its own commission to look into the mercenary issue. The result was the Diplock Report, which examined the involvement of Britons in foreign wars. Chaired by Lord Diplock, the commission examined the records of mercenaries in the Congo, Rhodesia, Angola, and elsewhere. These activities were then balanced against the historical penchant the British government had always displayed for mercenary services. The commissioners were most interested in the aspect of motivation. What motivated British citizens, among others, to go off to fight in foreign wars?

The commissioners decided that, based on the records, a few "mercenaries" did indeed fight in foreign wars strictly for financial gain, but this was certainly not exclusively their motive. More importantly, it seemed they confined their activities to either supporting pro-western causes or attacking openly socialist states. There are almost no examples of communist nations hiring western mercenary soldiers. The idea of paying professional soldiers a handsome wage doubtless flouted the basic tenet of communism that each individual has a duty to serve the Mother State without thought to financial compensation.

Lord Diplock's commission therefore decided, at least in the case of British citizens, that potential mercenaries were motivated by a diverse range of factors, including anti-communist sentiments, a desire for adventure, a hope for escape from the depressed British economy, and a simple wish to make something of themselves.

Certainly, years of NATO propaganda had convinced most western military veterans that communism was a scourge that must be eradicated at all costs. The very psychology that the West had carefully instilled in its fighting forces to give them the determination to fight the Warsaw Pact permeated so deeply that many ex-soldiers saw it as their duty to fight communism everywhere. Invariably, when mercenary recruiters approached potential volunteers in the West during the 1960s and '70s, the sales pitch included a speech about how they would be fighting the "evil" of communism abroad.

It would hardly have been politic for the British commissioners to discourage such a fervent belief in western democracy. In fact, from a foreign policy viewpoint, having Britons voluntarily head off to fight communism without a potentially embarrassing involvement by Her

Majesty's Government was not an entirely undesirable situation. Consequently, when the Diplock report offered its final definition of a mercenary, it specified only that: "... mercenaries can only be defined by what they do, not why they do it."

The one theme common to all of the post-colonial African wars was the almost mandatory involvement of foreign troops. In the Congo, Belgian, British, and South African mercenaries supported the Katangans. United Nations forces from Ireland, Sweden, Canada, and India fought for Lumumba. In the Simba war, the same mercenaries came back to fight for the Congolese government, while Chinese and Russian advisors supported the Simbas. In Angola, the MPLA government used Cuban, East German, and Russian support, while UNITA used South Africans and the FNLA used mercenaries. In Biafra, Guinea, Mozambique, Sudan, Ethiopia, Algeria, Chad, and virtually every other African state, no war was fought without foreign help.

In some instances, aid was supplied by foreign bodies of national troops such as the Cuban forces in Angola and Ethiopia or the British army in Kenya and Sudan. In other cases, mercenaries were used when western money was available, but not western soldiers. Regardless of the distinction, the Western powers were completely unwilling to allow either the OAU or the communist world to dictate the terms for their interventions. If mercenaries were a useful tool, then any attempt to outlaw them would have to be discredited.

The Americans embraced this idea wholeheartedly. During the late 1970s and early '80s, the U.S. government institutionalized the mercenary as a foreign policy tool. From 1979 to 1983, Colonel Oliver North ran his own private army of mercenaries for the U.S. Defense Department. Unknown to the White House, the Pentagon or even the CIA, a small group of mercenaries called the "Activity" carried out deniable operations around the world.

The "Activity" was actually the Intelligence Support Activity (ISA) and was a product of the U.S. Army's loss of faith in the CIA to provide useful intelligence in a timely fashion. One of the Activity's most famous operations occurred in 1979–80 when revolutionary Iranians overran the U.S. embassy in Tehran. The CIA's complete inability place an agent forced the

Activity into action. Dick Meadows, a retired special forces officer, was hired by the ISA to sneak into Tehran with a small team of mercenaries and provide intelligence for the planned rescue attempt. These men were the only human sources of reliable information the Pentagon had with which to plan its attack.

Later, the Activity placed agents in Grenada and Panama during those conflicts and conducted reconnaissance missions into Laos to look for American POWs. It was a typical example of a western power using professional soldiers to carry out military missions in support of foreign policy objectives. Some of the operatives were retired Americans, but many were foreign nationals.

The ISA's existence was "discovered" in 1983 when financing irregularities in the U.S. Army's special forces were investigated by Congress. With official knowledge of the ISA came an investigation into its activities. The American government decided that it was an incredibly effective tool and made it into an official agency reporting to the Defense Intelligence Agency (DIA).

The next year, 1984, the DIA prepared a report for the U.S. government looking into the official use of mercenary troops in foreign policy. Titled "Mercenary Troops in Modern Africa," it outlined the controversy surrounding mercenary forces and examined in detail how the United States should approach the use of their services. After the debacle in Angola where the U.S. threw millions of dollars into supporting Holden Roberto's incompetent mercenaries, a new set of criteria for selecting suitable groups in the future had to be established.

The organization, doctrine, tactics, leadership, and capabilities of mercenary groups were reviewed and assessed. Within the document, author Lieutenant Commander Gerry S. Thomas looks at the difficulty in defining the mercenary. Although he did not attempt to establish a clear definition, he did lay down some organization to the debate. He stated that there were five categories of individuals who, in 1984, were sometimes considered in the popular mind as mercenaries. These were:

1 Standing armies
2 Auxiliary troops
3 Partisans
4 Agents
5 Mercenaries

In Thomas's organization, standing armies are the regular bodies of national troops common to all states. They may retain a mercenary tie when bodies such as the French Foreign Legion are included in regular armies. The Legion, which is based on the concept of hiring foreign volunteers, is essentially mercenary in nature, but because it exists only within the larger framework of France's regular army, it is considered part of a standing army.

Auxiliary troops are bodies of regular national troops sent to aid a foreign power. This would include the Americans in Vietnam, the British in Kenya, the Cubans in Angola, and any other similar arrangement. Mercenary associations in this category are usually politically or ideologically motivated. Hitler's dispatch of the "Condor Legion" to support Franco in the Spanish Civil War would be a typical example of such a deployment.

Partisans are essentially groups opposed to ruling powers. They may include local citizens of the state but also may include foreign volunteers. The large numbers of ethnically linked volunteers that flowed into every side of the Balkan conflict would be an example. So, too, with the volunteers for the 1999 war in Kosovo. In 1970s Angola, the FNLA and UNITA would fall into this category after the MPLA was recognized by the OAU as the legitimate government. Foreign volunteers in such conflicts are rarely well paid and are motivated by ideology rather than more typically "mercenary" motives.

Agents are individuals sent by a foreign power to support movements within a state in conflict. During the Egyptian war with the Royalist Yemeni army in 1963, the British government sent ex-SAS legend Johnny Cooper to aid the Royalists and gather intelligence for the West. Agents can also include small teams of special forces soldiers or intelligence operators to support insurgency movements or rebel movements abroad. American special forces support to various groups

in Nicaragua, El Salvador, and Honduras during the 1980s would be
an example. The East German and Russian advisors sent to support
the MPLA in Angola would also fall into this category. Such individuals
and groups are never really mercenaries but are often accused of being
such for propaganda purposes.

Thomas's final category is the mercenary himself. His distinction in
this arrangement comes from the fact that the individual in question is
not an official representative of any foreign government and is paid for
his service. Colonel Mike Hoare's 5 Commando in the Congo would
be a prime example, according to this definition. The farcical group
hired by the FNLA in 1976 would also fit into this group.

The report goes on to specify what mercenaries are not. According
to Thomas, they cannot be:

► Members of a standing army;
► Auxiliary or seconded troops;
► Citizens or natives who conduct aggressive insurrection against their
  own nation; and
► Agents acting under orders of their government in support of insur-
  gents in a second country.

Thomas, despite a clearly western bias, made a great contribution to
the overall argument with his position paper. His initial characteriza-
tion of five categories of soldiers involved in foreign conflict begins
the process of dividing the various groups who regularly fall under
the mercenary banner into definable categories. He also attempts to
separate elements that, in the West's eyes, are legitimate bodies from
those who are more rogue in nature.

However, his report definitely suffers from a Cold War bias. Just as
the OAU's 1972 convention reflects an eastern bloc influence, Thomas
invests concepts of western ideology into his document. For the West,
the fight against communism was only partly a policy of "Mutually
Assured Destruction" (MAD). Nuclear deterrence was an appropriate
policy in Europe but had little application in Southeast Asia, Africa,
and South America. In these regions, a more conventional solution
had to be devised to repulse Soviet expansion.

Where the Russians and their allies had an advantage was in quantity of military technology. All Warsaw Pact military hardware reflected a concept of simplicity and mass production. Therefore, shipping huge quantities of arms from state-owned factories to backward revolutionaries was an easy process. Combined with communist ideology that emphasized personal sacrifice against capitalist oppressors, it was an effective foreign policy.

For the West, however, military technology was invariably high-tech, expensive, and produced in significantly smaller numbers. Western arms were built by private corporations and then sold to the various western governments in an exceptionally profitable arrangement, for the companies. Therefore, for a western government to ship large quantities of arms to their supporters around the world was not a viable option. This, combined with a political policy that emphasized personal freedom of choice and human rights, did not allow the West the same intervention alternatives as their eastern enemies enjoyed.

To counter the Soviets, then, a far different strategy had to be devised in the West. To intervene in African, Asian, and South American civil wars, a policy of covert financing and military aid was chosen. Thomas's DIA report reflects this reality. The British policy of "seconding" officers and NCOs to command the armies of friendly nations was not a mercenary venture, in Thomas's terms. Nor were special forces teams sent by the Americans to help pro-western guerillas fight communist governments. If the U.S. government hired retired soldiers from any nation and sent them to a foreign country to conduct military activities, this was not mercenary in nature.

Essentially, if a western government backed a venture, covert or not, the personnel involved could not be considered mercenaries in any way. This clause is very similar in concept to the OAU's argument that any insurrection supported by the OAU would by definition be considered a movement by the people for national liberation and self-determination.

Therefore, in Thomas's eyes, only groups that operate without any official sanction of any kind can be considered mercenaries. This means that the French Foreign Legion, the Gurkhas, the Papal Swiss Guards, Air America, and the many Canadians who volunteered for

Vietnam fall outside his parameters. Certainly, such a situation benefits mainly the West and legitimizes almost any use of foreign professional soldiers in supporting anti-communist struggles around the world.

In 1976, the Americans hired French mercenary Bob Denard to advise UNITA in Angola and teach the Angolans to use modern surface-to-air missiles against Russian-supplied jets. In Vietnam, the Americans hired Chinese Nung mercenaries to help them fight the Viet Cong and North Vietnamese army. In both cases, foreign professional soldiers were hired to fight a foreign enemy in a foreign state. By any other definition, these were mercenaries. The DIA document, although far superior to previous initiatives, definitely fell under the sway of politics and ideology.

Since the end of the Cold War in 1989, these various partisan attempts to define and regulate the mercenary have lost some of their relevance. The arguments surrounding the issue still center on left versus right politics, but the specter of communism fighting capitalism has disappeared from the equation. Now it is the liberal left versus the conservative right. In this New World Order, as the phrase goes, peace should be triumphant and old-style militarism should be dead. However, as even the casual observer of international affairs has realized, the world is a no less violent place then it was forty years ago. It is only the politics that have changed.

A perfect example of this fundamental change in global thinking occurred in 1992. In what must be the ultimate irony, Angola hired white South African mercenaries from 1992–94 to help defeat the still-fighting UNITA movement. To further add to the irony, this time the MPLA were supported by the Americans and the British. This change in policy was motivated by the huge quantities of oil and diamonds in that country that were being exploited by western companies. UNITA had become a clear threat to those interests. That such a move should come from Angola of all places bears testament to the realities of our New World Order.

Another strange post-Cold War reversal occurred recently in the Congo. This time, the West supported a coalition under the unknown Laurent Kabila in his attempt to overthrow the Mobutu government that the West had helped install in the 1960s. When the Congolese government hired French and Serbian mercenaries to defeat this insurrection, as they had done with American support in previous decades, Mobutu was widely criticized.

There can be no doubt in this instance that Mobutu had become a despotic tyrant who suppressed his people and resisted any attempt at a change in government. However, he was clearly non-communist and pro-West in his foreign policy. Under the New World Order, though, he had to go. What makes this case so unusual is that, for probably the first time, the capitalist right and the liberal left both condemned the use of mercenaries in an open fashion. Of course, the motivations of each group were quite different. For the right, the Congo represented huge natural resources that had remained under-exploited under Mobutu. For the left, the dictator definitely suppressed his people's rights to self-determination.

While all of this was going on, the United Nations had not been idle in the debate surrounding mercenaries. In 1989, the General Assembly produced the International Convention against the Recruitment, Use, Financing, and Training of Mercenaries. This document has never been widely accepted. It suffered from the same generalities and ideological bias as its predecessors. As of 1997, only eleven countries had become signatories to the convention.

To look into this issue in more detail, the U.N. appointed a Peruvian, Enriques Bernales Ballesteros, as a special rapporteur on the subject of mercenaries. Throughout the 1990s, Ballesteros examined this topic and produced periodic reports for the General Assembly and the U.N. Commission for Human Rights.

Unfortunately, the special rapporteur has contributed far more to the confusion surrounding the issue than he has toward a solution. From the outset, Ballesteros never made any attempt to define his subject matter. Instead, he chose to accept the 1949 Geneva Conventions definition of the mercenary, which he himself admits, in his 1997 report, is completely insufficient. Consequently, all of his subsequent research efforts suffered from the diverse personal and ideological opinions of his contributors as to what constitutes a mercenary.

This problem was clearly evident in his 1996 report to the Commission on Human Rights. To gather information for this document, Ballesteros sent out a questionnaire to the member states of the United Nations. In it he posed seven questions which I will summarize here. He asked them for:

1 Information relating to the possible existence of mercenaries in their territories;
2 Information relating to the possible activities of mercenaries in another country which interfere with that people's right to self-determination;
3 Information relating to mercenaries in their territory or elsewhere who are associated with terrorist attacks, drug/arms trafficking, and smuggling which impair the enjoyment of human rights by that population;
4 Information on the existence of mercenaries in another country who are used to impair the sovereignty of a third state or sub-region and interfere with rights to self-determination;
5 Information on domestic legislation to outlaw mercenaries;
6 Their position on the 1989 Convention; and
7 Suggestions that might be useful in eradicating mercenary activity.

The response to these questions was predictably political. Cuba made a positive reply, citing American support for groups of anti-Castro Cubans in Florida who continued to pose a threat. Chad explained how they had suffered from the predations of Libyan-backed mercenaries for years. The most motivated response came from Belgrade and the Federal Republic of Yugoslavia. The Serbs were highly concerned about the large numbers of Islamic fighters who had been arriving from around the Muslim world to aid their religious peers in Bosnia. Naturally, Belgrade saw this as an undesirable interference in its internal affairs by outside influences.

From these replies, Ballesteros prepared a document that highlighted the somewhat tired line that mercenaries were active around the world suppressing peoples' rights to self-determination. What went largely unsaid in the document was that, in the three cases I have mentioned, the groups in question are poor candidates for inclusion in any definition of mercenaries. Anti-Castro Cubans have existed for decades and generally support themselves through their own devices. Although no friend of Castro's, the U.S. government stopped financing these groups after the Bay of Pigs in 1962.

Chad, while complaining about Libyan interference, has been defended by the French Foreign Legion since the 1970s. As for the Serbian government in Belgrade, interfering with a people's rights to self-determination is their stock-in-trade. As well, there has never been any evidence presented that the Islamic extremists active in Bosnia were ever well paid for their services.

In summary, because he did not clearly define what constitutes a mercenary for the purposes of his research, Ballesteros's results were largely politically colored and not particularly helpful. The remainder of the 1996 report was even more perplexing. In paragraph 34, the special rapporteur suggests that:

> To prevent mercenary activities, States should consider, inter alia, the possibility of withdrawing the operating licenses and permits of entities that have hired mercenaries to engage in illegal activities, refusing to issue passports and visas to mercenaries, prohibiting them from passing through the territory of other states, declaring illegal and closing down associations and organizations that under various guises freely promote and offer training and contracts to mercenaries, etc.

The implication of this recommendation is that the basic human rights and freedoms of individuals accused of involvement with mercenaries should be suspended. All without ever offering direction as to who legally qualifies as a mercenary. That such a suggestion should come from a representative of the United Nations is deeply alarming.

In 1997, Ballesteros released a second report. Once again, in conducting his research a questionnaire was circulated to the member nations for perusal and reply. This time around, an additional question was included, asking for:

> (g) Information and views on the existence of security service, consultancy and military training companies offering their services to

Governments in order to intervene in internal armed conflicts with the assistance of mercenarized military professionals, for the purpose of improving the military effectiveness of government forces, in exchange for cash benefits and shares in the country's investments and economic ventures.

This particular request and the subsequent comments were the primary focus of the 1997 report. This question was obviously aimed at exploring the activities of the soon-to-be-dissolved Executive Outcomes and Sandline International, among others. The responses to the 1997 question were similar to those reflected in the previous report. Colombia denied any knowledge of mercenary activities. Cuba elaborated on its anti-Castro problems. Finland responded that it was reviewing the appropriateness of the 1989 Convention against mercenaries.

The remainder of the document read basically as an incrimination of any state that would surrender some or any of its responsibility for defense to a private company. Ballesteros seems to consider the idea of retaining military consultants to either improve military capability or advise on strategy as an abdication of control over internal conflict. Although I applaud him for directing his attention to this subject, because it is essentially the topic of this book, I find his stance on the subject peculiar and contradictory.

In his 1996 report, Ballesteros considered the greatest threat posed by mercenaries to be their penchant for interfering with a people's right to self-determination. In the 1997 document, however, he attempts to suggest to sovereign nations how they should conduct their internal affairs. Using Sierra Leone as an example, he suggests that the first democratically elected government that the country had ever seen was foolish to rely on South African mercenaries to provide interim national security while a new infrastructure was created.

If one accepts that a democratically elected government is the voice of a people, Ballesteros takes on quite a task in suggesting how they should conduct their internal affairs. I would think this is clearly a form of interfering with the Sierra Leonean people's right to self-determination. Whether or not the use of Executive Outcomes by the

Kabbah government was a wise choice, it really is their own affair.

If EO had been accused of murder, rape, torture or other human rights abuses, then certainly it should have been held to account for such actions, along with the Kabbah government. However, no such accusations were made in the U.N. report or elsewhere. In fact, other than the reality that EO consisted of military professionals who received pay for their work, the report makes no real case for why such groups should be the object of condemnation.

In Sierra Leone I spoke to some of the United Nations staff and many members of the more prestigious international aid organizations. While I can't name names because my sources would probably be drawn and quartered by their peers, each lamented the departure of the mercenaries. One individual who held an important role told me:

"If you could bring back EO or find another battalion of mercenaries, this war would be over in a week. Then we could finally help these people. As it is we sit around here [the hotel bar] while people are starving everywhere." Another aid worker I talked to mirrored his feelings of frustration.

"When EO got here, I was standing on the street and they had a parade! An actual parade through the streets. Here are all these white South Africans driving through the streets and everyone is cheering. As far as the Sierra Leoneans were concerned, these guys were their saviors. When EO left, it was a tragedy, a real disaster."

The one aspect of the 1997 report with which I firmly agree is Ballesteros's suggestion that a properly mandated commission needs to be set up to consider this entire issue. Such a commission needs to first define the mercenary, then attempt to remove the stigma surrounding some groups while targeting others, and, finally, deal with the issue of legislation and regulation. My one fear with such a commission, though, is the selection of its constituent members. If the historical record of such commissions is taken into account, the commissioners will probably be chosen so that a "suitable" set of recommendations is produced. This will then only have the affect of sending the global community into another decade or two of confusion and indecision.

This brings us into the twenty-first century. After forty years of attempting to come to terms with the issue of mercenaries, the world has not made any significant progress. Mercenarism still remains an emotional issue and one without clear definitions. From the early socialist-backed attempts in the Organization of African Unity through to the more recent confusion within the United Nations, the topic has defied solution.

Therefore, in a somewhat daring move, I am going to attempt to define the mercenary. I will do this for several reasons. Obviously the first is personal. Despite my recent near brush with the trade, I do not appreciate being labeled a mercenary and do not accept such a title. The second reason for attempting a definition is related to the larger issue of this book. If I am to examine the issue of international security from a private-sector standpoint, I must be able to differentiate military advisors from security consultants from terrorists. I have to be able to draw a line that clearly shows when a private security firm crosses the line and becomes a mercenary company.

The next reason is a matter of international law. Because mercenaries tend to enjoy some official status, especially with their home governments, they are very often repatriated and released after they have found themselves on the losing side in a war. This legitimacy as combatants has been seriously abused by criminal elements around the world. Right-wing paramilitaries, terrorists, religious extremists, and other unsavory criminal characters often claim mercenary status to avoid incarceration in countries where they have committed crimes. A prime example of this can be found in the large numbers of terrorist groups that have plagued various regions in the former Republic of Yugoslavia. Having committed rapes, tortured civilians, and supported ethnic cleansing activities, many of these individuals could only be expelled by the Balkan governments after capture rather than facing their crimes in a domestic court.

It must also be made clear that very few of these individuals pretending to be mercenaries were professional soldiers. Most were convicted criminals, the mentally disturbed or religious fundamentalists. In his 1996 book *War Dogs,* Keith Cory-Jones follows a group of these characters to Bosnia and records their activities. His tale highlights the worst type of self-described "mercenaries" who are essentially roving bandits who enjoy no official sanction. By defining the mercenary clearly, these illegal elements will be stripped of their ability to masquerade as professional soldiers.

The final reason for such an ambitious attempt is related to the profession of arms. It is my belief that there are some very noble men and women who have served their country in uniform and have gone on to equally noble activities in the mercenary field. Count Carl Gustav von Rosen, the Swedish hero and Biafran adventurer; Colonel David Stirling, founder of the SAS and loyal British patriot; others such as Johnny Cooper, Dick Meadows, Ron Reid Daly, and Mike Hoare equally deserve to be well remembered. To recall these men as no better than petty terrorists and murderers demeans the profession of arms as a whole.

In creating a definition, I offer my credentials. I am now employed in the international security field. I have been a NATO cold warrior, but I have also served shoulder-to-shoulder with former Warsaw Pact soldiers as a United Nations peacekeeper. I have even served under the command of a Russian paratrooper. I have worked in Africa and have seen the horrors of civil war with my own eyes. I have been involved in projects that, at some point, have clearly crossed the line between acceptable security services and outright mercenary adventures, and I have drawn a moral line accordingly. These are my qualifications. So, with a courageous heart, I step forward.

To begin, I have taken a page from Lieutenant Commander Gerry Thomas and organized the mercenary industry into five categories of activity. This is a perfect first step because many of the states that object to attempts at banning or regulating mercenaries have national interests to protect. The French with their Legion, the British and Nepalese with the Gurkhas. Even the Roman Catholic Church and their Swiss Guards. By clearly separating such respectable organizations from the less respectable categories, any future attempt to regulate or ban the trade can see its target more clearly and win more support in doing so.

I have taken Thomas's original five categories and updated them, removing the Cold War bias and adding the privatization of the indus-

try to the equation. I have also changed some of the terminology to
better reflect a more modern situation. There are the five categories,
including a brief explanation of each with examples:

1 *Regular Foreign Units.* These are long-serving regular formations that
   exist integrally within a larger national military structure. They are
   volunteer in nature and are primarily foreign in composition. Examples would be the French Foreign Legion, the Gurkhas, and the Swiss
   Guards.

2 *Auxiliary Foreign Units.* This category would include formations created
   for a specific duration that would recruit foreigners for military service.
   Units would typically be formed during a conflict and then disbanded
   on an end to hostilities. A critical element with this category is that
   the unit must be formed as integral to the national military structure
   and be subordinate to the founding national government. Examples
   would be the King's German Legion (Britain, 1780s–1820s); the Polish Parachute Brigade, the (British) West African Division, the Kachin
   Rangers, and the Flying Tigers (all during World War II); and more
   recently 5 Commando (the Congo), Katangese veterans in Angolan
   service, and the Chinese Nungs in American service during the war in
   Vietnam.

3 *Private Military Companies* (PMCS). These are privately run mercenary
   organizations that conduct combat or combat support operations. They
   are officially unaligned, although they may prefer to serve in a particular geographic or ideological arena. They can provide front-line combat troops, but normally they supply technical expertise or professional
   advice. In a historical sense, these would be the specialist groups of
   archers, for example, in medieval Europe who were hired for their special skills and experience. In a modern sense, they are the commanders,
   shock troops, pilots, logistics experts, planners, and the specialists of the
   modern military companies. Examples would be the Italian condottieri,
   the Honourable East India Company, Chennault's post-World War II
   CAT (Civilian Air Transport), David Stirling's Watchguard, Keeni-Meeny
   Services, Sandline International, and the former Executive Outcomes.

4 *Foreign Volunteers.* This category would consist of foreign soldiers who
   are not formed specifically into foreign units but are incorporated

into regular national formations. Their mercenary status would derive strictly from the fact that they are serving in a foreign army. One vital factor is that they must receive pay and recompense to do so. This group would include some members of both the historical and the modern British army whose ranks even now contain a significant number of foreigners (mostly from Commonwealth countries), the Israeli army, the Rhodesian army of the 1970s, and the American army of the Vietnam era. This category would also include individuals seconded to foreign armies, such as British officers in the Sultanates of Oman and Brunei.

5   *Freebooters.* In this category we would find the really objectionable elements of the mercenary trade. This group would include any individual or faction that operated strictly to achieve its own ends. Where all the above categories work only for recognized governments (with the possible but unlikely exception of PMCs), this would be the group who would serve drug smugglers, terrorist groups, and other illegal clients. It would also include elements that conduct military-style operations for their own personal gain, such as Frenchman Bob Denard's obsession with the Comoros Islands. It would also include many of the small groups of foreign "mercenaries" operating in a freelance fashion in the former Yugoslavia. It would include the random groups of Libyan and Ukrainian fighters who have been active in Sierra Leone's diamond regions on behalf of the rebels. Basically, individuals or groups who were not officially contracted to or under the command of an internationally recognized government would be considered freebooters.

Having selected these five categories, I have replaced Thomas's sections on partisans and agents. Partisans, in my view, are either the rebellious citizens of a region in conflict or altruistic volunteers who do not fight as paid professionals. As for agents, this term normally refers to intelligence operatives, who I consider to be outside the mandate of the mercenary. Spies do not fight. They are not directly linked to combat or combat support operations and as such cannot be considered mercenaries. As for teams of special forces sent by major powers to regions of conflict, these are national soldiers of a regular army and therefore do not fit under the mercenary banner. Whether their use is legal, justifiable or proper is an argument for others to consider.

Likewise, Thomas's "auxiliary troops" are regular soldiers of national armies sent to support allies in need. There is really no basis here to consider such groups as mercenaries. Considering the modern propensity for coalition warfare internationally, such a category has no real significance in the twenty-first century.

Now that the larger topic has been broken down into manageable chunks, it can be seen readily that some mercenaries are "legitimate" military organizations, such as the Regular Foreign Units. Others, such as the PMCs, bear close supervision. Finally, the Freebooters can be clearly held up as illegal and easily condemned.

However, all we have done is provide five categories into which individuals or groups can be placed for reference. There still remains the very real problem of identifying the mercenary in the first place. What separates an altruistic volunteer from mercenary Foreign Volunteers? What separates a civilian advising a foreign government on military matters from a PMC consultant? To complete a definition of the mercenary, the concept of military activity must be examined carefully.

The first issue that has to be dealt with is the question of mercenary services. With the sole exception of the Ballesteros report, all attempts to define the mercenary have accepted as a common platform that the mercenary is a soldier. His duties are those of a combat soldier. This includes activities such as logistics and the supply of combat support. Combat support can mean everything from piloting of military aircraft to providing ground maintenance for such aircraft or other high-tech equipment. Basically, mercenary services can be any duty typically assigned to a regular national soldier up to and including combat. This is the first clause in the identification of a mercenary.

This issue of tying the mercenary to the regular soldier is critical in terms of creating a legal definition. One of the few internationally accepted legal documents with regard to identifying soldiers is the Geneva Conventions of 1949. Within these conventions is a protocol that allows the international body to separate "legal" combatants in a conflict from illegal and criminal elements. The separation of the two groups is essential to determining who is guaranteed protection and rights under the Geneva Conventions and who is not.

Essentially, the dividing factor is the uniform. Any soldier who operates in the recognized uniform of his nation is entitled to protection under the Geneva Conventions. This article even applies to guerilla movements who wear a common identifying article of clothing such as a colored scarf or an unusual headdress. If a soldier operates without his uniform, or in an enemy's uniform, he is no longer protected as a legal combatant and has no rights under the Conventions.

This, in effect, is the legal definition of who is a soldier and who is not. Using such an article as a precedent, the mercenary can then be tied to the function of a soldier by a similar condition. To be accepted as a mercenary in a legal sense, a potential candidate must operate in a recognizable uniform. This can be either the uniform of his employer's state or a uniform specific to a recognized body of mercenary troops. For the Regular Foreign Unit, the Auxiliary Foreign Unit, and the Foreign Volunteer categories, this is already the accepted practice. These groups, integral to regular national armies, wear the uniform of their employing state. As such, these units still retain a status as soldiers with the International Red Cross. There is a possible exception with the Auxiliary Foreign Unit, but that is usually dealt with on a case-by-case basis.

The PMCs can also be fitted easily into this condition. Despite a wide freedom of choice as to personal preference in combat clothing, all modern free companies do wear uniforms. In Angola and Sierra Leone, EO personnel wore a variety of camouflage uniforms, but each was recognizable as a soldier. In Papua New Guinea, Sandline's contract with the government specified that both the national army and any applicable civil agencies would be required to both recognize and respond appropriately to the mercenary rank structure.

For the Freebooters, this clause is immaterial. Since the object of these conditions is to distinguish clearly the true mercenary from an armed international terrorist such as Bob Denard, the wearing of a uniform is irrelevant. Several of the following conditions will clarify this point.

The third condition that must be applied in defining the mercenary is the matter of pay. In his Report, Lord Diplock offered that payment for services was usually a motivation, but not exclusively so. In his 1997 report, Ballesteros suggests that "altruistic volunteers" must be ruled out as mercenaries. Certainly the many groups of Islamic volunteers who were active in Bosnia or Kosovo in 1999 cannot realistically be called mercenaries. Therefore, to separate the mercenary from the simple volunteer, the question of pay must be considered.

It is my contention that the mercenary is either a professional soldier or one who wishes to become a professional soldier. Regardless of his motivation, he chooses the profession of arms to earn a living. In this respect, to be considered a professional, he must receive suitable remuneration for his services. Such a clause in the definition would separate the "altruistic volunteer" from the ranks of the mercenary. Within the categories I have outlined, all five can and do receive pay or reward in return for, or as a result of, their activities.

The fourth condition in the definition would deal with the question of nationality. In every colloquial expression of the term "mercenary," it is accepted that the person in question is either a foreigner in domestic service or is serving in a foreign land. In many of the official attempts at a definition, this clause appears as well. The one exception to this rule is Ballesteros, who in his 1996 report suggests that individuals who commit crimes in their own nation but are paid to do so by a foreign state are mercenaries. I find such a description difficult to justify. Traitors, saboteurs, spies or terrorists perhaps, but not mercenaries.

Therefore, under my proposed definition, the candidate cannot be employed in his own state of birth or naturalization, regardless of changes in government in that state. Therefore, the French partisans in occupied France during World War II cannot be considered to have been mercenaries, even if they were supplied and financed by the British. The homeless Kurds in northern Iraq who were trained and supplied by U.S. special forces in 1994 cannot be considered mercenaries. Similarly, neither should the Palestinians of the West Bank, the Contras in Nicaragua nor the Afghan mujahidin in Russian-occupied Afghanistan.

The fifth condition in the definition concerns activities, or as Lord Diplock put it, "what he does, not why he does it." In every war zone or area of instability there will invariably be large numbers of foreigners looking to profit from the conflict. Arms dealers, combat "journalists," foreign intelligence operatives, political advisors, ideological extremists, terrorists, altruistic volunteers, corporate raiders, NGOS, and a wide assortment of others can be counted upon to show up.

If the mercenary is to be linked with the profession of the soldier (condition one), then his primary activity must be either combat or combat support. To clarify, combat support is any type of function that is essential to operating an army and is routinely conducted by regular soldiers. This could include functions such as command and control, communications, reconnaissance, intelligence, fire support, logistics, maintenance, transport, combat engineering, military police duties, and medical support.

Therefore under this heading, pilots who carry soldiers or drop supplies, naval vessels that move military personnel or equipment, or foreign advisors to combat headquarters can be considered candidates for mercenary status.

The sixth condition would be that the candidate must be engaged by an internationally recognized nation, or in the event of a civil war, a legitimate entity that is supported by a significant portion of the populace and has been officially recognized by at least one international government. This is where the five categories of mercenary service come into force in a significant way. The first four categories are all normally employed by the governments for which they serve. The Regular Foreign Unit, Auxiliary Foreign Unit, and the Foreign Volunteer all serve exclusively within the framework of a national army. The PMC is normally only employed by a government client because of the considerable expense of its operations.

The final condition I would impose for defining the mercenary is an ethical consideration, rather than a practical one. Because a mercenary is a professional soldier, he should be held to accepting and conducting himself according to the Laws of War, the Geneva Conventions and the International Declaration of Human Rights and Freedoms. Should an individual meet all of the other conditions laid out here but conduct himself in a fashion illegal under international law, then he should not be granted any special protection as a combatant in a foreign conflict. Carrying the label of mercenary has never historically been a license to operate outside either domestic or international law. This situation should not be allowed to change either in the present or in the future.

So this is the definition that I offer. The occupation of mercenary covers four legitimate categories of combatants who can and should be recognized as mercenary forces. Terrorists, drug smugglers, arms merchants, and international armed criminals are clearly distinguished from the concept of the mercenary by identifying the category of "Freebooter." Within the four legitimate categories, there are seven conditions that also must be met to discern the true mercenary from the legions of security companies, consultants, intelligence agents, and criminals often associated with this term.

To review, then, here is the complete definition. The four legitimate, acceptable categories of mercenary are:

1   Regular Foreign Unit;
2   Auxiliary Foreign Unit;
3   Foreign Volunteer; and
4   Private Military Company.

The seven conditions are:

1   That the occupation of mercenary must be directly linked with the occupation of soldier;
2   That the candidate must operate in either a uniform common to a body of mercenary troops or in the recognized uniform of the client state's armed forces, including insignias of rank and unit;
3   That the candidate must be paid for his services;
4   That the candidate must conduct his operations in a nation other than that of his birth or naturalization regardless of changes in government to the home state;
5   That the candidate must take a direct role in either the conduct of combat operations or in supplying combat support (as listed above);
6   That the candidate must be engaged by: (a) an internationally recog-

nized nation; or (b) in the event of a civil dispute, by a legitimate interim government that represents a significant portion of the population and has been recognized by a minimum of one foreign nation;

7 That the candidate must be seen to recognize and conduct himself by the Laws of War, the Geneva Conventions and the International Declaration of Human Rights and Freedoms.

Having been placed into one of these four categories and meeting all of the seven conditions, the candidate can then be classed as a mercenary, in my view. Should the candidate fail to meet any of the seven conditions but continue to conduct armed acts of aggression in a foreign state, he can be considered a Freebooter and an armed international criminal.

So that is the definition. Using these criteria, the international observer, military analyst, journalist, and political lobbyist can now make an informed decision on who can qualify as a mercenary. Should such august bodies as the United Nations or the OAU ever accept such a definition as feasible, it would support their investigations of the mercenary issue by finally establishing clear parameters. For the armed criminal or terrorist, it would eliminate any claims to legitimacy as an ideological or religious combatant.

The definition would achieve these aims in one very clear fashion. In three of the acceptable categories, the mercenary is a full-fledged member of a national army. He is in either a regular foreign unit or an auxiliary foreign unit or is an individual foreign volunteer in a regular unit. All three are directly commanded and supported by a national government or an interim government with clear international support. The fourth category, the PMC, is a licensed and registered business. It is subject to the regulations and controls of its home country and the host country in which it operates. In this fashion, the terrorists, drug smugglers, arms merchants, and armed criminals of this world can be decisively denied any legitimizing claims.

Where this definition becomes really interesting is in the category of the PMCs. The regular and auxiliary units, along with the foreign volunteers, are fairly acceptable groups that have been widely written about to date. Quite a bit of information is available about these categories from other sources. The one group that has begun to dominate the world's mind in the past few years, and about which very little is understood, is the Private Military Company.

The recent trend toward the privatization of international security has become a central focus for media essays and strategic think tanks around the world. The fact that a private company such as the former Executive Outcomes could achieve peace in record time in two African conflicts, when all attempts by the international community and the United Nations had failed, is an explosive issue.

That the PMCS are shaking the foundations of current thinking on international security is a given. However, now we have also identified that there are other elements of the international security industry, outside of the Military Combat Services, that are having a growing impact as well. The Security Services and Military Security Services are far more numerous and, as we shall see in subsequent chapters, are actually having a far greater influence on world affairs.

However, in looking at security companies and military consultancies, we can now differentiate between who works in what field and what services they should be offering. We can also look at those groups that seem to walk the line between mercenaries and other security professionals; an important first step in unraveling the mystery that is the shadow profession.

4

THE SECURITY SERVICES

IN MID-1998, I received another call from Alan Bell concerning an international project. It had been roughly one year since I had last been involved with Globe Risk during the ill-fated Sierra Leone project, and I was looking forward to another challenge. This time, there would be no mercenary overtones and the contract would be a straightforward security project.

This task was going to take place in a southern European country, bordering the Mediterranean. For reasons of client confidentiality and the personal safety of those involved, I can't disclose the exact location. This project is still underway and many of the security issues involved are still present. As you read on, you will understand the situation better.

This time, the client was a well-established North American mining company whose international reputation was of the highest caliber. The previous year this firm, which I shall call the ABC Mining Company, discovered an amazingly profitable gold opportunity on the site of an old mining project. Using new processing techniques, ABC Mining could smelt down raw ore to produce gold at well under US$200 an ounce.

Unfortunately, nothing was going to be that easy. The first obstacle that ABC ran into was a small group of "entrepreneurs" who recognized an opportunity. During the late 1990s there was a spate of major international mining projects that went astray based on a simple ploy. When a major mining house announced a new project in which it was going to invest millions of dollars, it became inevitable that some individual or other small mining company would contest title to the property.

The method was simple and ingenious. An out-of-luck mining house or opportunistic individual would dig up some former landholder or a relative of a deceased landholder and "buy" from them a decades-old agreement between the landholder and the first exploration company to have come through the region years before. Armed with such a document, the enterprising group would then make a legal challenge to the major mining house's clear claim to the property.

The mining house then had two choices: either pay off the annoying challengers and "buy" the rights back; or give the challengers a percentage of the overall project. On more than one occasion courts ordered the major to surrender as much as twenty percent of the title to the challengers.

ABC was now faced with the same problem. A small group had filed a petition in the national court claiming ownership of the property based on an outdated agreement from years previous. However, the identity of these individuals was never clear. They filed the petition under an offshore numbered company and provided few details about themselves.

ABC Mining turned to Globe Risk to investigate this group to find out who they were and any other information that would be pertinent to the upcoming legal battle. Globe Risk accepted the project and produced a report several weeks later. However, that was only the beginning of the security problems ABC was facing.

Within days of taking possession of the property pending the outcome of the courts, ABC came under attack from what appeared to be a local group of protestors. Soon, violent demonstrations were breaking out and ABC staff were even shot at by masked men armed with automatic weapons. Equipment was sabotaged and employees assaulted. Once again, Globe Risk was asked to investigate the problem.

Alan Bell and a small team from Globe Risk flew to the region several days later and conducted a security audit of the mine and its environs. They also spent a great deal of time researching the history of the area. What they found was some real evidence as to the nature of the problem.

Historically, this country had been wavering between socialism and democracy. Some regions were even openly communist. As it happens, the region surrounding the mine was of the latter category. The local politicians were becoming increasingly loud in their complaints about "rich foreign capitalists coming in to rape their land and steal their jobs."

While the ideology was easy to understand, the motivation was not. The area was horribly depressed economically; without the mine, the local economy was dead. The national government had no interest in developing the properties, and no local mining companies had the high-tech know-how to make the mine profitable. Surely, even a communist could see the logic in letting a big western company invest millions in their constituency? No, there was something else at work here.

After returning from the U.S. and some high-level meetings with the client, Bell received authorization to investigate further. He also got the company to agree to begin creating a crisis management capability. In the event of more attacks, the company needed to have plans in place to protect their people, their equipment, and their investment. Our firm was tasked to provide a consultant to develop those plans.

As part of this process, Globe Risk was to design a security program for the mine. A security guard force consisting of locals would be hired, and then Globe Risk would set up a training program to make sure they could handle the challenges ahead.

To implement this program, Bell brought in four consultants, myself included. The first consultant was to investigate the local opposition. The second was tasked with developing a crisis management plan and setting up the company's security program. The final two consultants were then to be deployed to train the security guard force. While I was first offered the crisis-and-security-planning task, I chose the training assignment. As a former sergeant in 3 Commando, training was what I knew best and enjoyed the most.

Before I could do my job, however, the other two consultants were going to have to do their part. The individual tasked with investigating the local opposition was "Mike L." After much thought, Mike decided to try to penetrate the opposition group using a cover story and discover what was going on from the inside.

Calling himself an independent journalist, Mike began a correspondence with the well-known members of the local community. He forwarded copies of articles he had written that were very sympathetic to the local cause. Soon enough, he was invited by the leaders of the opposition groups to travel to the area and see for himself the damage the "capitalists" were doing.

Mike flew to the region and began by conducting his reconnaissance. He rented a small apartment in a town near the area, but not too near. He also rented a car for emergencies and parked it at a garage in a village halfway between his apartment and the area. Then he rented a second car of a completely different model and drove to the town in question to meet his sponsors.

Over the next few weeks, he was slowly brought into the inner confidences of the opposition groups. He was shown bunkers full of automatic weapons and explosives and told that they would be used if ABC ever tried to start mining in their backyards. He listened to long-winded exhortations on the evils of western capitalism and drank to the success of the revolution.

One night, at about midnight, Mike was awakened by a knock on his door. He was immediately suspicious as this had not happened before. At the time he was staying in a little apartment belonging to the local mayor. Every few days, he drove out of town "to look around" and would travel to where his second vehicle was located. Parking a distance away, he would take a cab to the stashed car and would then spend the next couple of hours driving around to ensure he wasn't being followed. When he was satisfied he was safe, he would go to the safe house and report on his activities and results.

When the knock came, his first thought was that somehow his cover had been blown.

When Mike opened the door, his suspicions only got worse. Standing in the hallway was a group of three big bruisers who acted as the local mayor's muscle. They told him quite brusquely to get dressed; they were going for a ride.

While trying to remain outwardly calm, Mike was trying to figure out if there was any chance he had been found out. With no clear answer, Mike decided to play along and see what was up. Maybe it was just a test?

Pushed into the back of a car, Mike had no choice but to join his silent companions as they raced down the dark streets and out of town. Soon they were winding up a small dirt road into the mountains. With every mile, Mike was getting more and more worried.

"I was definitely starting to sweat," Mike told us later. "I thought, okay this is it, I'm finished."

"They drove me up onto the top of this mountain and it was pitch black – there was nothing there. The driver pulled over and then the two guys in the front got out. The guy in the back with me held my arm, so that I couldn't move. I must have looked pretty upset and they were getting off on it.

"Then the door opened and I was motioned out. I immediately thought, 'Okay, here we go,' and began looking around for some way of escaping. About twenty feet away was a wall of brush that led down the side of the mountain. I figured that at the first sign of trouble, I was going to make a run for it and dive through that stuff. There might be a cliff, but hopefully not.

"The next thing I know, I'm being shoved out into this orchard. Then out of the dark I hear this voice…

"'Ah, Mike, Mike, come here!'

"Turns out it's the mayor, stinking drunk. He is waving and calling me over. He's gotten plastered and wanted me to see this spot where his valiant countrymen had fought the Germans back during the war. Some hero statue or something… I never noticed, I was just so relieved that I wasn't going to get a bullet in the back of the head that I don't remember a word he said."

Mike came back to Canada soon after that incident where he reported to Bell and then was taken to see the clients. After detailing his activities and what he had found out, Mike delivered the real piece of intelligence. After assessing the whole situation, it appeared that the local opposition groups were only pawns in a larger game. Someone else was pulling the strings, issuing the orders, and paying for the whole intimidation campaign. Whoever it was seemed to have elements in the federal government and the local police in their back pocket because there seemed to be a lot of official resistance to probing too deep.

As security people with international experience, we immediately
recognized the classic cell structure of a terrorist organization. A "cell"
system is a method used by groups like the Irish Republican Army or
the Hezbollah to prevent security forces from ever catching an entire
organization. Each cell only knows its own local members. Direction
from the next-higher level in the organization comes by mail or letter
drop. No one ever knows who the next level is. They won't even know
who is in the next cell working in the same area. If the security forces
catch one cell, the rest of the organization is warned and can disappear
for a while. The captured group can't finger the next group because
they don't know who they are.

Mike was convinced, as were the rest of us from Globe Risk, that we
were looking at a well-organized cell system, and that upped the ante
significantly. Mike was asked to go back and see if he could penetrate
the next level of the organization. Despite the risk, Mike agreed.

While the details of the story could fill their own book, in the end
Mike was successful.

What he found was that the next level was a group of local businessmen who were pursuing a grand plan to get control of the mine, but
only after ABC Mining had spent nearly $10 million to renovate it. Mike
was wined and dined on yachts in the Mediterranean, surrounded by
prostitutes, and treated as a co-conspirator. The head of this group
bragged that the local mayor was his tool and, when the time was right,
he would unleash him on ABC. When ABC finally began looking for
a way out of the mess awaiting them, this group of "concerned local
citizens" was going to step in to take control.

While Mike was busy with his investigation, "John C." was busy
working out the crisis management and security plans for ABC. If
another attack did take place, John was to make sure that no one got
hurt. One thing that he was really concerned about was the tailings
ponds. These are artificial ponds where water used during the ore-
extraction process is pumped. The problem is that these waters are
highly contaminated and potentially lethal to the local environment.

In 1998, a broken dyke at a tailings pond in Spain spilled thousands
of gallons of contaminated effluent onto the local farmlands, killing

the plants, poisoning the soil, and causing health problems for local residents. In ABC's case, the tailings ponds sat at the head of a wide valley that led down to a coastal village. If the ponds' containment were breached, the effluent would flow right into the town and the ocean.

Were the local opposition groups capable of ruining their own homes to protest the company? Probably not, but the businessmen pulling the strings probably were. In fact, it would be an ideal move. It would cause international embarrassment to ABC and truly enrage any locals who were wavering in their opposition of the mine. The local government would penalize ABC, and it might very well be the deciding stroke in the game plan. John's job was both to try to prevent this crime and to come up with a workable plan of action in the event it did occur.

Later, I deployed to the region with another consultant and trained the newly hired guard force in their duties. The training focused on preparing the guards to address the issues John was covering in his master response plan. I spent two months there training, and it was a challenging and rewarding project for me.

ABC was quite worried that the shadowy group of businessmen challenging the company for title to the property in court might turn out to be either the same as the local businessmen preparing the terror campaign against their project or others allied with them. Globe Risk carried out further investigations and discovered no apparent link.

In the end, after nearly a year of hard work and no few dangers, Globe Risk completed its work and left the area. We had helped ABC prepare a "hearts-and-minds" campaign with the local population to win their support. We had used some political leverage the company had to let the local businessmen know that ABC was on to them (without letting anyone know how). John and I had put together a good security-and-crisis-management capability to deal with any future trouble.

All in all, it was a good project. The cost? While that is confidential, I can say it was less than US$200,000. Compared to the $10 million the company was investing or the potential lives lost and ecological damage that could have been caused, I think it was a small investment.

This is a perfect example of the types of work in which the shadow professionals of security consulting firms can be involved. Using their knowledge and skills built up over long careers in western military units, Globe Risk's consultants were able to use those skills to have a profound impact on an international business project. In this case, Globe Risk was able to take on activities that at first glance probably should have been the responsibility of local police forces but were not being properly addressed. We filled the void between potential disaster and law enforcement.

Actually, the last point brings up an important factor concerning the private security industry. Almost all international security consultants are ex-military, not law enforcement. There are very few former police officers who succeed in this line of work. The reason? It has a lot to do with the different job descriptions and the psychology involved in each trade.

First, police forces are domestic in nature. Very few have an international portfolio. Being a ten-year veteran of the Atlanta police department does not develop the skills and experience necessary to deal with guerrilla armies in central Africa. That is not to say that such an individual could not adapt to that environment, but the security companies hiring consultants prefer someone with an existing international portfolio.

Military units, on the other hand, are international by design. Every western army spends a great deal of time and effort sending its troops far and wide around the world to gain experience. Most soldiers are trained in intelligence gathering, survival skills, strategic thinking, and security techniques. Combine this with peacekeeping experience that puts a premium on security functions and low-level negotiations, and you produce the perfect candidate to be an international security consultant.

The different psychology of police versus military is important as well. Police forces are reactive in nature. While they try to discourage crime by their presence, they normally do not become involved until after a crime or incident has occurred. Security personnel, on the other hand, need to be proactive. It is their mandate to prevent crimes or incidents before they happen. This is their primary value, especially in regions where law enforcement is not particularly efficient to begin with.

Alan Bell puts it this way:

"We do not employ retired police officers in Globe Risk. The reason we don't isn't out of some petty jealousy between military and police veterans over who is better qualified. In reality, the whole psychology of police people is defensive.... They have a stringent set of laws, or rules, to work from, and when a rule is broken, they are authorized to respond. They can't act until a law is broken.

"Military people, on the other hand, are proactive from day one. Everything in the army is about outguessing the other guy and getting there first, or hitting before your opponent is ready. Surprise is your ally and deterrence is more than half your job.

"That difference in psychology between military and police mind-sets makes military people the better choice. That's why we don't hire former cops."

Bell's opinion is widely shared within the rest of the international security industry. In talking to many of the other international security consulting firms during the course of business or while researching this book, I have come across few former police officers. That is not to say that they are not out there. In fact, there are quite a few trying to break into the market, but to date they are not having much success.

A key illustration of this is a company known as Protection Concepts out of Calgary, Alberta, Canada. "Procon," as it is known, is the brainchild of a former member of the Royal Canadian Mounted Police (RCMP). The remaining members of the company are former members of the Calgary city police force. This group realized that there was a dynamic market in Calgary that was not being served: the many large petroleum companies that had started out drilling in Canada and had in recent years expanded onto the global scene.

Together, this group of retired law enforcement officers set up Procon to provide security consulting to companies active in Africa, South America, and Asia. However, they quickly realized that they were operating way out of their depth. A decade of service on the streets of western Canada had not prepared them for the terrorist-filled oilfields of Algeria or the jungles of Colombia.

Glenn Reierson, a vice-president of Procon, admits: "We realized pretty quickly that we needed some help. So we have been using military guys on a lot of the away jobs. We have an ex-JTF [Joint Task Force 11, Canada's counter-terrorist unit] guy who does most of our overseas work."

Another company that has built an impressive international reputation using primarily ex-military personnel is the Control Risks Group (CRG) of London, England. Created in 1975, CRG is probably the best example of an international security consultancy. Its website claims that it has served more than 3,500 clients in seventy-five different countries. I spoke with Christopher Grouse about his company and its market in mid-1999.

Located a short walk from Buckingham Palace in London, Control Risks is ensconced in offices in two unassuming buildings on Victoria Street. On one side of the bustling English thoroughfare are the corporate offices and their operational departments. There is no sign, no logo. In fact, if you weren't invited, you would never gain access to their offices.

Across the street and down a side alley is a glass-and-steel door with an intercom built into the brick wall. Upon buzzing the intercom, you are greeted by a secretary's voice that asks you to state your business. If you have an appointment, you will be buzzed in and can ascend a set of stairs with a sharp left angle into the secretary's lobby area. Upon passing muster with the secretary, you are shown to the Control Risks offices down the hallway. Here is a small series of conference rooms where clients are met and discussions held.

Christopher Grouse is one of the founding members of the firm. A former tank officer with the British army, Grouse retired in 1977 after thirteen years in uniform to join the Control Risks team. Back then, Control Risks was still struggling to establish itself in a new and poorly understood market. The other team members were military officers as well.

"Yes, we started out as a group of former soldiers and it remained that way for a long time," he explained. "I served for over a decade before I started wondering if there wasn't a better opportunity out there for a former military man."

Control Risks got its big break from none other than that icon of the insurance industry, Lloyds of London. Back in the 1970s, Lloyds decided to take on a new form of high-risk insurance, the type of business that has made that company so successful. This time, it offered Kidnap & Ransom (K&R) insurance to anyone who felt he or she was a likely target. The premiums were high, but many corporations and wealthy individuals who possessed great wealth in assets but not cash found the opportunity worth it.

However, after the first few incidents, Lloyds realized that forking over millions of dollars in ransoms was likely to prove bad for business. It needed to hedge its bets somewhat. To accomplish this, it instituted two conditions on each policy. The first is that the existence of the policy must be totally confidential. Public knowledge of a policy might encourage kidnappers. If confidentiality were broached, the policy would become void.

The second condition is that, in the event of a kidnapping, Lloyds would be represented by a highly trained consultant who would ensure that ransoms were not agreed to too easily and amounts would be negotiated as far down as was possible. To fill this role, Lloyds turned to Control Risks. After a contract was negotiated, Control Risks consultants were written in to every K&R policy Lloyds wrote. This agreement has continued until this day. With numerous kidnappings occurring every year, it has proven a lucrative market for the company.

"That was a big part of business," Grouse told me, "but we have grown way beyond that point now. We're much more focused on more business-related activities such as international investigation, crisis management planning, and security consulting."

According to Grouse, the company has evolved into an entirely new animal. Where once Control Risks was a collection of ex-soldiers providing security advice, now their offices are filled with young, eager university grads who work as information analysts. The bulk of the company's business is now handled by these non-military, non-law-enforcement types.

The Control Risks model is now much more directed at providing business intelligence to clients. Teams of analysts search the Internet,

the media, and other reports and collate them into information sum-
maries that are then sold to clients. The only military personnel left on
the team are the few original plank-owners such as Grouse.

"It is a new business now," he said. "I'm one of the few left."

That is not to say that Control Risks does not still hire ex-soldiers on
short-term contracts.

When a kidnapping occurs or a security audit needs to be done, the
company still maintains a large database of ex-soldiers who can be hired
to conduct the groundwork. That part has not changed. But in the British market, there's a plethora of ex-special forces soldiers on "the circuit"
waiting for contracts to come up. Control Risks no longer needs to have
these resources on staff; they can hire them at competitive rates for
small projects and then send these individuals back to the circuit.

I would like at this point to discuss how Control Risks might conduct a kidnap and ransom project. I could give you a true situation that
has occurred recently – there are many examples of which I am aware
– but if I were to name names or companies, their policies would be
voided. So instead, I will describe a fictional situation that is based on
an actual event. The details are fairly well known to me because, at
the time of this incident, the company involved was Canadian and the
Canadian Security and Intelligence Service (CSIS) had actually recommended that the corporation in question contact Globe Risk for advice
on how to handle the kidnapping of its employee.

The event occurred in a South American country. A Canadian natu-
ral-resource worker was driving down a country road in a pickup truck
when his vehicle was stopped by a group of armed masked men. The
Canadian was dragged out, had his hands bound, and was marched off
into the jungle. Another company employee later found the vehicle
and called the local police.

By the end of the day, the company back in Canada had been
informed that one of its employees was missing. As of yet, there was
no information that suggested a kidnapping; it could be just a random
crime. However, because kidnapping was endemic to this region there
was a pretty high probability.

Over the next two weeks the company waited for news. Company reps flew down to the region, the local police investigated and turned up nothing, and there was generally an increasing sense of doom.

Finally, a priest from a local mission in the area received a note. Members of the Peoples Revolutionary Army (PRA) had delivered to him a handwritten note saying that they had the Canadian and demands would follow. The company breathed a sigh of relief; at least their man wasn't dead and they could probably get him back safe. They had K&R insurance, after all. They placed a call to the insurance company informing it of the situation.

The insurance company immediately informed a security company, and the response plan was initiated. The security company, which had already been following the situation anyway, had a consultant on standby, and he was dispatched to the country in question within hours.

On arrival at the kidnap victim's company headquarters in the region, the consultant briefed the local manager and a corporate vice-president flown down to the region to oversee the ransom payment. He told them that there would be no ransom payment – not anytime soon, anyway.

The consultant explained the facts surrounding kidnappings and ransom payments. The first thing to be done was to establish who actually was holding the victim. It is quite common to have one group kidnap a victim and, while the first group is on the run in the jungle, another group claims responsibility. The second group negotiates a ransom, is paid, and then disappears, leaving the company broke and without their victim returned.

The second condition to be met was to establish proof of life. Once the kidnappers identified themselves, the consultant had to establish that the victim was still alive. This process would be ongoing. At every stage in the days ahead, the kidnappers would have to prove to the consultant that the victim was still alive or negotiations would be called off.

The final condition was that whatever ransom the kidnappers demanded, it would be refused. If ransoms are paid too easily, kidnappers are often encouraged to try for more. Instead, ransoms must be negotiated. On average, ransoms paid are less than fifty percent of the original demand. Kidnappers know this and will always begin with an extremely high first demand. Naturally, since the consultant was representing the insurance company, not the natural resources company, negotiating the lowest payout possible was part of his job.

Finally, the consultant explained that everyone might as well go home. This process takes weeks at a minimum – often months. He explained that this is a business transaction. It might go quickly, but that would only be suspicious. The longer the deal is negotiated, the better the deal.

Over the next weeks, notes are delivered and responded to through the village priest. The consultant is relaxed. He is in no hurry. When this project is over, he is unemployed again. For now, he is earning up to US$8,000 a month and staying in a nice hotel in the tropics. The longer this goes on, the better for him.

Back in Canada, the spouse of the kidnap victim is going crazy. The company won't tell her anything. She knows her husband has been kidnapped and the company is negotiating, but it won't let her have any of the details. Of course, the company can't, because it would void the insurance policy if its existence were disclosed. Finally, the wife has had enough and calls the local news station. She tells her story that her husband has been kidnapped and neither the company, the police, nor the Canadian government will tell her anything. Suddenly, the company is swarmed by the media and finds itself in deep trouble because it has no crisis communications policy to handle this event. The situation grows worse when shareholders discover that all operations in the region have halted due to the crisis, and suddenly share prices start to fall. Pressure increases for the company to explain the situation, what it is doing to resolve it, and when the victim is expected to be released.

The problem continues to worsen when the Canadian government informs the company that, unfortunately, the country where the kidnap has taken place has a law preventing ransoms from being paid to kidnappers. It is part of that country's efforts to halt the plague this crime represents. Therefore, any settlement would be illegal, and thus the Canadian government can't get involved.

Meanwhile, the consultant continues to send messages back and forth. A real problem occurs when the kidnappers demand large quantities of U.S. bills in small denominations. The problem is that neither the local government, the local banks, nor the U.S. Treasury like large amounts of small-denomination bills traveling with private citizens. In most countries, traveling with more than $10,000 can get you arrested. Also, since paying the ransom is technically illegal, having the local government agree to the plan is not likely. Negotiations continue.

Finally, after nearly three months, a price is agreed upon. The money is to be a combination of local currency and some U.S. bills. The ransom will be delivered to the priest, who will relay it to the kidnappers. Directions on how to recover the victim will follow. The money is quietly assembled over the course of the next two weeks using a combination of couriers and creative banking arrangements that the consultant has organized. The money is handed over to the priest.

After receiving the ransom, the rebels march the victim down to a nearby cart track and tell him which way to walk. Then they disappear into the jungle. The victim, dehydrated and weak from dysentery, manages to walk several miles before collapsing on the side of the road. Fortunately, he is found by a farmer and taken to the nearest village. Unconscious, it takes several days before he is well enough to explain who he is. Then word goes out and the consultant travels to the remote village and collects the victim. He is taken to the capital city and quickly flown out of the country on a chartered plane. Remember, everyone involved has now broken the law. While the government of the country in question knows full well what has just transpired, it can only look the other way for so long. The victim spends the next week in a hospital in a neighboring country. The local Canadian embassy must arrange for a new passport to allow the victim to travel, and the seriousness of the situation places a delay of several days on the processing of the document. As soon as everything can be arranged, he's put on a plane and returned to his family.

In the coming weeks he files a lawsuit against the company for the suffering he and his family endured – especially after he discovers that the company had Kidnap & Ransom insurance and he can't understand why the ransom wasn't paid after the first couple of days.

The consultant flies home after spending a week relaxing in a nearby resort to find himself back on the circuit and wondering when the next call will come. The natural resource company continues to suffer low stock prices and employee complaints from the staff remaining in the country who want protection, and it is forced to make an expensive out-of-court settlement with the victim.

The insurance company bills the natural resource company for the consultant at US$10,000 a month for four months and then ups the premium on the policy.

While no two kidnappings are alike, the above example gives a fair account of what goes on behind the scenes. There are essentially five elements involved: the victim, the company, the insurance company, the kidnappers, and the security consultant. The key player in the entire affair is the security consultant. He is the expert on how best to resolve the crisis so that all parties have the greatest chance of survival. This includes the insurance company, which could not pay out every ransom at full value and expect to be in business very long.

The consultant is also the victim's best, and sometimes only, chance at surviving the ordeal. If the consultant has the moral courage to negotiate hard and continually demand proof of life, it forces the kidnappers to keep their victim alive. They will realize they are dealing with a professional, and it keeps them honest. During these crimes, many participants react from the strong emotions and desperation they feel. The company, the victim, and his family just want it over and everyone home safe. The kidnappers are always afraid that they will be caught and either killed or imprisoned. In the midst of this sea of fear, confusion, and anger the security consultant must remain in control.

Another common activity for security service companies is in providing close protection. In North America, normally only government and media personalities retain bodyguards on a full-time basis, but in the rest of world, they are quite common. In the Middle East, South America, Africa, and Asia having a professional VIP security detail is not only a wise precaution but is de rigueur for the wealthy and powerful.

Many of my acquaintances in the international security services community spend a great deal of their time on close protection assignments. Donna, my partner in Vancouver, is one of the industry's most professional bodyguards. She has worked in the Middle East, in Ireland, on the European continent, in Washington and New York, and in many other areas. She has protected royalty on the slopes of Switzerland and looked after diplomats in war zones. As a woman, she is often not considered as a bodyguard and consequently can be more successful than her male counterparts.

Many clients don't want big, burly ex-paratroopers following them around. They especially don't want these individuals beside them in the corporate business environment. Donna, on the other hand, can pass as an executive secretary, a business consultant or any other business professional. She has on more than one occasion been thought of as a call girl.

"Sometimes I have to follow the client into these men-only clubs for the rich and powerful. I sit at the bar and watch what is going on. Everyone in the room knows I came with my client, but most think I'm some hired escort or something," she explains. "I don't mind, but I do get a lot of propositions from doddering old farts who are looking for some fun."

Dan, another security consultant with whom I have worked, has had equally strange experiences.

"I recently finished this project for a Saudi Prince," he told me. "I was looking after his family and usually ended up with the nine-year-old daughter. I didn't mind because I have two daughters of my own and it was pretty easy work. We would go to movies, play video games, and eat ice cream.

"The week before the project ended, I bought the daughter a little figurine from Harrods' as a gift. She was a great kid and I had a lot of fun on that job. She was pretty thrilled by it and thanked me in the strangest way."

Dan and I were sitting in the lobby of the International Hotel in London when he told me the rest of this story. I was in London on business and he had called me and told me the story up to that point over the phone. Then he told me he could only tell me what the "thank you" was in person. So off I trekked down to the hotel to meet him. Here he smiled and finished the tale.

"Okay, here's what happened," he said, as my curiosity was clearly piqued. "On the last night before the job was up, I get invited to dinner with the whole family. The Prince is there, his wife, everybody ... but I am the only guy from the team." There were ten other men on the team with Dan, and he had the least seniority.

"So I'm sitting there feeling pretty uncomfortable when the daughter announces she has a gift for me. She pulls out this little case and hands it over. Inside is a silver Rolex. On the face of the Rolex is the Saudi Royal Family crest and on the back it is numbered. I was totally choked!

"But then she says that this is only the small present! Then the whole family gets up and leads me outside the restaurant. Sitting there in front is a brand new Porsche 930 twin turbo. The daughter says, 'I remember you telling me how much you liked sports cars, so I asked my mother if I could buy you one. Do you like it?'"

Dan just sat there smiling at me as he tells me the story. I recall a long pregnant pause while I waited for him to tell me the punch line. I had to draw it out of him, as he was quite content to just sit there and let me hang.

"So, what happened?" I demanded.

"Well the Prince turns around to me and asks me, 'Where do you want it delivered?'"

To be perfectly honest, I have to say that Dan's story is not typical. I don't recommend rushing out and becoming a bodyguard so you can get free Porsches from your clients. In fact, being a bodyguard is probably the least glamorous and most difficult job a security consultant can do.

In most cases, the hours are long and unpleasant. If you're alone with the client during the day, there is no break for lunch or supper. If he eats, you have to watch him. If he wants to work late, you have to stay with him. If he wants to go out to the clubs or the opera, you have to stay alert. You can't even go to the bathroom unless he goes.

Most clients other than the very rich won't pay for a full team. Instead they hire one or two bodyguards. That means that the team is on twenty-four hours a day. One is on duty at the residence and the other is with the client. Rest means only having to do the administrative functions for the team. You have to stay well dressed and keep your suits pressed and clean. You need to exercise to work out the inevitable kinks that come from standing still for hours a day. Invoices need to be paid; electronic searches need to be done. Vehicles need to be fueled and washed daily. All the while, the client breezes through his day knowing his bodyguards are looking after him.

For the most part, it is tiring, demanding work. Your status is one of a servant, and that is often grating for former soldiers who have commanded men and braved dangers. Dan's experience is the exception, not the norm.

Another issue to understand is that, unlike the Hollywood image of bodyguards, in real life these men and women do not carry arsenals of handguns and machine pistols. Very few countries allow private citizens to carry concealed firearms, and even fewer are pleased when a bodyguard mows down civilians.

Neither Dan nor Donna has ever carried a firearm while working as a bodyguard. While they were in the military, yes, but not as civilians. Dan was a member of the SAS and had done VIP details as a soldier where he carried weapons, but not anymore.

"The trick now is to use our brains, not our guns," Donna says. "We tell the client where to go, what to do when he gets there, and what poses too great a risk. If we have to travel, we hire local armed guards who are licensed in that country. If any shooting goes on, it's them pulling the trigger, not us."

When I was protecting Saxena in Vancouver in 1997, there was a real threat from the Thais. We could very well have been facing an armed hit team. Donna and I briefly considered placing shotguns on every level of the house and one at the office, but we changed our minds. Facing years in court and possibly jail for killing a group of local teenage thieves who broke into the wrong house was not worth it. Instead we came up with a series of plans for what we would do in case of an attack.

Therefore, the task of the close protection specialist is not a Hollywood-style guns, glory, and hero job; it is hard work, strategy, planning, and drawing upon your experience to ensure you and your client avoid trouble before anything happens, not afterward.

As soldiers, Dan and Donna were among the best in their fields. Dan had conducted covert operations in Africa and the Balkans. Donna fought terrorists on the streets of Northern Ireland. Both are shadow professionals now who are putting that experience to use in the private sector. However, neither provides military service to military clients. They don't even use weapons any longer. Their tools are their experience, training, and unshakable self-confidence. They are both perfect examples of Security Services professionals.

Why is their type of experience so critical? Another security consultant I know conducted a project that demonstrates this requirement quite clearly.

I will refer to this individual as "Steve W." Steve is another ex-member of the SAS and has been working in the security services field for the last ten years. In 1998, Steve was retained by a client to conduct a consulting project in Congo-Brazzaville. The region had just experienced a bloody civil war that was easily the equal of the nightmare that gripped its neighbor, the Democratic Republic of the Congo (formerly Zaire). The client had a major mining project in the Congo and had been forced to flee during the fighting. Now the owners wanted to know if the government was going to honor its licenses.

Steve was asked if he would go to the Congo and find out who was in charge and who the power brokers were. If he was successful, the plan was for a team of lawyers to fly in and meet these officials and confirm the old deal or negotiate a new one. The problem was that the country was still in nearly a full state of war. The "Ninja," "Cobra," and "Cocoye" militias roamed the streets, shooting anything that took their fancy. It was certainly going to be dangerous, but: "That's what I get paid for," Steve likes to say.

Steve flew into the Congo three days later and found himself a hotel in Pointe Noir. There was still a small European community there and some semblance of order. Over the next couple of days, Steve met with several local officials who were willing to introduce him to the new mining minister ... in return for a new Land Rover or first class tickets to Paris.

"I told them that I was just a consultant. I had no authority to do any such thing. However, I agreed to tell my client that these guys were most helpful and when the contracts were signed, there would be a reward in it for them, " Steve told me. "Actually, I had no authority to offer any such thing, but such is Africa."

While waiting for a meeting to be arranged, Steve needed to get out into the hills and have a look at the concession area. After several days of waiting for official permission, Steve finally just rented a taxi and had the Congolese driver run him out into the countryside. He timed his trip into the war zone for early morning. Most of the local soldiers were passed out in a drunken slumber at six AM and the risk was minimal.

"I had been watching the local troops. They were drunk by mid-afternoon each day. Every night, they had roamed around looting and shooting in the air until about four in the morning. Then you didn't see any sign of them until noon. That is when all the locals got their business for the day done and then hid indoors."

After a successful recce of the property, Steve sat around for another week waiting for the chance to speak to the mining minister. One day, he was having lunch in an outdoor cafe frequented by westerners when an incident occurred close by.

"A gang of youths were walking along the far side of the street. They stop in front of this store and pull out bricks and smash the windows. Quick as lightning they're in the store looting it.

"Sitting a couple of tables away is this Congolese colonel. He gets up from his lunch, walks across the street and catches this teenager coming out of the store with his arms full of stuff. The colonel pulls out a pistol and shoots the guy right in the temple!

"All the Europeans in the restaurant with me just stop what they are doing to watch ... like it was on TV or something. Here is this kid lying in the street with his brains blown out and these people just think it's entertainment.

"I immediately threw some francs down on the table and started walking down the street. The hairs on the back of my neck were standing up. I just had the feeling that things were about to happen. Sure enough, I don't get three hundred feet when a bunch of the kid's friends come

running out from somewhere and start spraying the cafe with automatic
gunfire. I turned the corner and headed straight back to my hotel room.
The firing went on for nearly an hour. Later, soldiers are going around
the neighborhood beating people up, torching buildings, and shooting
anyone they think was involved in the whole affair. I just stayed in my
room with the lights out.

"Two days later, I got lifted by the local police. They showed up at
my hotel room and dragged me down to the local police station. I was
interrogated for about six hours. They already knew my name, who I
worked for, and how long I had been in the country. They wanted to
know what the "real" reason I had come to the Congo was. I figured
that French Intelligence had tipped them off. The French government
had a big influence there and was suspicious of any Anglo westerners.
They probably wanted to know what I was up to.

"When I got back to my hotel room, a message was waiting for me
to meet a local government official that afternoon. It turns out that
this guy is the new minister for oil and gas. The area where the mine
is going to be is in his riding. When I told him my clients wanted to
spend about a billion dollars in development, the guy was all smiles.
The very next day we were on a flight to Brazzaville to meet the mining minister.

"We flew into Brazzaville and it was a mess. As the plane landed
there was this horde of people waiting to get out. At the time, there
was only one flight in the morning and one at night. A Land Rover was
waiting to pick us up and it turns out it belongs to the new minister of
defense. Everyone is saluting as we go by.

"Eventually, we get to the presidential palace and it is in a terrible
state. Bullet holes and shell casings everywhere. I grabbed a couple
of shells and stuffed them in my pocket. I wanted to know where the
locals were getting their supplies. We went up into the palace and sat
down in this big foyer with about fifty other white guys. These guys
were all French and, all day, they keep getting called to go in to see the
mining minister. I ended up waiting all day. The plane out was at 5 PM
and I didn't want to miss it. Here I was dressed in a suit and there were
definitely no hotels in Brazzaville at that time. There was no way a

white guy in a suit was going to survive the night there.

"Eventually, it's 4:30 and I finally get dragged in to see someone. Turns out to be the vice-president. He asks me what I want and I tell him: I'm here to find out if the new government is going to honor my client's licenses.

"The Vice-President says, 'Une moment...' and walks out. Next, he returns and tells me to follow him. Next thing I know, I'm in the offices of the new president. Again, I'm asked what I want. When I explain, the president says something and an aide rushes out. Five minutes later he is back with some documents. The president stamps them and hands them over. What he's given me are the new ordinances signed and approved! Then he asks me if there is anything else. I tell him that it's five o'clock and I'm about to miss the plane out. He gets on the phone and then tells me the plane will wait.

"Five minutes later, I'm back in the defense minister's jeep and we're racing through the streets for the airport. The plane was waiting and I got the last seat out.

"The next day, I'm going to fly out and I'm walking through the airport. Armed guards are everywhere with AKs and FNs. As I'm heading for the security check, I suddenly remember I've got a pocket full of bullets! I pretend to kneel down to tie my shoelace and while I'm doing that, I slip the shells out of my pocket and put them down at my feet. One of the buggers starts rolling across the tile floor and every guard in the place turns to look. Suddenly, I'm hauled behind this big curtain and strip searched while an AK is jammed in my nose.

"Finally, I'm let go and get on my plane out. What a trip! That was the first time a client has met me at the airport. When I called him and told him I had his ordinances signed by the president, he was blown away. The moment I was off the plane, there he was. I thought he was going to hug me."

Steve's experience highlights the dangers that often face security professionals abroad. The only school in the world that provides the type of training one needs to survive in these environments, while accomplishing a job, is the military. One of the critical survival skills the military can give you is that sixth sense for your environment. I can personally recall times in my military service when I would be out on patrol or just driving along in a jeep and suddenly would get a very strong sense that something was not right. Sure enough, just around the bend would be an ambush or, in Yugoslavia, some drunken Croats with a machine-gun.

Feeling your way through situations like the one Steve encountered in the Congo is a matter of being able to assess risks and judge when a particular risk is worth taking. Or, knowing from experience what the consequences of certain actions are. It is not something that can be easily taught; it is just one of the by-products of a long and active military career.

Another peculiar feeling that comes from such projects is the sense of nakedness that accompanies consulting work. While in the military, we all carry weapons, knives, bayonets, grenades, and radios for calling in support. As a master of the weapons in your hands, you don't feel invincible, but you do feel you have at least some ability to influence events around you. There is also the confidence that behind you is a whole army of support that will come running if you get in trouble. As a security consultant, however, when you step off that plane in some war zone, you have no weapons, no back up, and only your wits and experience to see you through.

In essence, that is the value of the shadow professional. In the role of a security services consultant, all of the skills and experience built up over a career in uniform make for a flexible and effective tool. A tool that is not only trained to kill, fight, and destroy, but a precision instrument that can save lives, protect properties and investments, and advise clients in how to safely go about their affairs.

5

THE MILITARY
SECURITY SERVICES

FOR THE RETIRING military veteran looking to get involved in the international security industry, one of the first choices he must make is whether he is going to join the circuit of all the other ex-soldiers out there looking for contracts, or is he going to form his own company? The next question he should ask himself is what area of the industry he wants to get involved in. Does he want to become a security consultant? Perhaps he wants to train counter-terrorist units for Third World countries. Maybe he even wants to become a mercenary.

Whatever choices he makes will probably force him into one stream or another of the industry for the rest of his career in the shadow profession. If he chooses the security services sector, it is very competitive, but it is a growing market. If he chooses the military security service world, that is fine as well, but he cuts himself off from the security services market. Most of the major security services companies like Control Risks or KPMG will not hire anyone who has just returned from training a crack special forces unit in the Congo.

If he chooses the military combat services market and becomes a mercenary, he may be able to slip into the occasional military security contract, but only if the company hiring him isn't too choosy. The better military security companies like Defense Systems Limited or MPRI won't touch a mercenary.

One individual who faced this choice was Alistair Morrison of the SAS. His military career and subsequent move into the shadow profession set the standard for military security companies in the early 1980s.

Major Alistair Morrison became famous in 1977 when the SAS sent him to join the German counter-terrorist unit GSG9 for the storming of a hijacked passenger airliner in Mogadishu, Somalia. In October of that year, four Palestinian terrorists hijacked a Lufthansa passenger jet and demanded the release of several members of Germany's Baader-Meinhoff gang from prison and US$20 million in exchange for releasing their hostages. Germany, unwilling to give in to the terrorists, sent their counter-terrorist commandos, GSG9, to arrange a rescue.

The unit's commander, Colonel Ulrich Wegener, first went to London to ask for any assistance that might be available in terms of expertise, equipment, and political support. Since it appeared that the rescue would happen in an African country (unless the hijackers forced the Lufthansa crew to move the airliner elsewhere), Britain was well positioned to influence regional governments to let the Germans conduct an armed assault. The British agreed to help and sent Major Alistair Morrison and Sergeant Barry Davies, both of the SAS, to join GSG9. Morrison brought along a goody bag of SAS tricks, including the newly invented "flash-bang" concussion grenades to try out.

After the hijacked plane landed at the airport in Mogadishu a hostage was executed and dumped on the tarmac. This forced GSG9 into action and, with the two SAS men tossing the flash-bangs to disorient the terrorists, the commandos stormed the plane. Eight minutes later it was all over, with three of the four terrorists dead and four hostages slightly wounded.

In the years following the rescue, Morrison spent a great deal of his time singing the praises of GSG9 and Ulrich Wegener. He encouraged cross-training between the German unit and his own SAS, the Americans of Delta Force, and other similar units around the world. It was these efforts that brought him to the attention of the giant German arms manufacturer Hechler & Koch (H&K). At the time, H&K was producing a line of submachine guns known generally as the MP-5. This was a very reliable 9-mm weapon with several variants that was quickly becoming the weapon of choice for counter-terrorist units around the world. H&K wanted to hire Morrison away from the British army and use him to help market the MP-5 line and various other weapons systems.

Eventually, Morrison relented and retired from the SAS. His decision to join H&K was conditional on one other factor. He wanted to bring in another British soldier, Patrick Grayson, formerly of the Irish Guards. Together, these two spent several years working for H&K, marketing the company's products around the world. Eventually though, the desire to strike out on their own took them out of H&K and into the private security industry.

However, the decision facing the pair was what area of the market to target. David Stirling had retired by this point and Watchguard had departed the scene with him. In its place another company had popped up, registered in the Channel Islands. The creation of retired SAS Colonel David Walker, Keeni-Meeny Services (KMS) took on the projects that David Stirling was unwilling to accept. Even the name chosen for the company, "keeni-meeny" is Swahili for "slithering snake," became an apt description for the firm's activities. KMS took private-sector international security to a far more aggressive level.

It was David Walker's intention to put together an agency that would supply ex-SAS soldiers to clients around the world. This time, there would be very little concern for the political niceties of the contracts. KMS basically became a mercenary supply service sending professional soldiers around the globe to help clients fight communist insurrections, train special forces units and conduct intelligence missions. In some cases, the company would accept the contract and run the operations, or it would simply provide a recruiting service if the project was seen as a little too dodgy. In the latter case, KMS would make the introductions and then allow the individual men to make up their own minds as to whether or not to take the contract. Except for those in the industry, very people knew about KMS. The company definitely chose to cloak its actions in secrecy.

There were other companies in existence at the same time, some even less reputable than KMS. The shameless self-promoter John Banks still ran Security Advisory Services, despite the chaos and tragedy he created in Angola in the late 1970s. Like KMS, Banks's company was a mercenary supply agency for clients who weren't particular about the quality of the people they hired.

After looking at the market, Morrison and Grayson decided that, when Stirling departed, much of the credibility of the British industry had gone with him. Her Majesty's Government might just be looking for a company that provided quality service but steered clear of mercenary work and the political ramifications that went with it. To this end, they recruited ex-SAS Sergeant-Major David Abbot, and together the three formed Defense Systems Limited (DSL).

"Actually, I was the one who thought of the name," Grayson explained to me in his London offices. "Alistair was the famous one ... but that was fine with me."

DSL's corporate profile included providing military skills to clients up to, but not including, mercenary work. They would train, equip or advise, but not fight. KMS had that market, and they were welcome to it. After forming the company and setting up their offices, the three entrepreneurs sat down to wait for the phone to start ringing. However, even Morrison's reputation wasn't enough to land the first contract.

"After some long weeks of waiting, we finally got our first job. However, it wasn't the one we had really planned on," said Grayson with a smile.

While having a beer in a London pub one night, Grayson met a movie special effects man who was working on a new movie out at Pinewood Studios. The movie was about an SAS operation to infiltrate a terrorist group that was planning to force the British government to detonate a nuclear weapon in Scotland. Several weeks after the conversation, Grayson got a call from his new friend at Pinewood.

"It seems their stuntmen were refusing to rappel from the helicopters with a rope bag. Since this is how the SAS actually did rappel at the time, they felt they needed to do it this way to get the realism the director wanted."

Grayson was asked if he could put together a group of ex-SAS soldiers to film the dramatic final sequence in which SAS soldiers storm an embassy to rescue a group of important hostages. So, in a rather tongue-in-cheek fashion, Defense Systems Limited was launched onto the international security market as they rappelled out of helicopters before the movie cameras. The result was the 1984 movie *The Final Option*.

Soon afterwards, DSL won its first true security contract with their former employers, H&K. Morrison, Grayson, and Abbot were contracted to provide training teams to instruct counter-terrorist units in the Middle East in the use of H&K weapons systems. From there, the firm won another contract to train Dubai's U-Force in all facets of counter-terrorist and special forces work.

This experience in the Arab world led to their first big western contract as well. The United States government hired DSL to review its embassy's security arrangements in Bahrain. After examining the facility, Morrison and Grayson came up with an entirely new concept in diplomatic security. According to Grayson:

"Like most embassies, the Americans had two levels of security. They had the building itself with Marine Corps guards controlling access. Then they had the second ring of security, which was the wall around the compound and more Marine guards at the front gate. However, what we noticed was that their security had a major weakness. They had no ability to control what went on outside their walls. Since that was where the threat came from, they needed some ability to influence what went on out there."

Of course, the Marines could not legally operate outside of the walls of the embassy. The solution DSL came up with was what was known as the "third force concept." The idea was to hire a private company to patrol outside the walls of the embassy and provide early warning to the Marine guards inside when a threat appeared.

"So the arrangement we came up with was to put together a group of retired Gurkhas to provide this third force capability. It really was unique," Grayson explained.

Over the next decade, DSL went on to provide similar services to many government clients. They took their third force concept to other embassies and conducted training programs for military units around Africa. In the early 1990s, the company ran afoul of the media when it was reported that DSL personnel were training Colombian special police units. Human rights groups, citing the atrocious record of Colombian security forces for murder and torture, felt that it was morally objectionable for a western company to support Colombian security units. It is a claim that Patrick Grayson denies emphatically:

"That whole affair in Colombia... it never happened," he states firmly.

DSL had been hired by British Petroleum (BP) to provide advice on how the oil company could protect its personnel and offshore oil rigs in Colombian waters. BP had become especially worried after terrorists struck one of its rigs, and Colombian police units were too poorly equipped and trained to respond effectively. The situation was difficult for BP and the other oil companies in the region because they had been paying the Colombian government millions of dollars a year to protect their installations.

As unseemly as this arrangement may seem at first glance, it is actually a common practice globally. For sporting events, concerts, conferences, and other similar affairs, private companies often arrange for police coverage by paying fees to the local government. This "rent-a-cop" scheme is designed to allow police units to cover the extra costs and overtime pay associated with protecting large events. For BP, paying for police coverage was a far better option than hiring its own private armed security force and all the political ramifications that would go along with it.

Although the actual advice given to BP by DSL is privileged information under client confidentiality rules, I believe I can shed some light on the affair. I have no doubt that DSL would have advised BP that if it was going to pay all of this money for police security, it should probably try to arrange to get its money's worth. Although DSL would have been fully capable of providing that training, Grayson denies that either DSL or its local subsidiary, Defense Systems Colombia (DSC), had any further involvement.

What was unknown to reporters during this affair was that the actual SAS had been in Colombia in strength for some time helping security forces fight the drug cartels. They had been training local security units and going out on search-and-destroy missions with the Colombian army and police. Because they were already training the

Colombians in counter-terrorist tactics, the story of DSL's involvement is probably incorrect. If the SAS had been involved, they very well might have used DSL as a cover story to keep their own activities secret. Whatever the truth, it was a rough period for Morrison and his team.

In the late 1990s, DSL re-invented itself in the humanitarian aid support world. In Bosnia, DSL has had up to five hundred employees driving trucks, providing medical assistance, and handling logistics duties.

"When people see that image on television of the doctor treating sick and traumatized victims in a refugee camp, they rarely think about where that doctor is going to sleep that night, where her food is going to come from and how she gets her medical supplies. That's where we come in," Grayson says. "Since soldiers are the acknowledged experts in logistics and security, it is a natural evolution to involve us in supporting humanitarian aid missions." As we spoke in early 1999, DSL was gearing up to bring these same skills to the Albanian refugees in Kosovo.

When I asked Grayson to tell me where he saw DSL's place in the international security industry, he thought for a moment and then replied:

"DSL provides military-style skills for its various clients. We are experts at certain things – logistics, training – and, like most soldiers, we know how to handle ourselves under stressful conditions. That is, I guess, our real value. I would point out that I can only think of a couple of occasions when our personnel have ever carried weapons. We usually just conduct the training. We definitely have never taken any direct role in combat situations. That's where we draw the line."

In 1997, DSL came to the attention of Armor Holdings Inc. of Jacksonville, Florida. Armor Holdings was the name of a new public company that grew out of a small body-armor producer known as NIK Safety Systems. In 1996, NIK went public on the New York Stock Exchange and changed its name to Armor Holdings Inc. With this new revenue, the company went on an acquisition spree. One of the first targets was DSL. In mid-1997, Defense Systems Limited was acquired by the ambitious American company. Morrison and Grayson stayed on as advisors to the company, but the direction of DSL began to change rapidly.

In 1999, DSL ceased to exist and was renamed "ArmorGroup," the parent company's new security services division. ArmorGroup is now registered with the United Nations as a licensed supplier and has conducted de-mining operations in Angola and Mozambique. In an attempt to become more like Control Risks, ArmorGroup has signed on with Zurich U.S. as that insurance company's provider for security consultants for Kidnap & Ransom policies. Also much like Control Risks, the firm now sells competitive business intelligence services, product contamination prevention systems, and corporate consulting services. The company that Morrison, Grayson, and Abbot had set up in 1983 as a supplier of military skills to clients was no more

By the end of its third year in business, Armor Holdings had earned over US$120 million in sales and was listed as number twenty-two on Fortune's "500 Fastest Growing Companies." With a new name, new management, and new ownership, the company has managed to make the leap from military security services to security services quite smoothly. That is something that doesn't happen often in this industry.

Another company that clearly falls into this spectrum of the industry is Military Professional Resources Incorporated (MPRI). While it has been described all too often in various media articles as "America's mercenaries," the reality is quite different. In 1988, retired U.S. army General Vernon Lewis got together with a group of other retired senior officers and set up a company that would take advantage of the Pentagon's huge contracting budget. Since that time, MPRI has become one of the world's leading military security service companies with up to four hundred staff under contract, recording over US$48 million in sales in 1997.

According to the firm's literature, its business philosophy is that: "MPRI was founded on the premise that the retired military community is a national resource," and that "Our vision was to apply the extraordinary talents of this group in an effort to meet the needs of defense and organizational markets in both the domestic and international arenas."

For the first few years, MPRI's business was based on providing a baffling array of training to the U.S. Defense Department in systems integration, military strategy, information technology, and even recruitment strategies. Training programs were conducted at college campuses, military bases, and defense institutions. While it may seem unusual for the U.S. military to require private help in planning and organizing its affairs, remember that much of the West's Cold War strategies came from the Rand Corporation. This private strategic think tank was also filled with retired generals, politicians, defense contractors, and scientists.

In fact, the primary motivator in this new business market was just another by-product of the end of the Cold War. Back in the 1970s and '80s, retiring senior officers could take their pick of lucrative consulting and lobbying positions with the massive American defense industry. With the end of the Cold War, however, the bottom fell out of the defense contracting industry, and competition for these vacancies became very stiff.

At the same time, reductions in defense spending meant less ability to initiate new programs and keep the world's most advanced military machine working smoothly in concert with immense leaps in technology. Inevitably, the Pentagon began outsourcing more and more training and technology integration and development projects. The founders of MPRI recognized this trend and set up their firm to take advantage of the market.

On the domestic front, MPRI is involved in army recruiting programs to help fill the gap between manpower needs and enlistment figures. It also supports ROTC programs at colleges and universities. But it is on the international front where MPRI really came into its own.

One of the company's first major offshore contracts was the Democracy Transition Assistance Program (DTAP) for Croatia in 1994. Sponsored by the United States government, the program was designed to take Croatia's fragmented, soviet-style military structure and convert it into a modern military department based on the western model.

The interest of the United States was to ensure Croatia's new military was a product of, and loyal to, the new democratic system of government in that state. MPRI was also charged with teaching the Croatians about respect for human rights, the Geneva Conventions, and the laws of war.

MPRI's effort was both a terrific success and a horrible and critical failure. The year after MPRI began re-organizing the Croatian army a stunning campaign was conducted in the Serbian Krajina region. Known as Operation Storm, it was a precision operation that even the U.S. Army would have been proud of. The Serb command and control systems were eliminated in a series of lightning raids, and an overwhelming combined arms operations followed quickly on its heels.

The Krajina Serbs had known that an offensive was coming ever since the 1994 battles in the Medak pocket. They had been preparing defenses and stockpiling equipment ever since. Yet, despite mountainous terrain, fortified defenses, and reserves of ammunition, all elements that should have meant a disastrous failure for the Croats, the Serb defenses fell in less than forty-eight hours. Fighting continued for some time as Croats swept across the region, but with the command system removed, resistance was fragmented and doomed.

The stunning transformation of the Croatian forces from a rag-tag rebel faction into a modern all-arms force was due in large part to the splendid job done by MPRI.

However, this success had a terrible consequence. The moment the Serb military threat was reduced, the Croatian army began ethnically cleansing the entire region. Vast human rights tragedies were reported with bombardments of civilian targets, the torching of villages, and the dispersal of tens of thousands of Serb civilians.

Since 1994, MPRI has continued to work in Croatia, trying to turn that nation's military into an credible, acceptable, and sustainable military force. Croatia has petitioned to join NATO and, to do so, it must transform itself into a force acceptable to western sensibilities – an exclusive club that doesn't normally tolerate ethnic cleansing as a military function. The new contracts operate under the Croatian Armed Forces Readiness and Training Program (CARTS) and the Democracy Transition/Long Range Management Program (DT/LRMP).

Meanwhile, the company began looking for new markets. In 1995, Executive Outcomes was serving a two-year contract to help the Angolan government win a decades-old civil war with the rebel UNITA movement. The contract was worth US$20 million a year and EO was very successful. With the signing of the Lusaka Peace Accord, largely as a result of EO's efforts, the American government became very interested in the region.

President Clinton, in several speeches aimed at encouraging peace efforts in the region, suggested quite strongly that Angolan President Eduardo dos Santos cancel the contract with EO and send the mercenaries home. What he did not say quite as publicly was that he wanted to replace them with an American company. The State Department's African policy people were interested in getting MPRI to take over the contract and build U.S. influence in the area.

Why would the U.S. government work so hard to get an American military security company into Angola? The reasons were based mostly on a combination of business and political issues. On the business side, the majority of the major oil companies active in Angola's rich offshore oilfields were American companies, such as Chevron. On the political side, the disaster that was Somalia was only two years old and was still an open wound for the American people. Any official involvement by the U.S. military was out of the question. Yet, Angola was strategically placed, moving towards democracy, and had the potential to become a strong friend in southwest Africa.

The Angolan government was not too keen on MPRI. Where EO was hired for the specific reason that they would fight as well as advise, the Americans were only going to be very expensive policy consultants. The Angolans had been fighting their war for twenty years and had been unable to defeat Jonas Savimbi's powerful UNITA force. Their army was just not capable of accomplishing that task on its own. EO had tipped that balance by putting battle-hardened South Africans in the fight. MPRI, as a non-mercenary company, wasn't prepared to do the same.

The Americans kept the pressure on. There were even suggestions at times that aid shipments from the West might be suspended. Eventually, the Angolans caved and at the end of 1999 MPRI appears to have won a contract to train their army and police forces.

MPRI has also gone on to lucrative contracts back in the Balkan market. In Bosnia, they won part of a US$400 million deal to train the Bosnian army in 1995. In 1998 they won a contract to train the Macedonian army. In 1999, however, the company's wildly successful ride almost came to a shuddering halt.

Throughout the war in Kosovo in 1999, many observers around the world were quite confused and suspicious about the Kosovo Liberation Army (KLA). This group of "freedom fighters," who should have been a haphazard collection of peasants armed with hunting rifles, shotguns and ancient military surplus, were showing up on western news reports with brand new, matching camouflage uniforms, modern military weapons, and an efficient military structure. It was quite clear that there was money and professional help behind the KLA.

Many western observers claimed American mercenaries were training the KLA. Immediately, suspicion fell on MPRI. After its successful operations in virtually every other former state of the Yugoslav Republic, it was the likely candidate to be working with the KLA.

The situation worsened for MPRI when it became known that the KLA was being led by a Croatian mercenary trained by MPRI back in 1994. General Agim Ceku was a former Yugoslavian army officer who deserted to the Croatian cause in 1991. When MPRI began training the Croatian army in 1994, Ceku was one of the officers that received training. Ceku then went on to become a key planner in Operation Storm the following year in Krajina. Rumors even place MPRI consultants at a secret meeting with Ceku in the weeks before Operation Storm. When Ceku later turned up leading the KLA in Kosovo, it was too much for many observers. Despite the rather damning circumstantial evidence against them, MPRI almost certainly had nothing to do with the KLA. There would be no upside for a company like MPRI to take such a foolish risk.

In the U.S. system, companies providing any type of defense or military-related sales or services to foreign clients must be licensed by the U.S. State Department. In addition to being licensed, each individual contract must be approved by the State Department. With hundreds of millions of dollars in contracts to protect, MPRI would not have risked having anything to do with the KLA. There are numerous small military security companies and military combat companies run by retired special forces men who would have taken such a contract. MPRI would not be on that list.

As we enter the twenty-first century, MPRI is poised to make international security a corporate marketplace. With declining U.S. defense budgets contrasting with an increasing pressure for the United States to act as the world's policeman, there is an increasing gap between responsibility and capability. The Pentagon's budget is now largely committed to technology upgrading and maintaining that tremendously expensive advantage in equipment quality over the rest of the world. There is little money left over for deployments of troops all over the world. There is also much less political will to risk the lives of American servicemen after the horrors of Somalia.

The new president of MPRI, General Carl E. Vuono, is planning to fill this gap by bringing American military expertise and equipment to war zones around the world without having to be approved by Congress. If bureaucrats at the State Department give a project the thumbs up, MPRI is on the job.

Another company that has a similar arrangement with its government is Lordan-Levdan of Tel Aviv. This Israeli company is made up of former Israeli Defense Force (IDF) generals and intelligence officers from the Mossad. The company is owned by retired General Moshe Levy and is managed by General Ze've Zahrine. The company came to international attention when it was hired by President Lissouba of the Republic of the Congo (Congo-Brazzaville) to train a presidential guard unit for the paranoiac leader.

Levdan received a contract for US$40 million to train a 650-man unit and provide plans and procedures for its use. The Israeli defense industries also profited from the contract by winning an extra US$10 million in contracts to supply equipment.

However, it quickly became clear to Levdan that the country had no ability to pay such a tab for their services. After Levdan threatened to withdraw, President Lissouba was forced to offer new terms. The motivation for not losing the Israelis came from the president's lack of trust in his own army. He felt, quite rightly it turned out, that the army was loyal to the former president, Denis Sassou-Nguesso, whom he had deposed in 1992.

To keep the Israelis on line, the president offered them control of

Block III of the Congo's offshore oilfields. Levdan, not being an oil company, turned to Naptha Israel Petroleum to manage the project. In return for a reported US$300,000 payment and fifty percent of future revenues, the Israeli oil firm took control.

However, all was still not well with the security contract. Former President Denis Sassou-Nguesso was busy organizing his own private army known as "the Cobras." The Prime Minister, Bernard Kolelas, was also creating a militia loyal to him known as the "Ninjas." The force Levdan was training, to be known as the "Cocoyes," was not going to be large enough to fight the regular army, the Ninjas, and the Cobras. Seeing a civil war looming and not wanting to get involved, Levdan withdrew from the Congo in March 1997.

Sure enough, by June 1997, a bitter and brutal civil war broke out. This is the mess that Steve W. flew into in November, just a month after Sassou-Nguesso returned to power as President of Congo-Brazzaville. At the time he was in the country, the Cobras controlled most of the city, with the Cocoyes holding the north and the Ninjas the west.

Little is known about what Levdan might be up to now. It has managed to keep its name out of the press. Whatever new contracts it is pursuing will probably reflect the interests of the Israeli government.

The military security services category includes many other companies, but most of them are small, short-lived firms that last for one project and then dissolve. James Woods, a former Deputy Assistant Director of Defense for the U.S. government, describes the situation perfectly:

"Basically [these firms] consist of a retired military guy sitting in a spare bedroom with a fax machine and a Rolodex. They serve as a gateway to the large pool of retired military personnel. When they are in between jobs, there's not much to do."

The only firms that survive in this segment of the industry for any length of time are those that take on a proper corporate structure and ally themselves closely with their home governments. They usually consist of retired senior officers who can gain access to senior policy advisors for government and, as a consequence, become essentially a foreign policy instrument.

In turn, these generals don't actually get their hands dirty working on projects in some jungle somewhere. Instead, they turn to the legions of retired special forces operators sitting by their faxes and Rolodexes waiting for a call. The "circuit," as it is called. I will discuss the pros, cons, and concerns of this arrangement later in the book.

The conclusion to draw here about the military security services category is that it is most often inhabited by powerful, well-connected companies that can influence international policy through their contacts in government. The major benefit of this reality is that these firms are well supervised and well controlled by the home states that retain their services.

The concern with this segment of the industry arises when the majors won't accept a contract for one reason or another and the client turns to one of the small, one-man, spare-bedroom companies that aren't as well supervised or controlled.

In the next chapter I will look at the final category of the international security industry: the military combat services. This is another segment of the industry that is plagued by the same concerns. However, because combat services are included in the package, the consequences can be far more significant.

The company that most ideally represents this segment of the industry was Executive Outcomes, a firm whose roots went back seven centuries and which was as dynamic and controversial in its time as its ancestors were in the medieval world.

6

MILITARY COMBAT SERVICE

THE FREE COMPANY REBORN

"We are born of war, reared in war. War was our trade."
– John Kincaid, King's German Legion, 1814

IN THE MID-FOURTEENTH CENTURY, a middle-aged man by the name of John Hawkwood followed the Black Prince from England into battle on the European continent. The fighting was often fierce, but the Prince was unmatched in his day. With victory came the Treaty of Bretigny in 1360 and a temporary end to the war. Flushed with their success, the English soldiers who had followed him probably gave little thought initially to the fact that they were now unemployed and stuck in France. Victors in a foreign land, many sought out the booty that traditionally went to the successful army. Eventually, though, the foreign soldiers found that they were unwelcome in central Europe and, with their winnings spent, many began to wonder where they could find new employ.

John Hawkwood had been born around 1320 at Hawkwood Manor in Essex, England. One of seven siblings, he was a middle-child. When his father died around 1340, the estate and family wealth went to John's oldest brother, leaving John with nothing. The four sisters were married off and John's younger brother was sent into the priesthood. This left the young Hawkwood with no trade and no place in his own home. Although records are unclear as to what Hawkwood did for the next few years, it is believed that he tried his hand at several tradecrafts, but these positions would never allow him to regain the wealth and status to which he had been accustomed.

Eventually, like many of his aimless but ambitious peers, and typical of a middle son of the English gentry, Hawkwood became a soldier with the hope of winning wealth and glory in campaigns abroad. At the end of the war in France, however, Hawkwood had achieved fame as a soldier, but he had accumulated little wealth. Eventually, he headed south to the wealthy city-states of the Italian peninsula where he might find new employ as a mercenary.

Here Hawkwood founded one of the most famous free companies ever to exist: the "Compagnia Blanca," or White Company. There were several other free companies of soldiers-for-hire active at the same time, but Hawkwood used his experience with the Black Prince to form a mercenary unit that would become the best in the business. He used mostly Englishmen, whose longbows were more than a match for the local crossbows. His archers could launch twelve armor-piercing shafts for every crossbow bolt his enemy could deliver. When massed, his archers worked almost like modern machine-gunners, cutting great swaths into the ranks of his opposition.

Unlike his competitors, Hawkwood also increased his mobility by mounting every member of his company on horseback. In the fourteenth century, there was usually a clear division between mounted cavalry and the foot-borne infantry. This innovation allowed the White Company an unmatched mobility and strategic advantage.

Hawkwood's mercenaries took their name, the "White Company," from the fact that every man was ordered to polish his armor daily into a high sheen. With the sun glinting off the chest plates of its forces and into the eyes of the enemy, the White Company often struck fear into opponents simply by arriving on the battlefield. Combined with Hawkwood's brilliance in battle planning, the White Company became the unit of choice for the various nation-states on the peninsula.

During the next few years, the White Company would accept "condotte," or contracts, with the Pisan government and, later, with the Catholic Church. Hawkwood achieved many victories during this time, but not always by fighting. The White Company would often as not simply position their force to give them a tactical advantage and then negotiate for terms with his disadvantaged opponent. He often avoided fighting if at all possible.

He also broke with the standards of the day and used his company as an early form of special forces. Relying on the expertise of his men, he would devise cunning strategies that brought victory, even when the numbers were stacked against him.

In 1368, Emperor Charles IV decided to visit Rome. In this age, the Pope and the emperor were at best complacent enemies. Whenever any emperor decided to pay a visit to the historical seat of the Pope's power it was seen as a challenge to the papacy. Therefore, they were rarely welcomed. In this case, the Pope was for once on good terms with the emperor and did not challenge the visit.

At this time, the White Company was in the employ of the city of Milan. The ruler of that state was an egotistical tyrant named Visconti Bernabo. This Milanese ruler did not wish to be seen by his subjects to bow down to any visiting emperor from across the Alps. Bernabo decided to challenge Charles and prevent his access to central Italy.

Hawkwood was summoned and ordered to stop the emperor and his army. Not quite clear on how his small mercenary company was to achieve such a goal against the twenty-thousand-strong Imperial Army, he went with his company to take command of the defenses at the Borgoforte bridge over the Po river. Bernabo had recently constructed a fort there and he placed Hawkwood in charge of its defense. This was to be the bastion against the Imperial advance.

To defend this point and stop the Imperials, Hawkwood had at his disposal fewer than ten thousand mercenaries, including his White Company, some Germans and a few Burgundians.

Charles realized that trying to force the bridge would be a costly affair. He therefore set up his camp downstream where his navy could support him. Here Hawkwood saw a keen opportunity. He sent his sappers just downstream from the fort to breach the embankments and flood the Imperial camp. The swollen spring waters achieved a brilliant success. The tents and stores of the royal army were swept away, and Charles was forced to seek new terms with Bernabo.

Later, Hawkwood's brilliance came to the attention of the Pope.

A regular employer of mercenaries since the Crusades, the Catholic Church was the big league as far as mercenary contracts went. The White Company entered the Church's service, but the relationship did not last long. Strangely, it was morality that drove the mercenaries out of papal service.

Hawkwood found his papal paymasters to be rather forgetful with his pay on many occasions. At one point, he even kidnapped a cardinal and held him for the "ransom" payment of his company's wages. But it was the Church's dark side that finally drove Hawkwood out of its service. Some of the tasks he was asked to perform were just not honorable enough for the distinguished Englishman. The incident that drove the White Company out of Papal service forever was the siege of Cesena in 1376.

During most of the fourteenth century the Pope resided in Avignon in southern France, rather than in Rome. In his place, the Papal States were ruled by his Italian cardinals, who were always keen to increase their wealth and power base. These "Italian" church officials often resented having a French Pope and spent a great deal of time trying to increase their power to the point where they might one day challenge Avignon for control of the church. Chief among these was Cardinal Robert of Geneva.

In 1376, Cardinal Robert began a military campaign to win more lands in the region and, in doing so, increase his wealth and influence. To accomplish his aims, he hired a particularly bloodthirsty group of Breton mercenaries. The first town to fall in the path of this army was the walled city of Cesena. The cardinal's forces laid siege to it for many days but were unable to defeat the inhabitants. Frustrated in his attempts to take the city by force, the Cardinal blockaded the town and then waited to starve out the inhabitants. As the citizens of Cesena weakened, the cardinal offered his guarantee of safety to the citizens if they would lay down their arms. He swore that they would be spared any violence. Eventually, the town acceded to the Cardinal's force and opened the city gates.

Immediately, the Cardinal summoned the White Company, which was under contract to the Church at that time. Upon his arrival, Hawkwood reported for orders, believing he was going to assist in the disarmament of the population. Instead, to his horror, the cardinal explained that Hawkwood's men, along with the Bretons, were to surround the city and kill every living thing within its walls as an example of his power.

As the operation commenced, Hawkwood secretly ordered his men to hide as many of the inhabitants as they could. Additionally, Hawkwood gathered together more than a thousand women and children and put them under his own guard. These refugees were then marched under protection to Rimini where they would be safe from Cardinal Robert's predations. Immediately after the Cesena operation, Hawkwood canceled his contract and led his company out of papal service forever.

The next contract came from the state of Florence. There were rumblings of an uprising and a coup within the city's walls, and the leaders of the town needed someone they could trust to keep the peace. To prop up their government, the Florentines hired the White Company to put down the insurrection and restore order. To do so, the civic leaders took the almost unprecedented step of inviting the full mercenary company to enter the city bearing their arms. The threat that, with an uprising already underway, the mercenaries might be tempted to just seize power for themselves must have made the city fathers very nervous about this course of action. However, this was John Hawkwood, and the Florentines must have found some reassurance in his notable reputation.

Hawkwood's men entered the city and, moving about in formed squares, they convinced the inhabitants to return to their homes without any significant resistance. During the course of the emergency, the White Company continued to patrol the streets and maintain law and order. In doing so, they did such a good job that the city took the even more unusual step of offering Hawkwood a long-term contract to police Florence. Hawkwood accepted, and his mercenary company became a cornerstone of security for the leaders of Florence for years to come.

Hawkwood continued to accept other contracts with Florence's allies, and his reputation as a brilliant soldier, backed by an unbeat-

able company, ensured that his employers remained untroubled by any
enemy. In 1387, the Florentines "lent" the White Company to Fran-
cesco Carrera, leader of allied Padua, to fight their common Veronese
and Venetian enemies.

After years of skirmishes, the Paduans thought they would send an
army to capture Verona and end the conflict. Carrera's forces, however,
were not particularly impressive and not up to the challenge. They
would need assistance at all levels if they were to have any hope of
success. John Hawkwood was asked to provide a small contingent of
troops to "steady" the Paduan army and also to provide command
"advice" to the force. For the sake of appearances, the combined army
would be under the command of Carrera's son, Carrera the Younger,
but it was understood that Hawkwood would actually make all the decisions. The Paduan army being assembled consisted of 6,500 men-at-
arms and a thousand infantry. The White Company was to provide five
hundred men-at-arms and six hundred archers.

The Paduan forces marched in early fall and laid siege to the
city of Verona. The Veronese army was being commanded at the
time by another mercenary, Giovanni dei Ordelafi, and, unknown to
Hawkwood, his forces actually outnumbered the besieging Paduans.
Ordelafi was content to let his opponents lay siege to the city and wear
them down before he counterattacked.

As the siege dragged on into winter, the Paduans found themselves
in trouble. Ordelafi's forces were raiding their long supply line from
Padua and cutting off Hawkwood's forces from their support. Consequently, morale was beginning to suffer. Eventually, Hawkwood convinced young Carrera to pull his army back over the Adige River for
the winter and return in the spring. Carrera, seeing the wisdom of the
advice, agreed and ordered a withdrawal.

Immediately, Ordelafi launched his pursuit. With nine thousand
men-at-arms, 2,600 crossbowmen, some peculiar artillery rockets, and
several thousand citizen militia, the Veronese had superior numbers
and the offensive advantage. Ordelafi's plan was to pursue and harass
the retreating Paduans and then trap them as they attempted to cross
the river.

After several days of a fighting withdrawal, the Paduans reached the river, but Hawkwood forbade them to cross. This must have made some of the men uneasy because safety lay across the water and the Veronese army was not far behind. Instead, Hawkwood ordered the force to make camp.

In the morning, Hawkwood and Carrera moved through the army awarding promotions, making sure the men were fed, and generally raising morale. Hawkwood was now nearly seventy years old, and his grandfatherly appearance must have been comforting to the tired and worried Paduans.

When the Veronese arrived later in the morning they expected to find their enemy halfway through their crossing and vulnerable. Instead, they found their enemy drawn up and ready for battle. Perplexed for a time, Ordelafi was unsure about facing John Hawkwood on ground of Hawkwood's own choosing. After pondering his options for several hours, Ordelafi realized he really had no other choice and ordered the attack.

Hawkwood had chosen his ground well. To his front lay a deep irrigation ditch that paralleled the river. His men-at-arms were drawn up along its edge and his infantry positioned just behind to close any gaps. The archers, placed on the flanks, rained fire down on the approaching Veronese. Quickly the battle became a shoving match at the edge of the ditch. Every time the Veronese gained a foothold on the far bank, Ordelafi would rush in his reserves to try to exploit it. Finally, Ordelafi committed all of his men-at-arms and infantry.

The sheer weight of numbers began to force the Paduans away from the ditch and back towards the river. The moment of crisis had come. Both sides were fully committed. It was at this moment that Hawkwood told the Paduan commander to wait for his signal for one final effort and then rode off. Hawkwood gathered his White Company together, and they disappeared into the low ground on the riverbank.

The Veronese sensed victory. The famous White Company had broken and run and the Paduans were being crushed. Ordelafi was quite pleased. It seemed that he would be able to crush his enemy in one decisive battle. Also, his reputation and price would be greatly enhanced by defeating the famous Hawkwood and his unit.

All of a sudden, the Veronese heard the shouts of an old man scream-ing "Carne, carne!" (Flesh, flesh!) behind them. Turning, they found the White Company on their horses and at the full charge to their rear. At their head was John Hawkwood, swinging his great English broadsword.

As the mercenaries crashed into the Veronese rear, the Paduans real-ized the signal had come. They rallied on the riverbank and pushed their attackers back towards the ditch. The combined ferocity of the attack front and rear was too much and the Veronese broke. Ordelafi tried to call forward his own horsemen, but the human tide of his fleeing army made it impossible. Hawkwood's archers dismounted and fired shaft after shaft into the panicked ranks of Veronese. Finally unable to distin-guish friend from foe, they drew their own swords and joined the fray.

In the end, the Veronese army was smashed. It left over 1,600 dead and many more wounded spread across the battlefield. For Hawk-wood, his losses were less than a hundred and these were mostly Pad-uans. His White Company, using their professional skills, an excellent grasp of tactics, and no little amount of cunning, had won the day for his employers.

On his peaceful death in 1394 of old age, the city of Florence declared an official day of mourning. All shops were ordered closed and a grand state funeral organized. As he was borne through the streets by the men of the White Company, Hawkwood's procession was attended by many of the great mercenary captains of the day. Even the city's ruling Signoria council flouted tradition and attended the ceremonies. In the end, none other than King Richard II asked for Hawkwood's remains to be returned to England for burial in his home soil.

Nearly six hundred years later, another free company was formed that, although paling in comparison, essentially followed in the White Company's footsteps. This time the domain would be Africa and the company would become equally famous for its mercenary exploits. In this much more enlightened age, however, their condotte were no less successful but were far less welcomed by the world-at-large. This new-age free company's name was Executive Outcomes.

Luther Eben Barlow was born in South Africa and raised during the apartheid era. As a young man he joined the South African Defense Forces and fought in the ongoing border wars his country pursued. He rose to second-in-command of a unit known as 32 "Buffalo" Battalion, a special forces group composed mainly of black, Portuguese-speaking Angolans. His unit became one of the most famous and highly decorated organizations in the history of the South African army. Later Barlow moved into the innocuously named "Civil Cooperation Bureau," a covert intelligence and dirty-tricks unit for the apartheid regime. Inevitably, though, and justifiably so, South Africa's wars ended and the white-dominated government was replaced by Nelson Mandela's African National Congress (ANC).

As an apartheid warrior of a racist regime, Barlow was no longer welcome in the army of his home. Turned loose in this quickly restructuring world, Barlow wondered where he would find employ next. As Hawkwood had done before him, Barlow began to look for a new paymaster. Two other recently retired South Africans joined him in this search: Lafras Luitingh, a former major in the South African's tough recce-commandos, and Nick Van Den Berg, a lieutenant colonel from the paratroopers. Together these three in 1989 formed a new free company, which they named Executive Outcomes.

Using its links to the South African military community that still remained active, Executive Outcomes (EO) quickly won a contract to train the new special forces units of the completely renovated South African military. It also won a contract from the diamond-mining giant De Beers to investigate diamond thefts.

In its work for the diamond conglomerate, EO came to the attention of the British soldier-cum-industrialist Anthony Buckingham. A former officer in British special forces, Buckingham had bought up shares in several mining and oil companies on his retirement. As chairman of Heritage Oil & Gas, a company with extensive interests in Angolan oil properties, Buckingham's investments were being jeopardized by UNITA's military advances. To protect his business, Buckingham introduced EO to the Angolan government's oil company, Sonogal, in early 1993.

Angola's MPLA government, abandoned by its Cuban and Russian backers at the end of the Cold War, found itself incapable of defeating Jonas Savimbi's UNITA forces on its own. Without Russian money and Cuban military support, the MPLA was simply too poorly organized, trained, and equipped to pacify such a huge nation, more than twice the size of France. Having led the socialist charge against mercenarism in 1976, the MPLA government now found itself in the somewhat humbled position of having to replace the Cubans with another source of foreign military support. The MPLA president, Jose Eduardo dos Santos, was forced to look for mercenaries from his former enemies in South Africa and his former protagonists in Britain.

What issues were so pressing for dos Santos that he would consider accepting mercenary support? In October 1992, UNITA had launched a series of offensives that had captured most of the oil facilities and much of the diamond-mining regions. By September 1993, Jonas Savimbi's forces were marching on Luanda and had four-fifths of the country under their control. The Angolan army was defeated and victory was nearly his. To show his political savvy and statesmanship, as well as acknowledging significant pressure from the U.N. and OAU, Savimbi then declared a unilateral ceasefire in hopes of avoiding a bloodbath in the capture of the capital city. This moment of diplomacy was to cost him his victory and plunge the country into a new round of war.

Savimbi's offer of negotiation placed dos Santos in a difficult position. If he began negotiations now and the international community intervened, as he knew it would, the political lines in Angola would likely remain drawn where they stood when the ceasefire was announced. This would leave Savimbi with most of the country and all of its wealth under his control.

The situation was similar to that faced by Margaret Thatcher in 1982 over the Falklands Islands. Thatcher had to recapture the entire island group before the U.N. could force her government to accept a ceasefire that left the Argentinians in control of any portion of the islands. Otherwise, the future of the islands was in doubt. Dos Santos faced the same problem. If he chose to deal, given the circumstances, he would be negotiating from a position of extreme weakness. Savimbi had all the cards. This left dos Santos with a very slim opportunity to regain the advantage. The army was in tatters, his revenue-generating resources were in enemy hands, and his socialist brothers had abandoned him.

Initially, the Angolans might have looked at a company called Gurkha Security Guards Limited (GSG), which was already in Angola protecting diamond mines. The British and Canadian owners of the firm were Rhodesian veterans who were using demobilized Gurkhas to provide high-risk guard services for corporate clients. Two conditions made it improbable however. First, Gurkhas, while exceptional infantry, are not well known for their training capabilities or organizational strengths. Second, the company maintained a strict policy (at that time) that it wouldn't get involved in combat duties. Consequently, GSG withdrew from the mines when UNITA moved into their areas.

The situation almost turned around when a security firm known as International Defense and Security (IDAS) based in the Netherlands approached GSG to put together a force of two thousand Gurkhas to fight UNITA for the MPLA. The company's directors, Anthony Husher and Mike Borlace, weren't sure if they could find two thousand Gurkhas on short notice, and the negotiations with IDAS and the dos Santos government made little headway.

So, when Anthony Buckingham showed up and announced that he would partially fund a project to hire South African mercenaries who would actually fight and not just train, dos Santos saw the writing on the wall. Of course, the condition Buckingham lay down was that the first areas to be recovered would have to be his oil facilities. He also arranged that, in return for helping fund the project, his companies would be awarded some lucrative diamond and oil concessions. The MPLA leader accepted the terms, having no better alternatives on the table, and decided to use the South Africans as a first step in regaining the advantage from UNITA.

The first contract negotiated was fairly straightforward. EO was to provide two hundred mercenaries to attack and recapture the oil facilities at Kefekwena and Soyo from the UNITA occupiers. The contract was to last two months and was to be paid for by Sonogal and Heritage Oil & Gas in the form of Anthony Buckingham.

Barlow and Luitingh began recruiting in South Africa but managed to find only one hundred men. Recruiting was by word-of-mouth, and every recruit had to be known to someone in the organization. All were former comrades from South African special forces, and most had already fought in South Africa's border wars. Barlow led his new free company to Luanda where he set up a co-operative headquarters with their former enemy, General Joao de Matos of the Angolan Armed Forces (FAA).

The operation went ahead with the South Africans, supported by Angolan troops, storming the UNITA positions and initially driving them off. Unknown to EO, though, UNITA had moved several thousand troops into Soyo, and these forces quickly counterattacked. For several days, a pitched battle raged for control of the area. Several South Africans were killed and a large group, thinking the situation hopeless, demanded immediate evacuation. Buckingham, seeing his mercenaries falling apart, immediately offered a $3,000 bonus to any man who would stay on.

Luitingh, the force commander, announced he would stay and fight. Quite a few others followed their commander's example and chose to remain as well. After the dissenters were flown out, Luitingh got on with the job of securing his position with his remaining force. The South Africans and their Angolan troops doggedly held on, and over the next week UNITA was unable to dislodge the defiant enemy.

Eventually, the siege was lifted and Executive Outcomes had won its first victory. Outnumbered and cut off, it had managed a brilliant struggle. The fact that many of these mercenaries had chosen to stay on when the situation seemed hopeless and evacuation was available is particular surprising. While there was a cash bonus offered, that can hardly be considered a true incentive to surrender one's life. No, what EO had done was demonstrate a strength of character and reliability that was to become the framework for its future success.

UNITA, bloodied but unbeaten, now bided its time. When the mercenary contract ended after two months, EO was withdrawn. Immediately, Savimbi's forces swept in and recaptured the facilities from the hapless Angolan army. This lesson was not lost on President dos Santos. The South Africans had proven themselves capable of defeating the rebels and, with few other acceptable options available to him, he decided that this free company was once more his best option for saving his embattled government.

Like the Florentine city fathers before him, his choices were to accept defeat or to employ the best and most reliable mercenaries available to save his government. Having witnessed the disaster that befell Holden Roberto in 1975, dos Santos knew that the key was to hire only men of proven reliability and performance. Having fought against the South Africans for decades, dos Santos knew how good they were. He immediately offered EO a one-year renewable contract to support the Angolan army in its fight against the rebels.

This new condotta was to be worth US$40 million a year. Half of the fee was for weapons and equipment purchase and the remainder for EO's expenses. Although this may seem an extravagant expense at first glance, it must be noted that the United Nations was spending roughly $1 million a day to maintain its UNAVEM II observer force in Angola at the same time. For such a massive outlay of financial resources, the U.N. mission was having little success in achieving an end to the war. This was no fault of the U.N., however. Both dos Santos and Savimbi were not ready to accept a peace until one or the other was clearly defeated.

With typical military precision, EO immediately got to work. It began by selecting one brigade from the Angolan army and conducted an extensive training campaign with it. The 16th Brigade (16Bde) would become their ground force, and South African mercenaries inserted themselves into all levels of the formation's command structure. Like the White Company before them, they would be used to "stiffen" the ranks of their employer's force. They also took up an advisory role with the high command of the Angolan army to help steer its operations.

At the same time, EO began buying aircraft for the upcoming operations. Its acquisitions included Mi-24 Hind-D helicopter gunships purchased from the Ukraine, Mi-17 Hip medium transport helicopters, MIG-23 fighter jets, L-39 propeller-driven ground-attack aircraft, and even two Boeing 727s for logistics shipments.

In the model of the White Company, EO felt that mobility would be their greatest asset. Hawkwood had ensured that every one of his men was mounted, allowing them to move very quickly and appear anywhere on the battlefield while his enemies were forced to march on foot. For EO, its aircraft would accomplish the same aim. While UNITA was forced to march for days in the bush, EO could cover the same distance in minutes. Also like the White Company, EO-led squads would appear at these points with superior weapons and discipline. Together, these features would make EO unbeatable.

Barlow's plan for the campaign was based on well-practiced counter-insurgency strategies that had been perfected in Rhodesia, Mozambique, and Namibia. Using special forces reconnaissance teams and electronic intelligence, EO would locate UNITA units and headquarters in and around Angola. After building up a picture of UNITA's strengths and weaknesses, EO combat units would then commence a classic campaign of find, fix, and destroy.

Targets, having been located by reconnaissance, would suddenly be brought under attack by fixed-wing and helicopter gunships. This would serve to pin UNITA's forces in place. Artillery and mortars, flown into position, would then open up, furthering the process of forcing the enemy to seek cover. Then transport helicopters would place cut-off groups on routes out of the area to prevent escape. Finally, the main assault force of combined air and ground units would arrive to clear out the survivors.

In May 1994, EO and 16Bde captured Ndlatando city from UNITA in a stunning victory and went on to capture the Cafunfo diamond fields and recapture the Soyo oil region by the end of the year. These rapid victories against UNITA strongholds caught Savimbi off guard. Everywhere, his key financial assets were being seized by the South-African-backed MPLA. His drive to win a final victory was lost, at least temporarily. The pause to allow for negotiations outside Luanda had given his enemy enough breathing room to recover the initiative.

Savimbi was also suffering because the United Nations had lifted sanctions on the MPLA, but not on UNITA. Consequently, his forces were running short on all of their essential supplies. South Africa was no longer a source of support, due to the change in government there, and Zaire's contributions were simply insufficient. Battered on all fronts, Savimbi was even forced to give up his traditional stronghold at Huambo in November 1994, without a fight, to the advancing MPLA forces.

This, for Savimbi, was a difficult period. Like dos Santos only a year before, he was now watching as his forces were being pushed towards what might be a total defeat. Also like the MPLA president, he needed to find some breathing space to try somehow to regain the initiative. In late November 1994, after losing Huambo and retreating into his forest strongholds, Savimbi agreed to sign the U.N.-brokered Lusaka Peace Accord.

Throughout the campaign, EO mercenaries were at the forefront of the fighting. While they let the Angolans do most of the close-up combat work, the South Africans were never far away commanding the battles, co-coordinating air sorties, and directing artillery support. They also took a direct hand at critical moments using direct fire support from BMP-2 armored fighting vehicles and T-62 tanks to defeat UNITA strongpoints whenever the Angolan efforts faltered.

As a result of this successful relationship between EO and the MPLA government, the contract was renewed for a second year in 1995. By now, though, the work was far more training oriented as the ceasefire was technically still in effect.

For EO, this was a critical juncture. It had now come to the attention of the world, and questions were being raised about its mercenary activities. The United Nations, the OAU, and many world governments were starting to comment on EO's involvement in the Angolan war.

To counter this, EO went on the offensive. It began an intensive public relations campaign producing videos about its operations and inviting every major news organization in the world to come to Angola and see the work EO was doing there. Correspondents, investigative reporters, and photojournalists began to track the company's every move.

During this period, the international community made a few weak protests about EO's involvement in Angola, but there was a general sense of real confusion over the issue. A company like EO had been unknown for centuries, and there were just too many questions that needed to be answered. The situation was made even more complex because of the location of their success. Angola had led the world charge against mercenaries only twenty years earlier and had already signed the 1989 U.N. convention against mercenary activity. The world's leaders were uneasy about getting involved in any new debate on the issue, considering the complexities of the subject matter.

Also, it must be said that, since EO had been so successful in support of a legitimate government, any complaints against it would be difficult to support. UNITA was largely defeated, the internationally recognized MPLA government had been saved, and a previously ignored peace accord had finally been signed as a result of EO's involvement. The subsequent elections in Angola could also be considered a direct result of the successful military campaign EO had led. As a direct result of mercenary efforts, the political conflict-resolution agencies of the world community and various factions within Angola were finally in a situation where an end to the war might be negotiated.

During this period, EO was also moving quickly behind the scenes to consolidate its business position. Barlow and Luitingh had created a new holding company called the "Strategic Resources Corporation," registered in South Africa in 1995. Using this vehicle, the EO leadership either created or bought a large number of companies that would help make the firm more attractive to potential clients. By offering more than just mercenary services, EO ensured that it could dominate the market by providing a host of supporting capabilities. Strategic Resources offered medical services, construction and engineering expertise, and even a tourist agency.

One of EO's major investments was with Buckingham and his associate, another ex-SAS officer by the name of Simon Mann. This venture was Ibis Air and was the firm that would hold ownership over EO's new fleet of military and civilian aircraft. EO also maintained a close relationship with Buckingham's other ventures, including purchasing a share in Branch Energy (Angola).

Through 1995 and into 1996, EO continued to train the Angolan army. However, its time in that nation was quickly coming to an end. This came about for two reasons. First, Savimbi was openly critical of the MPLA's use of mercenaries in the most recent fighting. Although Savimbi had dabbled with mercenaries over the years, a good supply of battle-hardened UNITA troops had made their employment unnecessary in the latest conflict. The only exception had been in circumstances in which the purchase of high-technology equipment made their presence mandatory. With the loss of the diamond fields, Savimbi had lost most of his revenue and could not afford either the equipment or the manpower to answer the threat posed by the South Africans. It must have also been particularly galling to Savimbi that these same South Africans had been his allies in a common struggle only a few years before.

The second factor in EO's departure came from U.S. President Bill Clinton. In several addresses aimed at dos Santos's MPLA government in 1996, Clinton urged the Angolan leader to eject the South African mercenaries from his nation in the interests of peace and achieving a final resolution to the conflict. Of course there was also the less obviously stated intention of replacing them with American-owned assets.

EO made no public objection when it was asked to leave in mid-1996. Dos Santos expressed his appreciation for EO's efforts, but in the interests of reaching a lasting peace, the EO contract was to be concluded. For the South Africans and their British backers it had been a profitable venture. They had earned roughly US$80 million over the course of their two-and-a-half-year involvement for a cost of very few dead and wounded. In the history of the free companies, there were probably few condotte that were so successful in relative terms. Unfortunately, much of this income was to be eaten up in the company's next major project in Sierra Leone.

7

EXECUTIVE OUTCOMES
IN SIERRA LEONE

THE CONFLICT IN SIERRA LEONE had begun in March 1991. At this time, a Liberian-backed force of guerillas invaded areas of eastern Sierra Leone. Rebel leader Charles Taylor had all but won his battles for Liberia and his supporters were keen on adding the rich diamond mines in eastern Sierra Leone to their war chest. Unfortunately for the innocent populace, the Revolutionary United Front (RUF) was not concerned with winning the hearts and minds of the Sierra Leonean citizens. The rebels immediately began a program of intimidation and fear. They attacked the farmers, villagers, and miners in a horrible fashion. People were murdered or mutilated. Arms were amputated with machetes and women of all ages were raped. The rebels were thumbing their noses at the Freetown government, which was powerless to come to the aid of its people.

President Joseph Momoh, a congenial but entirely ineffectual leader, was running the country at this time. Having only a tiny, poorly led, and ill-equipped army at his disposal, Momoh and his cabinet had few options to deal with this armed insurrection. As the war worsened and the RUF became more bold, President Momoh began to look for help. The first place he turned was Britain.

The U.K. had held close ties with Sierra Leone since the early 1800s. The country had been a British protectorate and a strategic base in West Africa for many years. During World War II, the British government had recruited several combat units from Sierra Leone for the West African Division who went on to distinguish themselves in India and Burma.

During the Falklands War, British ships had used the port in Freetown as a logistical base. There was therefore a feeling in Freetown that the Sierra Leoneans had been there for the British when help was needed and now it was time to collect on those debts of friendship. However, Whitehall didn't feel the same way, and Momoh's request for military assistance was politely turned down.

By the end of 1991, Sierra Leone's token army was becoming demoralized. They could not defeat the rebels, and almost worse, President Momoh didn't appear to trust them. As morale sank, some army units began going over to the RUF. By early 1992, the Sierra Leonean army was broken and the rebels were approaching the capital.

Finally, on April 29, 1992, several junior army officers led by Captain Valentine Strasser forced their way into the president's offices and demanded some relief for the army. Momoh, thinking a coup was in progress, fled the building, leaving Strasser to wonder at his next course of action. Deciding that something needed to be done, and clearly the president wasn't up to the task, Strasser took control of the government. He declared himself head-of-state and formed a military council to run the country.

His first action was to open negotiations with RUF leader Foday Sankoh. However, the RUF could taste victory and were not interested in negotiation. The attacks on Freetown continued. In desperation, Strasser turned to Nigeria for help. The Nigerians agreed, if only to help contain the Liberians, who were becoming a threat to the stability of the entire region. Two thousand troops were sent to Freetown, and a few fighter aircraft were stationed at the airport.

To support his new foreign help, Strasser began a massive army recruitment drive. By late January 1994, the national army swelled in size from five thousand regulars to more than twelve thousand. Unfortunately, the recruits were not always of the highest quality. Street thugs, dope addicts, children, and released prisoners made up the ranks of the new Sierra Leonean army. Consequently, by early 1995, the military situation had not significantly improved. The Nigerians were hard pressed to do more than defend the airport and the capital. The army was proving entirely ineffective and the country was in ruins.

The atrocities committed by the RUF were mounting, and everywhere a sense of doom was rising.

Strasser finally decided that he needed professional help. As had many embattled African leaders before him, he turned to mercenaries to aid his struggling army. The first group he contacted was the British defense manufacturer J&S Franklin Limited. Strasser wanted someone to train his embattled army and give them an edge over the rebels. J&S Franklin accepted the contract and in turned hired Gurkha Security Guards, who had just left Angola the previous year.

The GSG team was led by Canadian-born mercenary Bob Mackenzie, who was a veteran of Vietnam and the Rhodesian SAS. Also on the team were ex-Gurkha officer James Maynard and a British ex-sergeant named Andrew Myres. The company brought in fifty Gurkha mercenary troops. This group arrived in Freetown during January 1995.

The project ended in disaster shortly afterwards. Major Mackenzie had decided to lead Sergeant Myres, five Gurkhas, and a platoon of Sierra Leone army troops on a scouting mission into the Malal hills to find a live firing range for the training. The group stumbled into a RUF jungle camp, and a fierce skirmish broke out. The Sierra Leonean troops immediately deserted Mackenzie, who had been wounded in the initial exchange of fire. The remaining Gurkhas and Sergeant Myres fought on until they were eventually overwhelmed and killed. With their leaders dead, the GSG company was left without the ability to carry on the contract. They quickly packed up their bags and departed Sierra Leone.

Strasser next turned to the new rising star in the field of mercenary operations: Executive Outcomes. The South Africans were just winding up their highly successful contract in Angola and were well positioned to bring critical military aid to Strasser and the Nigerians. The introduction was arranged once again by Anthony Buckingham, who had brought EO in to meet the Angolan government two years earlier. Buckingham was looking to expand his business empire out of Angola and into Sierra Leone. This time, he was in pursuit of diamonds. Here the entrepreneur found himself in the same situation he was in back in Angola. The rebel RUF forces had overrun the diamond mines, and the government was surrounded in the capital city. The Sierra Leonean army was defeated, and the situation looked grim. In fact, it was a direct repeat of the MPLA's situation in late 1993.

Given the situation, it was came as no surprise that Buckingham was willing to suggest to the Sierra Leone government that EO might be able to help. He arranged for the two groups to meet and, as a result of that meeting in April 1995, EO signed a contract to provide military support and training to the Sierra Leonean army. The price of the contract was to be US$2 million a month, and the mission was defined as one of providing assistance to the Sierra Leonean army in the conduct of its war with the rebel RUF.

Luther Eben Barlow had had been quite busy with building up EO over the past year. Based on their new financial position as a result of the Angolan contract, Barlow and Luitingh had invested most of EO's corporate profits into building a small but diverse business empire. They began to set up a corporate entity that paralleled a traditional national military structure. They had their flagship "army" company with EO. There was an impressive air force with Ibis Air. Trans Africa Logistics handled logistics. OPM Support Systems Limited employed retired military and police intelligence officers. Saracen International provided combat engineer duties such as minefield clearance and installation security. There was a medical company staffed by ex-South African Defense Forces doctors called Stuart Mills International, and communications were handled by Advanced Systems Communications. Altogether, the group appeared to have all the same assets and capabilities as any small western army.

The first contingent of fifty EO troops arrived in Freetown in early May and began to bring order to the chaos that was the Sierra Leonean army. EO took over a portion of Cockerill Barracks, the impressive headquarters building of the Sierra Leonean military, and began a restructuring process much as it had done in Angola the previous year.

EO immediately mapped out a three-phase campaign strategy. Phase one was to lift the siege of Freetown and give the government some breathing room. Phase two was to secure the diamond mines in the Koidu area. This was a crucial requirement because the diamond mines were the main source of revenue for the government. If Strasser was to have enough cash to run his country and pay EO's bill, he needed the diamond mines back. Phase three would be to hunt down and destroy the RUF.

The South Africans began by selecting a battalion of Sierra Leonean troops to train for the upcoming operations. Within the first month, however, they were forced to commence phase one because of the growing threat to Freetown. The operation was expected to last for nine weeks, but in fact it was completed in just ten days.

The RUF surrounding the capital were operating out of a main position in the hills just east of the city. EO began the operation by pounding the rebels' defenses with fire from Mi-24 Hind and Mi-17 Hip helicopter gunships. Then two BMP-2 fighting vehicles arrived to hammer the RUF with canon and machine-gun fire. Finally, EO-led companies of Sierra Leonean infantry stormed the position. The RUF lost two hundred dead in two days of fighting, and more than a thousand slave laborers, mostly children, that the RUF were holding were rescued.

With phase one complete, EO took two companies of infantry and the two BMP-2 vehicles and flew into the diamond areas around Kono. They met little opposition and, by July, the mines were back in government hands. That left only phase three to be completed. Using electronic intelligence and air-and-ground reconnaissance, EO located the RUF main headquarters fifty miles east of the capital and brought it under attack, killing many of the RUF leadership and destroying their ability to wage a concerted guerilla war.

Back in 1996, I had met with Ian Douglas, a retired Canadian general who worked in Sierra Leone in 1995–96 at the behest of the United Nations. At that time, I had just left the Canadian Forces and Douglas had offered to introduce me to EO if I was interested in becoming a mercenary. Knowing what I know now about the company, I often regret turning down his offer. Later, Douglas would write about his experiences in Sierra Leone and EO's successes in the 1995 campaign:

"The retaking of the mining areas demonstrated that a cohesive, well-trained organization, with appropriate intelligence and firepower, had the ability to defeat a force that outnumbered it significantly. The success of small-unit operations by the RSLMF [Sierra Leonean army] up to company level increased. This was particularly true when the organization had been trained by, and bonded with, similar EO elements. EO provided hard, combat-oriented training programs, supplemented by knowledgeable leadership – and leaders who led from the front, not the back...."

Through the rest of 1995 and into 1996 EO continued to lead select elements of the Sierra Leonean army against pockets of RUF fighters who had for the most part taken refuge in the jungle. As zones were cleared of rebels, the rest of the army began to settle in and reassert itself around the country.

Unfortunately, this wasn't a positive development. The army was poorly paid and was notorious for looting and robbery. The soldiers were often referred to as "sobels" (soldiers by day and rebels by night) due to their propensity to guard towns and diamond mines during daylight hours and then take off their uniforms and rob them by night. This made the army just as unpopular with the citizens of the country as the rebels were. Without a South African presence nearby and with no effective police force, the soldiers would terrorize the local villagers and then abandon their weapons and uniforms at the first sign of the RUF. Members of the military heirarchy itself were completely corrupt and were more concerned with their own private business ventures than with advancing the war with the rebels.

Witness to this situation, EO was introduced to a group known as the Kamajors. These were groups of traditional hunters who had taken up the struggle with the RUF when the army had been routed in the years before 1995. Unlike the army, who never left the towns and roads, the Kamajors took the war into the jungle and had been fighting a reasonably successful campaign by themselves against the RUF for several years. When the Sierra Leonean army returned to many areas where Kamajors were present, there was significant tension between the two groups. On more then one occasion, the Kamajors refused the army entry into towns and villages and were prepared to fight to keep them out. This situation naturally built up a significant amount of animosity between the army and the Kamajor militia.

For EO, the Kamajors were an intriguing new tool to employ in the war with the RUF. The South Africans began to train and equip Kamajor militia units and use them as scouts and raiders. Their ability to operate in the jungle, combined with a keen fighting spirit, made them good combat troops. Combined with EO leadership, they were an effective weapon against the RUF.

The fact that the majority of the rural populace supported the Kamajors while despising the army also made their employment crucial in the defense of the diamond mines and rural population centers. In 1996, the Kamajors were officially recognized and given the title "Civilian Defense Forces." Although this rankled the army, there was little that Strasser could do, since the Kamajors were his most effective troops and the South Africans preferred their involvement to army support.

The combined efforts of EO, the Kamajors, and to a lesser extent the army, broke and scattered the RUF in early 1996. Although they were not completely defeated, the rebel leadership under Foday Sankoh knew that their force was shattered. In April, Sankoh asked for a cease-fire and let it be known that he was willing to negotiate. However, neither Strasser nor anyone else who had been opposing the RUF was in a mood to discuss peace. The problem lay in the very nature of the RUF.

Much like Cardinal Robert of Geneva back in the fourteenth century, the RUF was an organization whose sole motivations were power and greed. In the pursuit of these goals, the rebels had used the most horrific and sadistic tactics imaginable. In a most random fashion, they would murder and mutilate anyone they came across regardless of whether they were pro-government, army, Kamajor or just simple villagers. Women and little girls were raped and then either murdered or had their arms hacked off with machetes. Young boys were forced to kill their friends and families and then were taken on as child soldiers. This pointless brutality made the RUF into true pariahs.

One of the South Africans told me of one brutal event. His helicopter patrol had spotted a group of Sierra Leonean villagers standing in a tight group on a stretch of highway. Nearby were several RUF fighters. The South Africans immediately set down their Mi-17 helicopter and several jumped out. Standing before them was a seven-year-old girl who just stood in the middle of the road staring at the white soldiers. All the while she was holding out two arms that had been amputated at the elbow only moments before. The South Africans were enraged and fired off burst after burst at the fleeing RUF. They then took the little girl into their helicopter and flew her straight to Freetown and the hospital there. For most of EO's men, the RUF were simply sadistic terrorists that needed to be dealt with in the harshest manner available.

When the RUF was initially founded in the late 1980s, it began as an organized movement for political change. The leaders of the core group were unhappy with the corrupt leadership in Freetown and the terrible standard of living in the rural areas. Many of these revolutionaries were university students with a socialist bent who had been trained in Libya. Their group was planning a well-managed movement to bring down the Momoh government and replace it with a new "people's government."

However, over time the RUF mutated, as the original ideological leaders were killed and new, more vicious and greedy elements moved in. Men whose only motivation was access to the diamonds and the riches they could bring. Many of the thugs that took control of the RUF had fought in Liberia with Charles Taylor and had come to Sierra Leone following the lure of the diamonds. The political platform disappeared as they fought purely to keep the government and the Sierra Leone people from interfering with their quest for wealth.

So initially there was no ceasefire. EO and the Kamajor militia continued to hunt down the surviving RUF elements, culminating in an attack on the RUF headquarters in October 1995. By various means, EO had located the main base in the jungle and a large force of Kamajors, army units, and South Africans attacked it. The base was destroyed and many of the RUF leadership were killed. This effectively finished the RUF. There were still many small roving bands around the country, but it would take a lot of time and money to rebuild the movement.

Having won the war, President Strasser announced a ceasefire in November, and it looked like the fighting might be over. EO moved into a defensive mode and took over guarding key installations and mining centers while the international community began pressuring Strasser to call a general election.

One real problem for EO was its pay. Under its initial contract, EO was to be paid US$2 million a month. The government, having no cash available in 1995, got Barlow to agree to accept a portion of the government's future revenues from mining operations in lieu of cash. The government normally taxed diamond, gold, bauxite, and rutile mines based on the volume of minerals recovered. Assuming EO won, the mines would reopen and it could then be paid. In the interim, EO was forced to take profits from the Angolan contract to pay its own expenses in Sierra Leone. Barlow threatened to withdraw his company if the situation wasn't soon resolved. Unfortunately, by the end of 1995 very few of Sierra Leone's mines were up and running and the Strasser government simply did not have enough finances to pay EO's bills.

This put the government in a very difficult position. Caving in to international pressure, the Strasser junta had agreed to call an election, which was scheduled for February 1996. The problem was that the Sierra Leonean army was distinctly unhappy about the prospect of a return to civilian rule. Having essentially run the country since the 1970s, many senior military officers had built lucrative empires that would be in jeopardy if they became accountable to an elected government. Knowing a coup was likely, Strasser needed EO to keep the army in line.

Financial pressure on Barlow made the possibility of keeping EO in Sierra Leone without any form of payment untenable. The South Africans met with Strasser in late December and announced that unless some payment system was organized, they were leaving. After some negotiating, Barlow accepted a plan that would see EO write off $2.5 million from the overall bill in exchange for a $3 million payment in January 1996. Subsequently, Sierra Leone would make monthly installments of $1.5 million against the balance owed. Strasser also asked Barlow if he could provide an extra two hundred mercenaries during the elections to make sure that neither the army nor the RUF disrupted them. Barlow agreed on a supplementary deal for the added manpower at a rate of $2 million a month.

With the finances temporarily sorted out, EO went back to work getting everything ready for the elections. Both the RUF and the army were likely to oppose the process, so EO stepped up Kamajor patrols around Freetown and other key centers. Inevitably, the worst happened. With only five weeks to go before the elections, Brigadier General Julius Maada-Bio staged a coup and took control of the government. Maada-Bio's sister was a key figure in the RUF hierarchy, and many observers began to wonder at the level of corruption and deceit that plagued the Sierra Leonean army command. Immediately, both the new junta and the RUF called for a postponement to the elections.

However, in a concerted display of the democratic process, the people of Sierra Leone held demonstrations and continued to press for the elections to go ahead. International pressure also fell upon Maada-Bio to make sure that the process went ahead on schedule. Eventually, the junta agreed and the elections where held.

Throughout all this EO remained largely uninvolved. With nearly three hundred mercenaries in the country and in control of virtually all of the heavy equipment, they could have intervened on behalf of Strasser, but chose to remain neutral. The idea of mercenaries toppling the new head-of-state to replace the recently dethroned military junta was simply too controversial to get mixed up in. Instead, EO just continued to watch the RUF.

Its vigilance paid off when Kamajor patrols found a large concentration of RUF fighters in a staging area north of Freetown in January. Obviously intending to conduct attacks during the election process, it was the largest gathering of rebels that EO had seen in months. A coordinated attack was launched, and the RUF were broken up with heavy losses.

The elections went forward with some disruption from the RUF and the army, but most observers felt that, as African elections go, it was fairly acceptable. Afterwards, the newly installed President Kabbah inherited a huge mess. The army, morosely unhappy about the new government, took a somewhat rogue attitude and began to operate almost as a private force. They controlled many areas and ran them as they saw fit. The Kamajors controlled other regions and were very pro-government. They continued to clash with the army and arguments often broke out into open fighting.

President Kabbah was faced with a rogue and coup-prone army that resented his presence, a civilian militia (the Kamajors) that wasn't really the army or the police but was loyal to him and could keep him in power, and a rebel movement that was still smoldering out in the jungles. On top of everything else, his country was being held together by a couple of hundred South African mercenaries.

The first thing that Kabbah did was to appoint a Kamajor, Chief Sam Norman, to the post of the acting minister of defense. This allowed the Kamajor Civilian Defense Forces to become the de facto army in Sierra Leone. Kabbah then chastised the actual army for a lack of loyalty and pursuing their own self-interests above the needs of the people. He would eventually fire nearly two hundred senior officers and NCOS.

His next act was to call in EO and explain that the country simply couldn't afford the present arrangement; he reduced the monthly payments to $1.2 million. The present contract was due to expire in December, and that would be the end of the project as far as Kabbah was concerned. EO could hardly complain. Out of the $20 million the government of Sierra Leone had been billed, less than $5 million had actually been paid. EO had no choice but to accept the new arrangement and hope the government would begin to pay its invoices. In the interim, it was to reduce its level of operations and focus on keeping the revenue-generating mine regions safe.

The situation changed dramatically in September when the RUF resumed its acts of random violence in the communities and returned to attacking government forces. Despite calls from Kabbah to enter into peace talks, Sankoh and the RUF persisted with a campaign of violence. Completely frustrated with the RUF's continued atrocities, the president summoned EO and ordered it to go on the offensive. Released from their monotonous security duties, the South Africans set upon the RUF. In a series of well-executed attacks, EO, the Kamajors, and ECOMOG forces (West African states' joint peacekeeping forces) smashed several RUF bases. EO had found the RUF's new headquarters at Zagoda and hit it, killing many of the surviving senior rebel commanders. Using intelligence captured in the raid, the government forces then hit an RUF battalion in its camp near Freetown. Another major RUF base on the Liberian border was flattened soon afterwards. The RUF was once again reduced to a few die-hard stragglers in less than a month by South African-led forces. Finally, Sankoh agreed to meet in Abidjan and sign a peace accord.

As part of the negotiations, however, Sankoh insisted that any cessation of hostilities must be conditional on the withdrawal of EO and ECOMOG forces from Sierra Leone. Like UNITA in Angola, his rebels had no answer to the professional mercenaries. If his movement was ever to have any long-term hope of success and even survival, a way had to be found to remove them from the equation.

Kabbah, despite his dislike for the mercenaries, was loath to do this. During September and October, there were three separate attempts at a military coup by senior army officers. In the days prior to the elections, Maada-Bio had held secret talks with the RUF, and Kabbah was suspicious that the army and the rebels may have come to some arrangement to cooperate in removing his elected government.

The key to the whole issue was the South Africans. Working as they were now for a legitimate, elected government, they were a major factor in Kabbah's grip on power. Because it was owed a considerable amount of money that it would never see if a joint rebel-army junta seized power, EO was expected to remain entirely loyal. The army may have been able to sideline EO if they were in command, but Kabbah's appointment of a Kamajor defense minister kept the army away from the mercenaries. The Kamajor militia was fiercely loyal to the South Africans, and together with EO this group gave Kabbah a force that could balance the army and the RUF. ECOMOG, though present in Sierra Leone, was not strong enough at that point to depend on alone.

However, the international community took up Sankoh's call for the removal of the mercenaries. Although most foreign observers acknowledged that EO was responsible for ending the war and for enabling elections to take place, it was just too morally difficult for them to accept EO's presence.

The weight that probably tipped the scales was the International Monetary Fund (IMF). In agreeing to fund President Kabbah's rebuilding of the country, the IMF had made strict stipulations about how the money should be spent. While being forced to budget under IMF-imposed austerity measures, the Sierra Leonean government just simply could not afford the cost of the South Africans. Kabbah was really left with no choice. EO had to go. In January 1997 EO withdrew from Sierra Leone.

As we now know, the Sierra Leonean army did stage a coup four months after EO departed in May 1997 and removed President Kabbah. We also know that the RUF seemed to know that the army rebellion was coming and moved quickly to join the rogue soldiers in looting and destroying Freetown. Kabbah must have known the coup was about to occur as well. When Alan Bell flew out of Freetown on his way to London the day before the coup, President Kabbah's wife was seated behind him on the plane. On either side of the first lady were two tough South African bodyguards.

A few South Africans had stayed behind when EO pulled out to provide technical assistance to the army. Of those who remained in government employ, most flew the new helicopters that had been purchased during the war. As the coup broke in the early morning of May 25, several of the pilots went to their aircraft and took off to lend support to the army in stopping what they thought was a rebel attack. When it was learned that the army was behind the coup and Kabbah had fled to the Nigerian-held airport, the pilots returned to base, collected the rest of their ground crews, and flew out to the Nigerian base at Luingi airport. Many of these men stayed on to fight with the Nigerians despite the fact there was no more pay. They had fought for Sierra Leone for two years and were reluctant to give it up to criminals and terrorists.

For EO, Sierra Leone was the beginning of the end. The money lost on the project put Barlow and his executives in a difficult position. International media attention hounded them, and the South African government was bringing into force new legislation to prevent South African companies from providing military assistance to foreign states without government permission.

When Tim Spicer won his contract to provide equipment and mercenaries to Papua New Guinea, he was going to subcontract most of the
work to EO, but that project ended in disaster and embarrassment.

EO went through a period of restructuring in 1997 and 1998 with
Barlow and Luitingh stepping down and relinquishing leadership of the
firm to the new CEO, Nick Van den Berg. Some of the sub-companies
were closed and much of the air fleet was sold off. Eventually, unable
to find any new contracts, the company closed its doors in December
1998, ending nine years of operations.

The various men who had worked for EO over the years went on to
other projects. Some stayed in Angola and worked for security companies. About twenty-five ex-EO men set up Lifeguard Security to guard
the diamond mines in Sierra Leone in early 1997. By 1999, however, Lifeguard was reduced to fifteen men guarding a hydroelectric dam in north-
central Sierra Leone and a few others periodically checking on abandoned mining equipment for the absent Sierra Rutile Corporation.

Unlike Hawkwood before them, there was no last great heroic
charge into glory. For EO, the end came without fanfare as the offices
were closed, the phones disconnected, and the website closed down.
However, few doubt that these men won't continue to show up in
other companies and other countries in the years ahead. For the
moment, anyway, their free company was at an end.

There's no point in glorifying Executive Outcomes. At worst, it par-
ticipated in the killing of many combatants in two vicious little African
wars that were not its own. It revived a model of warfare that had
pretty much ceased to exist over a century earlier. In doing so, it may
have set the stage for far more bloody struggles to come across Africa
and the rest of the world. EO's ability to wage successful military campaigns for very little money in the grand scheme of things may have
upped the ante and provided a dangerous precedent for other embattled leaders around the globe.

However.

The growing trend in civil warfare around the globe as we enter the
twenty-first century has shifted away from classic military combat in
which two opposing forces fight each other until one side is defeated

and the other claims victory. In its place, modern wars tend to disdain direct combat between forces and concentrate on targeting the civilian populations in an effort to destroy the political and ethnic power base of the opposing forces. In the former Yugoslavia, Rwanda, Sudan, the Congos, Burundi, Algeria, Liberia, Central African Republic, and a host of others, this "terroristic" approach to conflict has turned warfare into human tragedies for civilian populations, as opposed to focusing on victory through battlefield casualties.

During EO's involvement in Angola and Sierra Leone, its presence and leadership turned the campaigns back into struggles between military forces. At no time did EO ever specifically target civilian populations. In fact, it often supported NGO efforts to help civilian populations in these areas by safeguarding the delivery of humanitarian support. Against legitimate combatants, they were ruthless … and successful.

It cannot be denied that EO's involvement in a campaign increased the level of violence by using sophisticated air and ground hardware, but the accusation is irrelevant. There is no "nice" way to fight a war. Is it better to let various ethnic groups spray each other with rusty AK-47's or hack children apart with machetes with no end in sight or to employ modern combat systems and professional soldiers to bring about a resolution in a matter of months?

EO has never been accused of any atrocities. It has been identified as causing significant collateral damage, but that is what international guidelines for warfare are all about. After the Kosovo and Iraqi campaigns by the western world in the late 1990s there can be no argument on this point.

As a soldier I can appreciate what EO has accomplished. Having been part of the United Nations forces in Rwanda in 1994 and having felt the frustration that failed mission generated, I envy EO's ability to take direct action. In Rwanda, the U.N. had advance notice of the Hutu plans for genocide and had the forces available in the country to stop them. However, the U.N.'s unwillingness to take direct military action led to the execution of hundreds of thousands of innocent civilians and more than a few U.N. soldiers. In comparison, when EO deployed it was under no such constraints. Its very employment was founded on the concept of direct action.

I have to respect a group of soldiers who have had the courage to put their lives at risk when the rest of the international community just stood by and watched. In both Angola and Sierra Leone they fulfilled their contracts and won these dirty little wars for their paymasters. That in both cases the political powers could not capitalize on the victories won by EO with political settlements cannot be blamed on their mercenaries. Soldiers can't stop wars. They can only win battles, and EO did its part with élan.

In my travels researching this book I have met many people with similar opinions. A director for a United Nations aid agency with whom I spoke says that EO did a great job in Sierra Leone, and it was the doom of that country to let it go. In Sierra Leone I spoke with another United Nations employee working with the observer mission there. He had been witnessing the RUF's atrocities for many months and often felt completely frustrated.

"A couple of hundred good mercenaries could end this war in a month or two," he said.

"That has to be better than this endless horror."

The Sierra Leoneans I talked to were split on the issue. Most younger people felt that the South African had just stolen their diamonds, but the older Sierra Leoneans knew better.

"They came here and they fought for us when no one else would. It is a shame they are not here now," one middle-aged former miner told me.

In the French Foreign Legion, the concept of honor is based on one's contract. For the Legionnaire who deserts with his contract incomplete, there is only shame. If a man stays and completes his contract, then he is an honorable man. Whatever anyone can say about EO and the men who worked for them, it can never be said that they didn't complete their contracts.

8

THE BUSINESS OF INTERNATIONAL SECURITY

A Model for Success?

*"There are the modern private security companies which provide many
different kinds of service, economic advice and sophisticated military
training but which are covers for former professional soldiers and mercenaries offering themselves as a solution, in exchange for large sums
of money, to countries experiencing instability and armed conflict and
the consequent impossibility of developing their enormous natural
resources. Such companies, as will be discussed below, today represent
the biggest and most sophisticated threat to the peace, sovereignty and
self-determination of the peoples of many countries...."*
    – Excerpt from the 1997 Ballesteros Thematic Report
    on Mercenarism (E/CN.4/119/24) to the United
    Nations' Commission on Human Rights

AFTER LOOKING at the international security industry, defining its
membership, categorizing its component parts, and regaling ourselves with tales of their adventures, the question still remains: Is this
a viable business industry? Certainly some pretty significant numbers have been tossed around. Annual sales of US$58 billion in 1998.
Contracts worth millions of dollars, extending over several years, for
individual companies. Powerful western governments lobbying for
their own respective firms. Buy-outs and share strategies. Negotiations for ownership in diamond, oil, and other projects.

Yet, what about the cost of doing business? What does it cost to hire two hundred South Africans to staff a contract? What perks are offered? How about life insurance, performance bonuses or optional buy-ins? Not to mention ammunition, weapons, uniforms, radios, food, vehicles, spare parts, batteries, medical supplies, and all the other stores critical to any military campaign.

Another issue that seems to be of import is exactly how these companies are organized. Are they run like any other business, or do they move in the shadow of numbered offshore accounts, numbered companies, and corrupt Third World governments? In previous chapters, I discussed a few specific businesses by categories of what they do, but are they successful business ventures?

For the military security company which doesn't win gigantic government projects and must exist on smaller corporate contracts, how much business is out there? Why did one of the first and most respected firms in this market, DSL, sell out and convert to a security service provider? Perhaps the business model of the international security industry needs to be looked at nearly as much as what type of business these companies are doing.

The security services industry is probably the smallest and easiest-to-manage category. The conduct of security-only contracts can be accomplished by no more than a couple of consultants, a telephone, and a computer for each contract. However, this small-scale requirement can be both a strength and a weakness. Like any other business, there is a right way and a wrong way to run a company. Let's first have a closer look at the most successful firm in the category: the Control Risks Group.

Control Risks evolved out of another company known as the "Hogg Robinson Insurance and Travel Group." During the 1970s, this firm was supplying major corporations with specialized insurance, travel planning, financial consulting, and project support. One of the areas in which it provided advice to its clients was risk management. Hogg Robinson was known as a firm with an extensive knowledge of international markets, and it worked with its clients to help them operate safely and profitably around the world. This firm was also one of the first insurance agents to begin looking at arranging Kidnap & Ransom insurance for its corporate clients.

In 1980, five of the principal managers of Hogg Robinson's K&R division got together and decided that there was room to expand in the security market. They formed a business plan, raised some capital from financial institutions, and bought the risk management division from Hogg Robinson.

The new company was named Control Risks, and the founding members quickly began to bring in experienced military men such Christopher Grouse, who we met in Chapter 4. With an existing client base brought over from Hogg Robinson, sufficient working capital and some first-class staff, Control Risks was well launched into the international security industry.

The first thing the company did was define its market. Control Risks's competition at the time consisted of mostly fly-by-night, spare-bedroom companies providing security, military security, and military combat services, like John Banks's "SAS." Other more serious peers were the growing firms such as the fledgling DSL or Keeni-Meeny Services. However, both these latter two firms were working in the military security and military combat fields. Control Risks chose the security services category instead.

Hoping to steer clear of such shadowy firms and move primarily in the "corporate world," Control Risks took on all the aspects of a regular British business. It chose offices with an eye to prestige, maintained secretaries, and kept proper records. Meetings were held in a typical boardroom environment, which made clients comfortable with the "business" atmosphere of the firm. Being one of the few companies in existence with actual experience in Kidnap & Ransom response, Control Risks was a natural to win the Lloyds of London contract for K&R consulting.

Over the years, the company has pursued its market with typical British conservatism. Its members belong to all the right clubs, suits are Savile Row only, and controversy is avoided at all costs. This combination makes Control Risks the leading company in the field of security services. It has never dabbled in military-security services and has avoided mercenary services like the plague.

"We don't even use the 'M' word around here," noted Christopher Grouse.

As we enter the new millennium, Control Risks has offices in sixteen countries serving more than 3,500 clients with operations in 130 nations. Like any successful business in any industry, its success is based on running a well-managed agency that provides a high quality of service with a good degree of client satisfaction and the resulting repeat business.

If Control Risks is a model for success in the security services sector, a company I will refer to as the "Hammer Group Inc." reflects most of the rest of the industry. The Hammer Group was formed in 1989 by "Don Hammer," a former member of the British army. On retirement, Don emigrated to Canada and decided to set up his own security services company in the city of Toronto. To get started, the new entrepreneur came up with some marketing material and advertised close protection services to major clients. Quite quickly, Don won a contract from a wealthy family to provide quasi-bodyguards. The client owned several large businesses, and Don was tasked to provide drivers for the head of the family and for the key executives in the company.

For this first contract Don hired a couple of former security guards with no training or experience and made them executive drivers. The reason Don chose former security guards? The price, mainly. Highly qualified close protection specialists can demand up to US$10,000 a month for a long-term contract. Security guards, however, work for maybe $2,500 a month. The other factor in not wanting to hire well-trained professionals was that Don had no actual training in VIP security. The branch of military service he came from did not get involved in this type of work. Don probably felt that, as president of the company, it wouldn't do to have staff who knew the jobs he was servicing better than he did. Security guards, on the other hand, with no training of their own, could be more easily impressed by tales of their boss's military expertise.

With this first major contract Don immediately decided he was a success. On the strength of this early business, he went looking for partners who wanted to invest in his company. To get involved, the terms were a contribution of $50,000 for a fifteen percent share. Within a year, Don found three likely candidates who were willing to buy in.

With his new partners, some money in the bank and one major client, Don began to expand. He began looking internationally, primarily in Mexico, and at other opportunities domestically. Despite his desire to join the big leagues offshore, his next success was domestic. The Hammer Group had begun offering a night-response service. Wealthy clients were given a telephone number to call if they ever felt threatened in their homes during the night. Don had a pager attached to the number and put a security guard in a patrol car to respond. Whenever a wealthy client heard something that might indicate a burglar or intruder, he or she dialed the number and one of Don's guards sped to the scene to investigate.

This service was not widely accepted, but slowly Don managed to find enough subscribers to make it profitable. However, problems quickly began to arise with the new business. The cracks first began to appear with a contract in a city several hundred miles away. Don's task was to escort a client to a conference in the distant city. However, Don asked the two guards he was sending to drive their own cars, pay for their own food, fuel, and accommodations, assuring them he would reimburse them when they returned. His guards, happy to be out of their former mall security jobs, didn't complain and agreed. Naturally, on their return, they found Don difficult to get hold of, and, not only were they not paid, they weren't reimbursed for their expenses.

Why not? Don had taken all of the money in the business and purchased a grand, six-thousand-square-foot mansion in a trendy new community. The revenues from his major client, his night response clients, and most of the other small projects went to paying for the house, filling it with fine furniture, and paying himself a significant salary.

Don, realizing he was in over his head, began avoiding his partners, now that their investment had gone into his new home. His employees were completely ignored, especially when it came time for them to collect their paychecks. To resolve the situation, Don fired all of his guards and hired his son to service his major client. Don began doing the night-response patrols himself. His former employees were never paid or reimbursed, and his partners haven't received any return on their investment.

Where Control Risks is a well-run business first and a security services company second, Don's enterprise was a poorly managed business and a poorly operated security company.

Strangely, the Hammer Group is still in business after ten years. It continues to exist on the small night-response service and the driver-bodyguard contract. Don has pursued international clients, but largely without success. Periodically, he recruits new staff who have never heard of him and abuses their goodwill until they become fed up and quit. In this fashion, Don has managed to keep his fine home and has even kept his major client.

The Hammer Group raises three issues that, unfortunately, are typical of the security services sector. Like most business start-ups, more than eighty percent are doomed to fail in their first five years. The deciding factor is usually the lack of good management and business techniques. Soldiers do not acquire much in the way of business acumen while serving in the military and consequently have a difficult time managing their own businesses. This has the overall effect of producing volumes of small, short-life-span companies that promise much and then fail to deliver. The end result is a lack of overall confidence and credibility among the potential clients of the security industry.

One look at the local business phone directory in an average city will bear out this assertion. In every case, there are hundreds of companies advertising all manner of services, but phone calls to the listed numbers will show many disconnections, overburdened answering machines, and residential locales. Businesses that never got off the ground.

The second factor here is the inability of clients to investigate the credentials of companies offering a wide array of services that they may or may not be qualified to offer. Certainly, men like Alan Bell, Christopher Grouse, or Alistair Morrison are qualified to offer the services they do.

Don Hammer, on the other hand, is not. Military organizations are rarely cooperative when civilian companies want to call up and review the personnel files of retired soldiers, especially special forces soldiers. Therefore, just about anyone can claim to have served in an elite military unit, and the client has no way of verifying the information.

This is one of the reasons why within the industry it is so important to "vet" each other and find a common point of reference to verify claims. Working with someone who claims to be a highly qualified special forces operative who turns out to have been a cook or mechanic can be hazardous to your health. For clients, however, a judgment has to be made on character alone, and unfortunately a poorly qualified but charming individual like Hammer can do a lot of harm.

The third and final issue is the very service that security companies provide. Many clients trust their businesses, their property, and even their lives to security service companies. When an oil company is looking at a new project in Africa or South America, it may spend up to $100 million just in the feasibility, due diligence, and project start-up phases before the first liter of petroleum is pumped. If the security consultant hired to review security issues fails to note that a local terrorist organization is planning to target foreign oil companies as a way of striking at the national government's credibility, the potential for disaster can be immense.

When clients hire bodyguards, investigators or K&R consultants who are not qualified to handle these vital tasks, lives can be jeopardized. It is distinctly less worrisome if the local shoe store fails or a technology company goes bankrupt. Yes, a few jobs are lost, but the consequences pale in comparison to the damage an unqualified, poorly managed security services company can cause.

If the record of the small, spare-bedroom-and-a-fax-machine-style companies is so dismal, then why don't clients just stick to the majors such a Control Risks or KPMG? Christopher Grouse explains:

"We occasionally come up against the problem of the little company competing for the same contract that we interested in. Obviously, they do not have the business overhead we do and can underbid us significantly. On that basis, we can't compete with them. For Control Risks, our reputation for delivering a quality service often wins out, but a persuasive independent can often claim anything and bid lower. It is a constant problem."

The shadow profession is a profession, but the lack of a certification system makes the smooth-tongued independent a real risk for the majors. Checking the credentials of lawyers, doctors or nuclear scientists who claim to have graduated from Harvard, Oxford or some other prestigious academy can be a simple matter. For the retired military serviceman, the same does not apply. Therefore, the small security start-up is often willing to make any claim or offer a reduced billing rate to compete with the majors. The question then becomes: Can the small firm reliably service the contract? When it does not and the company goes out of business, it is inevitably replaced by a dozen other start-ups that repeat the cycle.

The military security service sectors face many of the same business challenges as the security services market. However, in addition to the pressure of operating a successful business, there is often the added pressure of navigating the political environment that goes along with these services. Companies like MPRI and Levdan work almost exclusively with the United Nations, national governments, and other international organizations. To be successful, these respective management teams must move in the complex and demanding waters of international politics and mega-project tendering processes.

The military security industry is therefore divided up into three elements that each target a different sector of this business category. There are the top-of-the-food-chain firms servicing the big, multinational projects – companies such as Levdan and MPRI. Then there is a mid-level of companies targeting the projects that are either too small or too controversial for the majors. Finally, at the bottom of the market are the one-man, spare-bedroom independents who will take any job that they can win.

The majors in the military security field are very similar to the major security services companies in that they are very much businesses first and industry contractors second. With hundreds of employees, tens of millions of dollars in revenue, and a large infrastructure to support, MPRI is truly a modern corporation like any other. The business model of this firm is the same business model one would find in any high-tech, multi-discipline corporate environment. The principal motivation is good business, not just the servicing of the shadow profession's market.

The Vinnell Corporation of the United States has maintained a decade-old, US$170 million contract to train the Saudi Arabian National Guard. This firm is partly owned by the Carlyle Group, headed up by former U.S. Secretary of Defense Frank Carlucci. DynCorp, founded in 1946, has provided technology and logistics support for the American army in Korea, Vietnam, Grenada, and the Gulf War. With nineteen thousand employees and over a billion dollars in annual revenues, Dyn-Corp is also a major international corporation. Its company web page declares that, "When the Department of State needs personnel to reconstitute, establish, and maintain rule of law in emerging democracies, they come to DynCorp."

These above companies, along with several others around the world, make up the industry majors. Some are publicly traded corporations and a few are employee-owned. Others are still privately held. These firms are business successes of the first order and are consequently often beyond the scope of any group of retired military veterans. They employ hundreds or thousands of full-time staff and have diversified investment holdings or multi-disciplined divisions. These firms, such as MPRI, are supported by major financial institutions and rely on the critical advice of experienced business managers who flesh out their management teams.

Operating on a much smaller scale are the mid-level military-security companies. These firms are more likely to be staffed principally by retired soldiers at the management level and have only a handful of full-time staff. The market these firms target is one that requires some level of corporate depth but not the massive resources of a major firm. The projects undertaken are ones that are profitable, but not to the degree that the majors will take notice. Also, the mid-level firms generally take on the projects that are too controversial for their more politically sensitive big brothers.

The most successful niche in the mid-size market is the provision of armed guards. Ex-soldiers are regularly retained to organize armed guard services in dangerous regions. The mid-level military security companies thrive in this area because in it there is always the ever-present association with mercenary services, and that keeps the majors away. While it is true that you will find well-armed ex-soldiers on these projects who are willing to fight in defense of their client's property, they do not fulfill the requirements for mercenary status. Their job is security, not military operations, and that is the critical difference.

In Angola, two companies known as Teleservices and Alpha 5 provide armed guards for mining and petroleum projects. Both companies are owned by senior Angolan army officers but are primarily managed by South African ex-soldiers. While most of the actual guards are Angolan, the South Africans manage all of the routine functions and provide direction during response incidents. Why the South African presence? Because these are the most reliable professionals available and western companies investing in Angola have little confidence in Angolan security forces. Just as EO mercenaries "stiffened" the Angolan army to produce effective results, other South African soldiers stiffen the security companies.

In the event of an attack, the guards are equipped and trained to defend their client's lives and facilities, but they will only do enough to discourage the attackers from pressing their actions. In the event of a major UNITA offensive in their area, the guards and their clients will pull out and wait for the army to come in and clear out the area before returning.

In the fall of 1998 UNITA rebels attacked a Canadian-run diamond mine at Yetwene in the Lunda Norte province of Angola. Here, about twenty guards from Teleservices were on duty protecting the mine and its staff. They were armed with automatic rifles and machine-guns and defended the mine for a time before finally withdrawing. The end of the battle saw eight dead, twenty-four wounded, and ten personnel hauled away as hostages.

In Sierra Leone, another military security services company known as Lifeguard was responsible for security at a diamond property in the Kono district. Here South African personnel built a complete military-style defensive position around the mine areas to protect their British and Canadian clients. There were sandbagged machine-gun bunkers, underground shelters, and helipads for re-supply. When the May 1997 coup erupted in Freetown, about fifteen South African Lifeguard employees found themselves cut off and surrounded by several hundred rebels. Trapped with the Lifeguard security personnel was a collection of miners, aid workers, and even a British soldier-of-fortune. With no means of escape and no desire to surrender, the security guards fought off the RUF for nearly a month before being evacuated.

An executive for a Toronto-based diamond-mining firm I spoke to recently was one of the men trapped in Kono with Lifeguard.

"I felt safer there than I think I would have in Freetown. Those Lifeguard guys were great. Very professional. Our only worry was how long we were going to be there. We heard about the evacuations and wondered how things were going to turn out. Eventually a Russian helicopter came in to fly us out," he explained.

The mid-level companies that supply these services are very much like any other small business. There is usually an office in a major city and a small staff responsible for reception, marketing, and day-to-day business management. The incomes for projects like Angola and Sierra Leone hover near the one-million-dollar mark annually. In Lifeguard's case, figures supplied to me in 1997 showed their billing rate as US$70,000 a month for fifteen staff. The actual manpower for these projects normally comes from the "circuit," either in Britain or South Africa. Shadow professionals are hired for four-to-six-month contracts and paid $5,000 to $8,000 a month.

The competition for these contracts is very stiff. There are only so many places in the world where the right combination of elements comes together to make these projects feasible. Normally, winning one long-term contract is the dividing line between success and failure for these mid-level firms.

The conditions that make a suitable market for mid-level companies are also the factors that make their employment so controversial. First and foremost, they operate typically in a country with significant internal risks – either civil wars in progress or terrorist factions that pose a threat to foreign investment.

This leads to the second condition: international investment. In countries where there is no international presence, there is also no need for expensive foreign security expertise, nor is there money to pay for them. Local resources can often suffice. However, introduce a foreign corporation into the mix and it will want a more reliable level of security. This means importing expertise.

Of course, to interest international investment there must be some type of resource that is valuable enough to gain the attention of acquisition-minded corporations. As the big multi-nationals move into these dangerous markets, they bring mid-size military security service providers with them.

This series of conditions is also the foundation for much of the controversy surrounding military security service firms. As evident in the quote that opens this chapter, many people are convinced that these companies are simply fronts for mercenary companies extorting riches from impoverished nations. It is this controversy that keeps the majors out of these projects. However, for the mid-size firms, these projects are their lifeblood.

To clarify the status of such firms, there are three elements to consider when discussing armed security guards. Does the company agree to fight to pacify the areas around the mine or oil well? Do the imported experts actually function as armed guards? Finally, do the imported experts function solely as managers and instructors, leaving the guard services to trained local workers?

If the company is contracted to fight to pacify a "safe" area around a mine or well, it is a military combat company and its employees can be considered mercenaries. Executive Outcomes' clearing and securing of the diamond mines in Sierra Leone or the oil tank farms in Angola would be an example. However, if the company only advertises and performs protective guard services, and is staffed by shadow professionals, then it is a military security company. Gurkha Security Guards Limited had the contract to defend the Angolan oilfields prior to the arrival of Executive Outcomes in that theater. However, GSG refused to conduct combat operations and withdrew from the country when the fighting overran its client's properties. In Sierra Leone, GSG was hired to train the Sierra Leonean army, but, as we saw, it pulled out when its officers were killed by rebels in an ambush.

In Algeria now there are several firms working for the industry giant Bechtel that provide this type of service. Guards are hired from the retired ranks of the French Foreign Legion or the British Army to patrol the massive pipelines that crisscross this embattled nation. They are given Land Rovers, a shotgun, and a couple of local guards armed with AK-47s and instructed to spend their days cruising over the desert plains and mountains. The task is not to fight the terrorists that plague the nation, but simply to protect the investment of the western companies involved.

The final category of contracted work in this discussion is a guard service in which foreign professionals are employed in a management role only. All of the actual manpower is hired and trained locally. This would be a security services project and could keep that status as long as the imported professionals never carry arms.

However, regardless of which category the armed guard service fits into, it is easy prey for the accusation of conducting mercenary services. This is especially true with the military security companies which arm their imported professionals and expect them to defend their client's properties.

For this reason, most of the mid-size firms in the military security category try to maintain close ties with the various governments with which they are involved, both at home and abroad. While they can rarely generate the political clout of a major, they need a least some "protection" to survive. At the very least, they need the active disinterest of their home government to avoid censure. Both Watchguard and DSL set a clear precedent in this regard.

Survival, therefore, as a business and at the political level for these firms is a difficult balancing act. Projects are invariably in war zones or other regions of conflict. Various companies vie for the few contracts, and none can rely on its home government to intervene on its behalf. At the same time, they have to count on the fact that their home governments won't stop the project either before it gets started or at some future point when the press discovers the story.

The final category of the military security services sector is the one-man, spare-bedroom operation. Much the same as their brethren in the security services sector, these individuals are often a major headache for the mid-sized and majors in this market. These are the "companies" that will take on the projects that are too small for the majors and too controversial even for the mid-size firms.

For instance, the contract to train the new counter-drug cartel team in Colombia did not go to MPRI, the Vinnell Corporation or DynCorp. It did not go to a mid-size firm like Gray Security, Alpha 5 or a Colombian version of a Teleservices. Not because these firms couldn't service such a contract, but because, after DSL's embarrassment in that region, no other credible firm felt the risk was warranted. Instead, the contract went to a retired U.S. Marine major whose reputation was expendable.

In the postwar Sierra Leone of early 1997, there was a significant requirement to support the training of the new military and police forces in that state. Executive Outcomes had gone, and the resulting vacuum made for an attractive opportunity. Did DSL, MPRI or Levdan look at this market? Probably, but they were not likely to pursue it because of several critical factors: the Sierra Leonean government had no money to pay for their services at that time; the media would immediately descend on any company trying to replace EO, and finally the lack of international interest in the nation made the chance of any mega-dollar project tenders unlikely.

In their place there assembled a collection of freelancers who were willing to take their chances. Will Scully, a former SAS sergeant and friend of Alan Bell, was one of these men. He traveled to Sierra Leone in April 1997 to join several other British ex-soldiers who were being promised a contract to train the new army. The project fell apart, however, when the May 25 coup d'état occurred, leaving Scully to fight a one-sided battle with the rebels while protecting European refugees hiding out in a cut-off hotel. His adventures are told in his gripping book, *Once a Pilgrim*.

These freelancers who work in the military security field are also trouble because they will rarely, if ever, have any political support for their work. It is doubtful that their home governments will even know they are operating in some foreign state. These are the individuals that are really worrisome because there is a complete lack of controls, checks or balances on their activities. The majors work hand-in-hand with national governments and can quite rightly be described as tools of foreign policy. There is a significant oversight capability with these companies through their home states.

The mid-size military security firms must operate with the knowledge of their home governments. Few modern states will tolerate for any length of time their nationals running around training foreign armies unchecked. In Britain, MI6 and the Foreign Office keep close tabs on what British-based military security companies are doing. In South Africa, the Mandela government passed legislation controlling the activity of all military services companies. In France, the intelligence services monitor everything French nationals are doing around the world.

The other issue that makes the activities of these freelancers so troubling is that, as independents, they may attempt to jump back and forth between categories, servicing a mercenary contract on one project and a security services contract on the next. Without any requirement for licensing or registration in the industry, the freelancers are the wild card of the shadow profession.

As a whole, then, the military security market is extremely competitive, stratified in terms of projects undertaken, and controversial in the types of projects. As to the businesses themselves, as in any other industry some are well managed and others are business failures. Defense Systems Limited, a mid-size leader in this market for two decades, has been bought out and is converting to a security services provider. In its wake, majors like MPRI, Levdan, the Vinnell Corporation, and DynCorp are taking the private military security sector into the lofty regions of major transnational business empires.

Finally, let's take a look at the military combat services market – certainly the most controversial of the international security industry's market sectors and the most written about. In this category, it is difficult to draw any broad conclusions because there are so few modern examples to look at. Executive Outcomes was the first and best example, but it went out of business in 1998.

How well did EO do during its nine-year run? The first large contract the company won was the Angolan project. The initial two-month contract ended up generating roughly $5 million in revenue (all figures in US dollars), but it was the long-term contract that was the real wage earner. At $40 million a year for two-and-a-half years, the final tally came to just over $100 million.

What is not quite so apparent is some of the built-in costs. When considering the annual contracts, a provision of the contracts terms that should be kept in mind was that EO should act as an arms purchaser and utilize a full fifty percent of the annual fees to supply the equipment of war. Over the period of the contracts, EO arranged for the delivery of relatively modern MIG-23 jet fighter aircraft, Swiss Pilatus prop-driven ground-attack aircraft, Mi-24 Hind gunships, and Mi-17 medium transport helicopters. On the ground there were BMP-2 Infantry Fighting Vehicles and numerous small arms, artillery, communications equipment, and ancillary gear. Although the total value of these purchases is unknown, a conservative estimate would place the total in the $30–40 million range.

EO personnel were also fairly expensive. The average wage of an employee was roughly $6,000 per month, with combat pilots earning up to $15,000 for the same period. With an average number of employees under contract at any given time hovering around one hundred, EO's annual salary expenses reached the $8 million mark. The purchase of two Boeing 727s for company use must also be added to the sum.

Still, all told, EO made a fairly comfortable profit margin on the Angola project. A rough estimate would place profits at roughly $30 million over less than three years, minus any taxes it may have paid. However, EO's next project, as we know, was to become a major liability and a drain against this handsome profit margin.

The Sierra Leone contract was worth $2 million a month. The contract lasted for twenty months, from May 1995 until December 1996, and was worth a total of $40 million. However, EO wasn't paid for the first eight months and had to accept a write-down of part of the total fees even before the first $3 million payment was made in January 1996. By the time the contract ended in December 1996, only a little over one-third of the balance owing had been paid. A plan for monthly installments was arranged, but with the May 1997 coup the payments ended.

EO ended up leaving Sierra Leone with nearly $25 million of its contracted fee in arrears. This loss went a long way to reducing the overall profitability of the firm by nearly wiping out the financial gains earned in Angola. As a consequence, over the next year the company was forced to go through a major restructuring to balance its books. The firm's president, Eben Barlow, was retired with a share arrangement, and so was his second-in-command, Lafras Luitingh. Many of the organization's assets were sold off, including the two Boeing 727s.

Much has been said about EO's "alternative" payments in the form of mining concessions or business privileges. Certainly in Angola many of EO's corporate management invested in shares of mentor Tony Buckingham's firm Branch Energy. In Sierra Leone, EO executives also purchased shares in the Canadian firm Diamondworks when Branch Energy financed the creation of that company in 1996. As active participants in the regions in question, the EO directors must have realized the profit potential of these mining and petroleum projects. When given an opportunity to get involved in these ventures on an individual basis, few executives in any profession would be likely to refuse. The portfolios of successful international business men or women everywhere are based on this type of shrewd financial activity. Any ethical indictment against EO's executives for this practice would really be an indictment against the entire investment industry.

For the average EO contract employee, other business opportunities usually presented themselves as a result of working on EO operations. In both Angola and Sierra Leone, major western investment in mining and oil projects was based on a belief in the high degree of security being provided by EO in these regions. Whenever EO departed, the security vacuum remaining was an attractive business opportunity for the wise entrepreneur.

It must be remembered that EO did not employ its soldiers full time. With the end of their EO contracts these men were looking at unemployment. To not take advantage of the opportunity to set up a security company to guard lucrative mineral concessions would be shortsighted. In Angola, ex-EO men formed the backbone of several new security companies, including Gray Security, Alpha 5, and Teleservices. In Sierra Leone, several ex-EO men put together the firm Lifeguard to fill the shoes left by the departing EO forces. These companies are still in operation, with Lifeguard managing to protect a hydroelectric dam deep inside RUF territory throughout the war.

Therefore, the accusations made that countries hiring EO have mortgaged their future by giving up rights to lucrative mineral resources are missing the mark. EO has in no way taken control of any country's natural resources. There have definitely been spin-off opportunities for individuals, but there is no evidence of any wholesale corporate strategy in this regard. If there had been, I doubt that EO would have been forced to close its doors and go out of business.

In the end, the Executive Outcomes corporation disappeared from the international security scene. This departure was not entirely due to financial considerations. On the two occasions when EO won major contracts, the broker for the deal was Anthony Buckingham. It is probably not a coincidence that EO's fortunes began to change at the same time that Buckingham formed his own private military company in England.

This brings us to the only surviving military combat company at the time of writing. Sandline International out of London openly advertises itself as a private military company and the successor to Executive Outcomes. However, the story and the business behind Sandline is as intriguing as this element of the industry itself.

The company was created in early 1996 when Tony Buckingham activated a numbered shell company in the Bahamas and renamed it Sandline International. The timing of the creation of this firm is significant. Remember that Buckingham had been EO's biggest supporter, bringing it in to Angola and Sierra Leone. The principals of EO had even bought shares in Buckingham's petroleum and mining companies. So why, then, did the daring entrepreneur suddenly decide to create his own military combat company which would in effect replace EO?

By incorporating a private military company within his own business empire, Buckingham could expect to not only earn money on his mining and petroleum operations but also take advantage of the lucrative security contracts that were ancillary to most of his projects. This all-under-one-roof arrangement would then become an attractive package in the high-risk type of environments in which Branch Energy specialized.

In middle of 1996, Buckingham invited retired Lieutenant Colonel Tim Spicer to a meeting at Branch Energy's corporate offices at 535 Kings Road, London, and by the time he left he had become the director of Sandline International Limited. This new arrangement coincided with the growing crisis in EO's financial situation in Sierra Leone and, considering the Buckingham link, it cannot be thought of as a mere coincidence. What the secretive Englishman's true motives were in abandoning his South African prodigy is open to conjecture, but there are some interesting facts to consider.

The first is Buckingham's choice of Tim Spicer. The private military corporation community in Britain is almost exclusively populated by retired special forces soldiers. The SAS, the Special Boat Service (SBS), and the Paras are normally the soldiers of choice for private enterprise. Even Buckingham was a veteran of the SBS. At any given time, there is a plethora of retired special forces veterans in the United Kingdom who would relish the opportunity to head up a fully financed PMC. Yet Buckingham's first choice was a retired Scots Guards officer whose only operational experience involved a routine tour of Northern Ireland, a supporting role in the Falklands, and a stint as a public affairs aide for General Sir Michael Rose in Bosnia in 1995.

I've asked a few of my contacts in the industry about this peculiar choice. One individual I spoke with, a former member of the SAS, commented:

"The fact that there are no SAS guys working for Sandline says it all. If this company was serious, they would have at least a few guys from the regiment in there. Maybe the word is out to avoid this group."

The Scots Guards are an old and well-respected infantry regiment within the British army. They are both admired and occasionally teased for their exceptional discipline and skill on the parade square. As a former colonel in this regiment, Spicer is probably qualified to lead a security company, but his lack of experience in the types of dirty little wars PMC's often find themselves involved in makes him an unusual choice. Especially when the SAS has specialized in dirty little wars for the last fifty years.

Shortly after forming Sandline, Tony Buckingham arranged for

Spicer to be introduced to the government of Papua New Guinea
(PNG). At the time, PNG was embroiled in a decade-old civil war with
independence-minded rebels on the island of Bougainville. The government wanted high-tech weapons, military helicopters, and enough
mercenaries to put an end to the uprising. In January 1997, Spicer
signed a contract for US$36 million to provide two Mi-24 Hind gun-
ships, two Mi-17 Hip transport helicopters, radios, satellite communications, and enough weapons and equipment for a one-hundred-man
special forces team. The deal specified nineteen mercenaries to fly and
maintain the aircraft, forty-two mercenaries for the special forces team,
and one ground commander. The contract also included the provision
that each Sandline mercenary would receive a military rank that must
be respected by the PNG army.

In an unsurprising turn of events, there have been reports published
that suggest Anthony Buckingham offered to pay half of Sandline's tab
if his company was given control of the giant Panguna copper mine,
which was sitting idle as a result of the war. The offer was turned down,
however, because the PNG government, already severely taxing the
national social service budget to pay for the project, needed control
of the mine and its revenue to pay its war debt when the conflict was
eventually resolved.

The whole project went down the tubes, however, when PNG Briga-
dier-General Jerry Singirok announced the terms of the contract publicly. The army, already starved for funding, revolted when the cost
of the mercenary contract was released. The resulting chaos brought
down the government of Prime Minister Sir Julius Chan. Fortunately
for Spicer, a payment of US$18 million had already been made, but
the remainder of his fees was held up for nearly two years pending an
inquiry by the Australian government. Spicer himself was arrested and
detained for questioning. His South African mercenaries, all EO veterans, were expelled from the country, and the arms already purchased
were impounded.

For Spicer the very real problem was that he had already taken delivery of much of the equipment specified under the contract. The aircraft alone came to over $15 million. After using his $18 million to pay

off his arms suppliers and the mercenaries from EO, Sandline would have little or no profit to show until the second payment was released in late 1998. Spicer didn't have time to wait.

Sandline immediately jumped on the next project to come along. In Sierra Leone, only a few months after the PNG debacle, Spicer chose to accept the contract that we at Globe Risk turned down. Spicer proposed a US$20 million operation to defeat the RUF rebels and reinstate the Kabbah government. Rakesh Saxena had proposed to fund half, but President Kabbah decided it was too ambitious and set the limit for the operation at $10 million. Saxena still agreed to pay half and delivered Spicer an initial payment of $1.5 million. With this amount, the Guards colonel began purchasing weapons in Eastern Europe. Unfortunately, before Saxena could pay the balance, he was arrested in Canada and placed in jail for trying to acquire an illegal foreign passport. Spicer was once again arrested, this time in England, and charged with weapons smuggling offenses. This left Sandline with a balance payment owing on the weapons impounded in Sierra Leone, his paymaster in jail, and President Kabbah publicly denying any knowledge of the entire affair.

For Sandline, the final numbers are not much better than were EO's. The only saving grace for Spicer was the final payment in 1998 of the remaining $18 million from the PNG project. Sierra Leone was a complete loss and resulted in significant legal costs in trying to defend Spicer's case. As a final nail in the coffin, Sandline had not managed to successfully complete either of its two major contracts. In an industry where reputation is everything, his firm will likely face an uphill battle to win any more contracts, even with Tony Buckingham's patronage.

Having now looked closely at the numbers involved in the PMC industry's two most famous corporations, we can see that claims of outrageous wealth are unfounded. Both EO and Sandline were not economically successful ventures. Despite the grand numbers involved in the average PMC contract, the potential for disaster makes these companies poor risks in the long run. Nor is this situation likely to change in the near future.

The immense cost of hiring a private military company makes it improbable that most wartorn and impoverished countries can afford these services. When there are natural resources to offer, the proposition still relies on the co-operation of a devil-may-care entrepreneur like Tony Buckingham or Rakesh Saxena who is willing to finance the project. The region involved must also be such a backwater in terms of international opinion that no major power is likely to object. This combination of elements necessary for the employment of PMCs is just too rare to support a large industry, especially when one considers international efforts to outlaw the PMC entirely.

EO realized this problem and closed its doors. Sandline, under Tim Spicer's dogged leadership, still clings to this idea of the successful PMC model. The fact that there is a market out there for the professional military company will ensure that the industry does not die out completely, but there is no getting around the fact that the EO / Sandline model does not work. A new approach needs to be found.

Now that we have looked at the business aspects of the international security industry as a whole, it is easy to see that the picture is not quite as clear as it may have seemed on casual observation. Just because there are highly skilled ex-soldiers running many of these companies does not mean that they are going to be business successes. As in any industry, there are a few success stories and there are legions of failures.

The markets these companies compete for are very competitive. The conditions required to make their use possible are not common. The majors count on the political muscle of their home states to win them projects. The mid-size firms live and die often by one contract. The freelancers constantly undercut the established firms which must maintain business overhead and operate by clear codes of conduct.

So what are the conclusions to be drawn? The first is that, regardless of the need for private military and security expertise around the world, the first principle of success must be good business practices. For the companies that don't respect this aspect of entrepreneurship there is only failure.

Because they work primarily in the corporate world, security services companies must become "corporate" entities themselves. Clients should conduct proper due diligence investigations before retaining security providers to ensure that they are what they claim to be.

Military security companies must all eventually gravitate to the majors to survive. To do this, they must work closely with their home governments and pursue exacting codes of conduct.

The smaller mid-size firms are exceptionally vulnerable to competition from smooth-talking freelancers who operate without any of the restrictions faced by the established firms.

Finally, the vaunted military combat companies are a clear example of a failed business model. Neither EO nor Sandline demonstrated that it could properly survive the imponderables of its chosen market. Clients either didn't pay or ran the company out of the country based on social or political pressure.

Having looked, then, at the business of international security, it is clear that there are success stories and failures. The point that is most clearly driven home is that security and mercenary companies must be good businesses first and effective operators second. No longer is it good enough to be a retired soldier with a good military record. Now you must also be a cunning businessman, an aggressive promoter, and a public relations expert.

We have also established that there is a market for all three types of international security services. Wishing these companies away, or even trying to make them illegal, will not prevent suppliers from meeting the demand. Therefore, I think it is important and inevitable that the question of how the industry should be approached and possibly regulated in the twenty-first century is examined.

9

THE FUTURE

THROUGHOUT THIS LOOK inside the international security industry there are a couple of constants that don't appear to have changed much in the last seven centuries. The first is that soldiers, whether in regular national armies or out of them, are a resource in constant demand. Sometimes they are needed as trainers for struggling new nations such as George Washington's hiring of the Prussian officer Friedrich von Steuben to train his new American army during the War of Independence. On other occasions, they are needed to support regular armies in times of need, such as the Gurkhas in mid-nineteenth-century India or the Polish Parachute Brigade in World War II. On a few occasions, but not as many as most critics would like us to think, they are needed to replace failing regular armies altogether, such as the White Company of Florence or Executive Outcomes in Sierra Leone.

The saying goes that "Those who forget history are doomed to repeat it." Certainly this is true for the issue of the modern shadow professionals of the international security industry. Their ancestors have played a critical role in the development of all of the modern "successful" nations.

England, France, Germany, Switzerland, Ireland, Canada, the United States, Japan, China, Mexico, Chile, Greece, and a host of others all had their emerging national destinies shaped by mercenary soldiers. There is no reason to believe that the future of other nations, both today and in the years ahead, won't also depend on such support during times of need when no other help can be found.

The second constant through our past has been the fact that no matter how much we pine for peace, we have never truly achieved it on a global scale. There have been and always will be for the foreseeable future regions of the world where competition for resources, ethnic and religious divisions, and a general thirst for conquest will drive human beings to conflict.

The world did make great strides in the latter half of the twentieth century to find solutions to this issue. The creation of the United Nations as a forum for world conflict resolution through dialogue rather than force of arms is a leap ahead in the quest for peace. Where negotiation could not immediately resolve a dispute, the Canadian statesman Lester B. Pearson conceived the concept of peacekeeping in the 1950s as a method of using soldiers to enforce peace, not fight wars.

Unfortunately, peacekeeping has been a complete strategic failure. From the first disastrous mission in the Congo in 1961 through to the present, the "Blue Helmets" have yet to end a war. In the Congo, the U.N. backed the wrong side and within a week of leaving their man was executed by his own government and a return to war ensued. In the Golan Heights and Lebanon no lasting peace has yet been reached. In Cyprus, both the Greeks and the Turks have been unable to resolve their dispute and will in all likelihood fall upon each other the moment the peacekeepers depart. In Croatia and Bosnia, I was personally witness to our failures. The horror of the U.N. "Safe Haven" of Srebenica cannot soon be forgotten. NATO eventually had to replace the failed peacekeepers when the U.N. finally admitted defeat.

In Rwanda, the U.N. had over a month's advance notice of the Hutu extremist-planned genocide and the resources were on the ground to stop it, yet they did nothing. In Haiti, there are more murders and cases of torture reported per week now than before the U.N. intervention. Angola has been a total failure, as were Vietnam, Somalia, and Cambodia.

Why have the U.N. peacekeepers been so uniformly unsuccessful? Because history has shown us quite clearly that soldiers and armies can win battles and defeat their enemies, but they cannot end wars. That must be a political function. A battlefield victory may lead to an end in

fighting, but that is not the same as peace. A surrender must be negotiated, a new government must be created or a reorganization of power
must be decided. These are not the mandate of the soldier, especially
in a democracy. These are matters of politics, negotiation, and govern-
ment-to-government diplomacy.

There has been a distinctive lack of success in the United Nations to
negotiate the end to conflicts – especially Third World conflicts. Why?
Most people tend to forget that while the U.N. Secretary-General may
plead for the world to respond to a crisis in Asia or Africa, the power to
decide any action lies in the Security Council, which is controlled by the
"Big Five." If Britain, France, Russia, the United States, or China does not
have an interest in these areas, there will be no U.N. intervention.

Why is all this important to the question of the international security industry? Well, the facts are that at the beginning of the twenty-
first century there are no fewer wars and violent struggles being conducted around the world than there were during the last century. The
U.N., though trying valiantly, has not proven capable of resolving
these conflicts.

For small, Third World nations with no powerful western benefac-
tor, the odds are that, because of the fashion in which the Security
Council is organized, they will probably not receive any support unless
CNN or the BBC popularizes their plight with prime-time reports.
Where else can these embattled nations turn when there is no one else
other than the private security industry?

The services they desire may simply be the provision of enough
security to make international corporations comfortable in investing
in their economies. They may want help training their own police
and military forces to provide their own internal security. They may
want help in defeating rebel forces that plague the nation and refuse to
accept democracy as the only acceptable method for social change.

Here lies the critical factor. Mercenaries, private military companies,
and military security companies cannot end conflicts. Like any military
force or soldier-related activity, they can only provide the conditions
necessary for a political settlement. Their critics are therefore missing
the critical point here. Mercenaries are simply a tool for achieving a

battlefield victory when no other resource is available. Due to their cost, they are rarely used when there is any other less costly alternative, such as negotiation. They are a means of last resort. If a war is not resolved in the aftermath of that victory, blaming the intervention of a professional private military company is like cutting the tail off of the Hydra and leaving its many snarling heads intact.

In Angola, UNITA was given opportunity after opportunity to decide the fate of the nation through democratic elections. Certainly this was the focus of the Lusaka Accord. The true desire of the people of Angola to choose between Jonas Savimbi and Jose dos Santos should have been decided by ballot, not bullet. When no other recourse was available to the government of Angola to stop the war, they turned to the mercenary services of Executive Outcomes. Within a year, UNITA agreed to end the fighting and sign the Lusaka Accord, paving the way for the first elections that nation had ever seen.

In Sierra Leone, when no other country, not even the United Nations, would raise a finger to stop the fighting, EO mercenaries ended the war and protected democratic elections. That nation then saw its first properly elected government since its independence.

The failure of peace to take hold in these nations after a mercenary battlefield victory cannot be blamed on the mercenaries. In both cases, the United Nations and political intervention were to blame. In Angola, the first demand of Jonas Savimbi after his defeat and forced arrival at the bargaining table was that EO must leave as a condition for peace. The United Nations, the OAU, and even U.S. President Bill Clinton took up this demand. Shortly after EO's departure, Savimbi ignored the election results, and the Lusaka Accord, which he had signed, and returned to the bush to carry on his struggle.

In Sierra Leone, after winning the war, protecting the elections and guarding NGOs as they delivered aid around the country, international political and financial pressure forced the new Sierra Leone government to send EO packing. Within four months, the rebels and the criminally minded army overthrew the elected government and returned the country to war and anarchy. All for a matter of $20 million. That price is less than what the U.N. would spend in a month in Yugoslavia.

Like the British and French at Waterloo, a war for the future of
these two nations was fought in a large part by mercenaries. But also
much like at Waterloo, the military campaign may have been decided
in that French valley, but the peace was decided in Paris and London.
In the cases of Angola and Sierra Leone, this should have been the
case, but the international community pointed its fingers at the wrong
target. As a result, peace was lost.

In the reports of Special Rapporteur Ballesteros to the United
Nations, in the publications of Pretoria's Institute of Strategic Studies, the International Commission for Human Rights, as well as a host
of other agencies concerned with international relations and security,
another common theme on this issue is that the employment of military combat companies and even military security companies prolongs
wars. They often even go so far as to suggest that private military companies use strategies that will ensure a long-smoldering struggle to
extend their contracts as long as possible, rather than a quick and decisive victory. While such a suggestion might in fact be a good business
decision on the part of the private companies, it has yet to occur.

Once again, both the record of the military companies and the
larger political factors are being viewed in a skewed fashion. As with
any army working for a government, directions, objectives, and time
lines are decided by the government administration. The military strategy to achieve these goals is then created by the mercenary commanders. In neither Angola, Sierra Leone, nor Papua-New Guinea did the
mercenary units dictate the objectives of the campaigns.

In Sierra Leone, President Kabbah both turned on and turned off
his mercenary company. On direction from the president, EO went
into a defensive posture guarding infrastructure and the diamond
mines. On order from the president, EO went on the offensive to
respond to an upsurge in rebel activity. On the completion of that
short campaign, it returned to its defensive posture. All this happened
on the orders of the president.

Alan Bell, who had a chance to meet with a former EO commander
in Sierra Leone, describes one such situation.

"I was asking Colonel 'White' about the RUF and he told me about the last EO offensive in 1996. He said that at one point they had the last remnants of the RUF leadership cornered in a small mountain reserve, and at that point, he asked President Kabbah what his orders were. The president decided to play peacemaker and diplomat and ordered EO to cease its attacks and let the survivors escape. That decision cost him his country."

In both Angola and Sierra Leone, EO's presence brought a quick and decisive battlefield victory. Remember that in Angola, President dos Santos ordered EO to halt its offensive to give the reeling Savimbi a chance to negotiate. That decision cost Angola another decade of war that is still ongoing as I write. The failure to win these wars or the decision to prolong these conflicts did not come from any mercenary commander. In both cases it came from the government policy makers. Once again, the political failure to take advantage of these offers of negotiation cannot be laid at the feet of the military combat company.

Did the presence of EO mercenaries as strategic assets convince the political masters to prolong the conflicts? By their simple presence, did they encourage more fighting? That assertion is also perplexing and difficult to justify. In both cases mentioned above, the mercenaries were a very expensive proposition. The hard but logical choice should have been to finish these campaigns quickly with a decisive battlefield victory. That would speed negotiations and a return to peace, a situation that would hasten the end of the mercenary contract. Yet in both occasions, the spirit of offering peace and reconciliation rather than destruction motivated these leaders to prolong the wars.

Yet what if EO had never gotten involved in either conflict? What if there were no mercenary companies to hire? Would that have made a difference? If the United Nations had ever achieved a single success in the final resolution to a conflict, there may have been an alternative. That is, of course, assuming that the Security Council could be motivated to become involved. Since the war in Angola had raged on since 1975 and the war in Sierra Leone since 1991, it can easily be argued that the U.N. was long past making a useful commitment in either case. The leaders of both nations could not foresee the future. For their nations, they looked at the options open to them at the time and chose the path that offered the best, and often the only, solution.

To sit comfortably in a leather chair, in an air-conditioned office in Geneva or New York and second-guess the decisions of these leaders who were trying to hold together their embattled and chaotic countries is not fair or just. To pass moral decisions on their choice is far less fair.

Whether you respect those decisions or even agree with them is immaterial. The facts are that in those circumstances, those leaders had the moral courage to make those choices. The men who served for EO also had the courage to take up the struggles of their former enemies and risked their lives to do it.

This brings us to another element that needs to be considered seriously for the future. Working for an international security company, one tends to meet all manner of people, from heads-of-state to major corporate leaders and to the various experts on international relations.

On the other hand, we also meet the villagers in Africa, the harried and always-frustrated aid workers, and the people who truly suffer at the bottom end of the human scale.

One factor that is becoming increasingly apparent is the growing chasm between policy makers and policy implementers. In my time in the industry I have run across many of the organizations primarily made up of university professors, retired politicians or bureaucrats and other assorted intelligentsia who move from contract to contract, producing reports and recommendations on various matters of international significance.

Using grants or funding from national governments, the United Nations, the IMF or the World Bank, they investigate regions of conflict, routinely from the safety of their western offices, and produce voluminous reports on the situation making extensive recommendations for action.

The reports are filed, and may even be read by the organization commissioning the study, and then they are placed into the vaults with a legion of other studies.

Anyone interested in this topic should visit the libraries of the United Nations, the World Bank, and the International Monetary Fund, or even their own country's foreign office. The effort and cost dedicated to building these massive libraries is enormous. For the organizations that conduct these studies, the measure of success with their peers is the number of grants they can win and the number of reports they can produce. This is now a major international industry valued into the tens of millions of dollars and producing reports in never-before-seen quantities.

While everyone in the world agreed the situation in Sierra Leone was a horrible tragedy, and the world's archives are brimming with reports and studies of it, what was actually accomplished? How many recommendations were ever acted upon? While this is an intangible in many respects, the groups who did take some actions were the dedicated volunteers for the aid agencies and companies like Gurkha Security Guards and Executive Outcomes.

Yes, the military services companies were paid to take action, but make no mistake, so were the aid agency volunteers. Every aid worker receives a paycheck for his or her efforts. The fact is, both are implementers. The general world opinion, fashioned by the numerous studies and reports, suggests action, and these are the groups that convert words into deeds.

As I found in talking to aid workers and U.N. people on the ground in Sierra Leone, both groups admire each other and have counted on each other to meet their separate mandates. Most aid workers felt EO's departure was the nail in the coffin for thousands of innocent lives. They wanted EO back.

Sympathy between aid workers and mercenaries should simply not exist, considering the type of people who inhabit both groups and the wildly different jobs they do. Yet, they are both there on the ground, risking their lives to make an difference while the rest of the world simply talks about it. This is the basis for a common bond.

The results of this bonding are becoming increasingly apparent. Virtually every major international aid organization now employs its own shadow professionals to organize security and logistics. While the advertising and fund-raising pitch may focus on the noble, neutral, and peaceful efforts of the aid groups in zones of conflict, the reality on the ground is much different. The days of the Red Cross moving across no man's land to serve both sides equally and impartially has long since passed. Now combatants in small, bitter, ethnic and religious struggles target aid workers along with anyone else. To continue to meet the humanitarian needs of civilians caught up in these struggles, the aid organizations are becoming increasingly security conscious.

In Somalia, Rwanda, the Sudan, Ethiopia, and numerous other African states, aid organizations must hire armed guards to defend them both while out in the communities and in their base camps. These armed guards are often hired, vetted, trained, and organized by shadow professionals hired by the aid organization to meet this requirement.

In Rwanda, I was asked by the organizers of a CARE feeding camp to organize their security. I had to travel to their facility and conduct a security review and then make recommendations. Base on my conclusions, we implemented a security strategy that would give them some level of security in the event of an attack. We also left them a radio to contact us in an emergency.

In Western Africa, a former Canadian soldier I served with is now the director of Security and Logistics for the U.N.'s World Food Program (WFP). Brian is responsible for organizing food convoys in Sierra Leone and conducting regular assessments of the security situation there.

He has on many occasions been sent to negotiate with rebel soldiers at roadblocks that interfere with aid distribution. His time as a U.N. peacekeeper in Yugoslavia makes him one of the best-qualified people on the planet to carry out this vital but dangerous task.

In speaking with the director of an aid organization based in Ottawa recently I asked about this growing trend.

"Yes, there is definitely a need," he acknowledged. "Our people have been beat up, raped, and even murdered while on duty. It really is open season. We need the security expertise that soldiers can bring, otherwise we can't do our jobs. I don't like it, but those are the facts."

He went on to say, "I even support the use of mercenaries. They definitely have a place because they will go where no one else will. It is an uncomfortable relationship, but there are many times when I've wished we had a good quality mercenary group working with us."

Perhaps by now it will have become increasingly clear why a poorly defined and confusing document such as the U.N.'s convention banning the recruitment, use, and support of mercenaries will never pass into law. Between their historical necessity in aiding the resolution of wars and their modern use as the implementers of last resort, mercenaries are simply too valuable a resource to throw away.

That is not to say that mercenaries and other shadow professionals should be given a free hand to do as they please. Like any other industry that has a major impact on international peace and security, there should be legislation, regulation, and oversight. The question is, how would such a situation work?

The first factor that should be considered in defining a method of regulation for the industry is the market it serves. Throughout the ages, there have been two pressing concerns for mercenaries and their clients. Mercenaries are forever concerned that they are not going to get paid. EO's misfortunes in Sierra Leone are a prime example. Clients, on the other hand, are always worried about the loyalty of their mercenaries and whether or not they will render a full measure of service commensurate with their cost. In other words, performance and payment are the two critical issues – essentially the same issues that are critical in any business enterprise.

The next factor that needs to be considered is the conduct of the contract. Mercenaries are always concerned about what their clients are going to expect from them. Hired soldiers are not suicide troops to be thrown away carelessly. Good mercenary companies, such as the White Company or EO, are best used to stiffen a regular army and provide decisive professional support at critical moments. As well, clients on occasion expect mercenary troops to carry out brutal functions that might not be safely entrusted to citizen soldiers. Cardinal Robert of Geneva's sack of Cesena or some of Hitler's foreign Waffen ss legions are an example.

On the other hand, clients are always worried, especially in the modern era, about what embarrassments or human disasters mercenary troops might inflict upon their administration and reputation. Holden Roberto's employment of criminals and thugs in 1975 produced massacres and effectively ended his hopes for power in Angola. When President Mobutu hired Serbian mercenaries to save his government in Zaire in 1997, the Serbs murdered so many Congolese that even the president's loyal army units turned on them. When the Chechens hired an eight-hundred-man battalion of Ukrainian Cossack mercenaries in 1998 to help fight the Russians, they may never have expected the ruthlessness of their employees. (Although, considering the recent history of Chechnya, it may also be the other way around.)

The final issue in the regulation of mercenaries and their clients is the issue of control and oversight. What are clients asking mercenaries to do? What are mercenaries doing that their clients don't know about? If the mercenaries are not paid, what actions might they take? If the clients murder their mercenaries, what action should the international community take? There clearly has to be some method of controlling mercenaries and their clients in a politically and morally effective fashion.

The key element here is the money. Like any business, the transfer of payment for services rendered or withheld for services not completed is the foundation for controlling mercenary activity. If one could find a way to control the money, mercenaries would behave and play by the rules – and so would clients.

How could such a scheme work?

The following is a suggestion for how to finally deal with the issue of mercenaries, military services companies, and freebooting criminals. It is based on my opinions alone, and to the best of my knowledge it has neither been attempted nor even suggested before.

To begin with, the United Nations should set up a commission charged with regulating the International Security Industry. This commission will be sanctioned and supervised by the U.N. but have a non-political mandate. In other words, it is a legal body with clearly defined rules, regulations, and operating procedures. Once established, it shall require a majority vote of the General Assembly to alter its charter.

Currently, all manner of companies who wish to bid on and service U.N. contracts must go through a lengthy and exhaustive licensing procedure. Every aspect of the company is analyzed, reviewed, and either passed, failed or recommended to comply with policy. This is essential to maintain the U.N.'s high standards of conduct for contractors and operations. Very few contracts pass by this process, and then only on the recommendation of a major power and only until the licensing process is complete. This usually occurs in an emergency when something like a water purification systems engineer or other technical professional is required promptly.

The International Security Industry Commission would act in a similar fashion. Companies such as MPRI, Sandline International, Globe Risk Holdings, Levdan, Vinnell Corporation or any successor to EO would be asked to register for an operating license from the commission. Compliance would not be mandatory, only encouraged. The reasons for this will become clear shortly. Once the firms apply, they must be vetted rigorously by a process similar to the current U.N. contractors process.

The commission would look at the following issues. First, what category of the industry do the applicants fall under? Are they security services, military security services or military combat services? Companies could be licensed in one or more categories, but the certification process must be separate for each. Naturally, the certification process will require a large fee to help maintain the costs of the commission. This would also limit the number of spare-bedroom-company applications. I would suggest something in the range of US$10,000 to $20,000.

The second issue the commission would look at is who are the principals of the company and what are their backgrounds. While this information can remain confidential, requesting it will compel any company claiming to employ the services of highly skilled special forces veterans to prove it. If the company's principals have criminal backgrounds or have belonged to internationally condemned organizations, or for any other significant illegal factor, they can either be refused certification or have their files noted in a public document.

Because these companies only maintain small administrative staffs and hire their employees for each project from a large pool of retired veterans, there would be a separate registry for contract employees.

For each contract, the licensed company must provide detailed lists of who their employees are, along with background information. Over time, the pool of freelancers on the circuit will become registered with the commission. Thereafter, companies selecting individuals from the pool will be required to hire only employees who are certified by the commission. This allows clients to know that the actual staff their security contractor brings in to service any contract is who they say they are, possessing the expected capabilities and experience.

Freelancers will be required to pay a professional fee to register that can either be paid by their employer or, if an individual wants to be certified independently, he or she can pay. On certification, freelancers are also expected to sign an industry "best practices" document and acknowledge that they are aware of the legal implications of the Geneva Conventions and the International Charter of Human Rights and Freedoms.

Once companies are certified, they can then be licensed for business with the commission. From this point on client states, non-governmental organizations, corporations or any other client can approach the commission to either identify a suitable short list of contractors for a particular project or conduct due diligence on any company bidding on a contract.

Here is where the concept gets into the real enforcement issue. For all contracts between licensed International Security Companies and their clients the fees agreed upon will become the responsibility of the commission's appointed agent. Remember that military combat and military security companies can often render a service and then either not get paid or spend years in litigation to win their due. Clients can hire a military services company only to have them not perform as expected or not complete the terms of the contract in some fashion. Both parties need assurances that the contracts will be honored in good faith on both sides. There may be mitigating factors on both sides, and those must be considered as well.

Therefore, the concept would be that any contract between a military security or military combat company and a client would be required by law to be filed with the commission prior to commencement. The commission would not have the legal authority to stop a contract, but it would be aware of the details.

To ensure both sides honor that registered contract, the client must do one of three things. It must deposit the full balance of the contract into an international financial institution authorized by the commission. This may include the World Bank or a major banking chain. If the client does not have the liquid assets to deposit the full amount, it must arrange financing with either a commission-authorized institution or another institution. This may include corporate financing. Once again, the full balance must be deposited in the contract account prior to commencement of the project.

If the client neither has the liquid assets nor can raise the capital in advance, it has the final option of negotiating an alternative payment system. This must be authorized and negotiated through a commission-authorized facilitator. Although the deal may include any type of payment, such as natural resource concessions, it must be approved by the commission's facilitator to ensure it does not significantly mortgage the future of that client. In other words, there must be a reasonable expectation of payment without undue duress caused to the citizens of that state.

The result of this system would be that, prior to a contract being undertaken, the contract terms are registered with the commission, the payment is guaranteed, and both the client and the contractor can proceed with some level of comfort with the outcome.

Once the full balance has been secured, the contractor may negotiate a release of up to fifty percent of the payment balance to cover start-up costs. The details of this requirement must be negotiated as part of the initial contract. Where this is not done, the contractor may also borrow against the total value of the contract to meet this need. If equipment is going to be purchased, a similar arrangement can be organized.

Throughout the course of the contract, say something similar to EO's operation in Sierra Leone or MPRI's activities in Bosnia, representatives of the commission can periodically monitor or accompany either the client or the contractor. If there is a question raised in the U.N. concerning questionable activity on the part of either group, the balance payment may be frozen until an investigation has been conducted.

On completion of the contract, both client and contractor would have a period of thirty days to raise protests concerning their contractual obligations or expectations. If protests are lodged, an appointed facilitator would intervene and investigate the complaints. His decision, on approval of the commission, can then award penalties to either the client or contractor as required. After a legislated period of no more than sixty days, the balance of the payment less any holdbacks for upheld protests is released to the contractor. An appeal process can be initiated, but penalties or awards identified in an appeal must be pursued in a national court under that country's applicable laws.

Could such a system work? Let's consider the various players and motivations. International security industry companies yearn for international recognition and approval. Every one of them currently operates under the cloud of the mercenary label. Every credible firm points to their record of successes and says, "See, we're not evil mercenaries. We're the good guys." Combine this with the fact that if they honor their contract and fulfill their obligations they are guaranteed payment and this becomes an attractive proposition.

Just the simple chance to clarify where in the industry they belong is advantageous. Currently in North America, the rage in business is to win an ISO certification. It is a way of announcing to potential clients that a firm is a well-managed and reliable company. Similarly, if clients looking for a military services contractor had a choice of a commission-certified contractor or an unknown, which would they likely choose? Especially, when they know they can get their money back if the contractor cannot fulfill its obligations. The chances of another Holden Roberto fiasco would be lessened.

On the international security front, supervision and oversight could be written in to the process. In the event of legally proven, properly documented evidence of a planned violation of the Geneva Conventions or the International Charter of Human Rights and Freedoms, payments can be withheld. If the crimes are committed by individuals working for a licensed company, the company can have the chance to prove it wasn't involved officially and disown the acts of the individuals involved. The level of cooperation inherent in the system will make the investigation of allegations much less difficult.

The corollary here is that the companies selecting personnel for projects will raise their standards significantly, knowing that collecting their fees may be dependent on the performance of their employees.

Earlier I mentioned that companies wouldn't be mandated to become certified. There will in all likelihood be many companies that either refuse to register or cannot register for a variety of reasons. The most likely motivation to avoid the process would either be that the company's principals have committed criminal acts in the past or that they are unwilling to operate under the dictates of international law.

With the freelancers the situation is similar. Those individuals who refuse to become registered are either likely not who they say they are or have other legal reasons why they will not join.

The end result is that any company or individual who operates unlicensed can be marked and monitored very closely. Governments of countries such as the United States, Britain, and France can use their political muscle to ensure clients hire only certified companies. Any client hiring an unlicensed company would have its motivation questioned immediately. Perhaps it wants its contractor to perform illegal duties. Perhaps it has no intention of ever paying its contractor.

Regardless of the reason, the entire process can be at first discouraged and then monitored closely.

Some critics may point out that these contracts may never become public knowledge. The odds of that happening in the twenty-first century are slim. The Internet is everywhere, the media can smell a controversy a continent away, and aid groups are wherever there is a market for military services. EO was hounded by the media from the first moment it set foot in Angola. MPRI has managed to keep few secrets. On a smaller scale, Globe Risk has completed over three hundred interviews in the last four years. On most occasions, Alan Bell's first question to any reporter is how he or she found out about the company.

In areas like Colombia or Chechnya, it may be possible in the short term to avoid discovery, but even the SAS in Colombia was discovered by reporters despite the total cloak of secrecy imposed on that mission.

The division between certified and unknown companies will only serve to narrow this focus.

Since we are discussing the future here, I feel it is only proper that I devise a fanciful scenario that could well reflect a future situation should these changes occur. Please understand that this is totally fictional and bears no resemblance to the plans of anyone I know or have ever met (including myself!).

One of the smallest states in the world is the tiny island nation of Nauru in the South Pacific. Located northeast of Australia, it gained independence in 1968 and has flourished ever since. The island has a shoreline of just over eighteen miles, and that is surrounded by an unbroken coral reef. It is at first glance a gorgeous island paradise that rarely sees any tourists.

What has made the island so prosperous if not the tourist industry? Essentially, Nauru is one big phosphorous rock sticking out of the Pacific Ocean. These minerals have been mined since the 1800s, mostly for fertilizer, and that trade has produced the nation's wealth. The nation's ten thousand or so inhabitants have enjoyed one of the wealthiest standards of living in the Pacific.

However, the ride was over in the year 2000. The phosphates ran out and the natural beauty of the island was spoiled by over a century of mining activity. Soil erosion and a lack of fresh water meant that the island was dying. Only the revenue earned in the mining trade provided enough wealth to cover the cost of importing all of life's essentials. Disaster was looming.

Into this dire situation step the principals of the First Independent Company (FIC).

This firm is a military combat services company that is looking to create the first full-time mercenary organization to exist privately in over a century. Rather than have a small administrative staff and rely on the circuit to fill contract positions, the directors of the FIC want to create a full-time organization with up to five hundred employees. The market FIC is looking to pursue is in United Nations contracting, as well as other regional peacekeeping and peace enforcement efforts. It will also consider military support projects for individual national clients.

Unfortunately, most countries in the world would frown on such an organization existing within their borders. The directors of the FIC have been searching the globe for a home base for their unit. They feel they have found it in Nauru.

In a well-publicized meeting with government officials, the FIC directors lay out their plan. The concept envisions a corporate headquarters in New York City to remain close to United Nations contacts. The firm plans to retain the services of several influential former U.N. bureaucrats and senior U.S. and British military officers as spokesmen to market the company's services there.

Meanwhile, the company's operations people are going to purchase a large ocean-going container ship. The ship will be modified to house, clothe, feed, and support the unit as well as moving a considerable amount of stores. It will have helicopter landing pads and will even support two seaplanes for local security.

The ship will be used to purchase and deliver the needs of the unit and the Islanders to Nauru, and also as a staging point for contract military operations. The ultimate intention is to purchase two ships, but that would be overly ambitious to begin the venture. While the costs of this logistic set up are quite high, there are few political entanglements associated with a home base in Nauru.

The local populace will all be offered employment in providing the logistics base for the unit. Raw materials delivered by ship will be processed into uniforms, munitions, rations, and other stores. Islanders would also be encouraged to set up recreational businesses to service the needs of the unit's professionals when they are home and to deliver every manner of consumer goods.

The soldiers themselves will be recruited primarily from the ranks of decommissioned Gurkha mercenaries. These hardy soldiers are the epitome of loyalty and dedicated service. They never commit atrocities and can be expected to perform any duty, no matter how harsh, boring or dangerous. In their off-duty time, they live quietly and rarely drink and are not expected to cause trouble with the Islanders. Yet, despite these ideal qualities, they will work for less than half what a western soldier demands.

The plan foresees creating three, one-hundred-man companies of infantry with the Gurkhas. There will also be a one-hundred-man combat support unit. Another fifty mercenaries will fill out the support duties such as operating the ship, the headquarters, and the unit home station. All additional support functions will be contracted out to Islanders.

The officers and senior commanders of the unit will be selected from around the world based on the strength of their individual resumes and not be limited in race or nationality. There will be fifty officers and NCOs, and they will be paid in a climbing scale according to rank. It should be noted that in time Gurkhas may also rise to fill these positions should they meet the promotion criteria.

The Islanders, for their part, have no better offers on the table and after a referendum agree to a five-year contract to house the company. The unit shall also be designated as the official Nauru army and receive complete government sanction in return for commitments to respond to natural and human disasters if required.

While the organization of the unit gets underway, the New York office is busy pursuing the certification process. The First Independent Company is one of the first applicants, and the checks are rigorous and thorough. As the application process nears completion, a major Asian bank agrees to finance the company. In return for a forty-nine percent share in First Independent Company PLC, registered in the Republic of Nauru, the bank agrees to invest US$25 million in the company. The terms are a ten-year commitment with no payments in the first year, a ten percent return in the second year, and a twenty percent return for every year after that, with a gross revenue bonus of five percent for every million dollars earned over ten million. As well, a lien on the ship to be purchased is included in the collateral.

With a certification and financing, the FIC is in business. The Gurkhas are recruited in groups of one hundred over the next year and are outfitted and trained at the Island basic training academy. The ship is purchased and begins the conversion outfitting process at a shipyard in Australia.

Meanwhile, the principals back in New York are aggressively pursuing the first contract. Somewhat surprisingly, it comes much quicker than anyone imagined. The United Nations has officially recognized the state of Kurdistan in Northern Iraq, adjacent to the border with Turkey. Finally, after years of living as the region's unwanted refugees, the Kurds regain their own home state. However, neither the Turks nor the Iraqis are giving their full cooperation. There is an urgent requirement for a U.N.-sponsored transitional force to secure the region until such time as a proper Kurdistan government and security infrastructure can be created.

Unfortunately, there is a distinct lack of nations volunteering troops for the mission. Canada has offered a supply-and-communications unit. The French have offered a unit of the Legion. There have also been motions made by a few Arab countries.

However, it is going to take up to six months to deploy the U.N. force. In the interim a few American special forces officers are on site, but no real military presence. Even policing duties are unknown. The Kurds have no infrastructure whatsoever and will need significant help in organizing a functioning government. Aid groups are starting to move in, but the Iraqis and Turks are blocking their movements wherever possible.

An additional problem lies in the remote nature of the region. Kurdistan sits in the northwest corner of Iraq adjacent to the Turkish border. There are few roads and the only rail line runs through Syria. The new capital of Kurdistan, Zakhu, is so difficult to reach it may be impossible to supply any large U.N. force by ground for a considerable period. Essentially, whoever goes in there will be cut off until such time as arrangements can be negotiated with the neighboring states. Considering the local opposition to the creation of the Kurdistan, this may take a while. This situation makes the member states even less enthusiastic about committing their peacekeepers.

Into the fray steps the FIC. It makes a presentation first to the Secretary-General and then to the Security Council. It can have its first units onsite in forty-eight hours and the main body in under twenty-one days. The plan is to stage out of Cyprus and insert the first units by parachute. Once a base has been established, the company's newly acquired Mi-17 helicopters will begin deploying food, fuel, vehicles, and equipment. The plan would see the company secure the city of Zakhu for a period of six months. From this secure base, the U.N. observers and aid agencies could launch their activities.

The proposed price of the project? US$3.5 million a month for six months, not including transportation costs for rental aircraft. Additionally, the purchase of all supplies will be the responsibility of the U.N. These additional requirements are budgeted at $8.3 million over the six months. The total anticipated price tag: US$29.3 million.

At the current time, there are three other companies undergoing commission certification. They include MPRI and Levdan. However, MPRI is not bidding because this project includes combat operations and Levdan, being an Israeli company, is unacceptable to the Kurds. The FIC wins the contract.

A contract negotiation process begins in which the FIC brings in the services of Airstar International Ltd., a Ukrainian company flying decommissioned Russian military transport planes, to provide logistic support. Three of the firm's aircraft will also drop in the company's first parachute unit.

Rules of engagement are negotiated that will see United Nations Chapter 7 intervention capabilities including offensive operations in support of mission objectives. The chain of command will include a Canadian major general as the mission commander. Under him will be a U.N. headquarters staffed by a variety of nations and a logistic unit from Canada. The mission will stage out of Cyprus initially, and a small U.N. headquarters will deploy with the advance units of the FIC.

The commission reviews the terms of the contract, and the mercenary company's full pay of $21 million is deposited in the contract account opened with the World Bank. Eight million dollars is initially released to the FIC to get its mission underway, and within the first forty-eight hours, a one-hundred-man company from Nauru is picked up by pre-positioned Airstar transports and flown to Cyprus. On D-day, the first hundred are parachuted into Kurdistan to the delight of the local onlookers. Over the next week, their position is expanded as more and more equipment is flown in. Meanwhile the company ship,

Fortune One, is on its way with the company's main body and the bulk of their equipment.

Over the next six months, there are several armed clashes with Iraqi rebel groups within Kurdistan, and the FIC takes thirteen dead and forty-two wounded as casualties. The biggest clash occurs on the Iraqi border where the rail line from Syria passes within artillery distance. A raid on an outpost near the border by Iraqi rebels and supported by mortars also kills five and wounds ten others.

Eventually though, NATO air cover provides enough security to begin moving peacekeepers into the region. By the end of the six-month contract, roughly four thousand peacekeepers and U.N. observers have arrived in Zakhu and deployed into the provinces. The U.N. headquarters moved in from Cyprus in month four, and the International Committee for the Red Cross established an NGO support center within the first two months.

At the end of the six months, the FIC withdraws by rail to the port of Latakia on the Syrian coast. There they board their ship and head for home. In New York, the FIC directors deliver three protests to the commission. The first is that, under the terms of the contract, combat air support should have been made available to the FIC if the need was urgent. However, the U.N. could not organize the proper agreements with the NATO forces stationed in Ankara until month four. The FIC's claim is that this oversight cost them fourteen casualties.

The other two complaints refer to directions received from U.N. Headquarters Cyprus to carry out reconnaissances to areas deemed too dangerous by FIC commanders. Without extensive air support, sending detachments to these remote locations would unnecessarily jeopardize lives.

These demands produced significant tension between the two groups for a period, and the FIC wanted the Facilitator to rule.

On the U.N.'s side, more than two dozen similar complaints were lodged when the FIC refused to undertake missions directed by U.N. headquarters. With the protests lodged, the Facilitator contacts three groups of military experts and asks them to review the individual situations and make recommendations.

In the end, six U.N. protests are upheld and a sum of $250,000 is deducted from the FIC's account. However, one of the FIC's protests is upheld, replacing a portion of the $250,000. The U.N. is ordered to pay an undisclosed penalty to the surviving families of the dead mercenaries.

The total net profit for the six-month mission for the FIC amounts to $9.3 million after all the costs are deducted. Some of this money is deposited into the company's accounts, but $3 million is used to buy a thirty percent share in Airstar International. Airstar has just won a $45 million contract to provide air supply services to the U.N. mission to Kurdistan for the next three years.

The FIC has less than three months of rest, however, before it is approached by the new government of Kurdistan to return and train the new Kurdish army. Unfortunately, while Gurkhas are excellent soldiers, they do not make great instructors. Their skills they are born with and cannot pass them on well. To send a large team of officers to carry out the contract would mean splitting up the now cohesive unit spirit the FIC has developed. The contract is turned down and goes instead to another military security services firm. However, a new intervention along the India–Pakistan border is in the works at the Security Council, and the FIC is poised to respond to any proposal.

So ends this rather fanciful scenario. In the fictional First Independent Company we see a management team that has as much business sense as military experience. The company hired only the best and most reliable staff, each of whom were vetted and registered by the commission. The function carried out was supervised and controlled by the United Nations, and the mercenary company provided a critical service, at a critical moment. The performance of the company was subject to review, and payment, less penalties, was made in full.

This describes an ideal contract in which everybody wins. Yes, there were some deaths, but that is what war and mercenary service are about. Each man was a volunteer and knew what he faced as a professional soldier. In reality, this type of contract might not go so smoothly. In any military action there are a thousand imponderables that can go wrong. Yet, the best defense against such problems is the use of trained professionals who can react with experience and confidence.

That is, in the end, what this book is about: the fact that professional soldiers are a valuable commodity to the world at large. Much like Lester B. Pearson first envisioned, they can be used to end wars, not to start them. Executive Outcome ended two wars in a professional manner that didn't target civilians and caused as little collateral damage as possible. It also did it without the supervision of global bodies such as the United Nations. If the opinions of EO's critics are to be believed, we should be hearing thousands of tales of looting, pillage, and rape by the mercenaries. Yet that has not happened. EO's men were professionals with a job to do, and they did it with élan.

For the military security service companies, their market allows nations that haven't collapsed into conflict to build the skills necessary to survive and prosper in a western model. The security services companies allow the global economy to enter confidently challenging new markets where the risks are high but the rewards are worth it. These investments are a cornerstone for building strong economies that can prevent wars from arising in the first place.

The shadow professionals are truly what they appear to be: soldiers who have made a life out of a trade that goes back through all the ages of modern man. Sometimes their work involved fighting. More often it involved presenting enough of a deterrent to avoid conflict. Occasionally, they advised and trained. The expertise they gained in the service of their nations became a valuable commodity in the larger world.

If you were to go back into our various national histories and pick out the great achievers, you would find that many of them were military veterans. Presidents, statesmen, kings, inventors, explorers, and poets all come from the ranks of military service. The self-discipline and confidence gained in uniform served them well in their chosen careers. That a few continued in military service as mercenaries should not divide them from the ranks of their peers, but should instead justify their existence.

In the end, probably the best thing you can say about these men is that, when the situation is desperate and the rest of the world can only write reports and make comforting noises, they are the ones who wade in and take action. Their job is dangerous, often bloody, and occasionally brutal. They witness things that most people cannot imagine from the safety of their First World homes. Sometimes they do a noble job. On other occasions they fail miserably. On still fewer they make matters worse rather than better. Yet, for better or worse, they are the ones who are on the ground trying to make a difference.

Some say they do it just for the money. However, I challenge anyone to find me a mercenary who has retired wealthy and content to grow old and die a quiet death in his bed. Most do it because that is what they are good at. Soldiering can be a rewarding and challenging profession. Especially mercenary service. They are professionals in one of the world's oldest professions: the mercenary soldier.

Epilogue

SIERRA LEONE UPDATE

AFTER GLOBE RISK walked away from the Sierra Leone project in the summer of 1997, I remained fascinated by that nation. I continued to follow on an almost daily basis the events there. I developed a distinct sympathy for the plight of the Sierra Leone people and an in-depth knowledge of the conflict. In March of 1998, the RUF and other rebel forces surrendered Freetown and allowed President Kabbah to return to power. I immediately got on the phone to Alan Bell.

"I'm going to Freetown," I announced. "Kabbah's back and I think there is an opportunity here if we move fast."

Bell, to his credit, was less than moved by my declaration.

"If you go, you won't be representing Globe Risk. You'll be on your own. Personally, I think you're mad."

Sobered somewhat by Bell's words, I spent the next few days considering. What would I do when I got there? What market was there for security services at the moment? More importantly, who had the money to pay for security services? The mining companies wouldn't be going back until the rebels gave up the diamond areas, and as yet there was no sign of that happening any time soon. While there were lots of Sierra Leoneans in need, I was an ex-soldier and an entrepreneur, not an aid worker. So, reluctantly, I went back to waiting and watching.

Finally, in 1999, I got my chance. In May of that year I had a fair idea what Sierra Leone needed in terms of investment and support, but I had no vehicle with which to make things happen. A Canadian Member of Parliament, David Pratt, had just returned from a fact-finding mission to Sierra Leone, and I had read his report eagerly.

His primary suggestion was that, until human and national security could be restored to Sierra Leone, the country would never truly
achieve a peace. I knew that the British army had sent in a training
team to begin the process of creating a new, more reliable Sierra Leonean army. What appeared to have been overlooked, though, was the
police.

I began researching the state of the police force there and found
little that was positive. Of eight thousand officers on the books, no
one even knew how many were still alive. Of those that were still on
duty, the average pay was $50 a month, not even enough to live on. So
far, there had been a few discussions in the multi-nation Sierra Leone
Contact Group concerning police support, but nothing concrete.

I also knew intuitively that the Canadian government wanted to
make a contribution. All the elements were there. Canada was at the
top of the U.N. list for the best nations in the world to live and Sierra
Leone was at the bottom. Both countries are members of the Commonwealth and the predominant language is English. Sierra Leone
was small enough to have some hope of effecting change there, and
it could be accomplished without a significant price tag. All Canada
needed was some way to be seen to be helping out the poorest and
most destitute nation on earth.

Therefore, I sat down and drafted a proposal to rebuild the police
academy at Hastings, just west of Freetown, and staff it with Canadian police officers to work as instructors. The plan called for a five-
year program to train a revitalized police force and then, in a gradual
process, hand control of the school back over to the Sierra Leonean
government.

Once complete, I delivered copies of the document to the Director
for West Africa at Canada's Department of Foreign Affairs and to David
Pratt, M.P. I also contacted the Sierra Leonean embassy in Washington
and discussed the proposal with the number-two man there, Mr. Has-
san Conteh.

Two weeks later, I was in Ottawa to meet with a team from Foreign Affairs and discuss the proposal. In that meeting were Mr. Jacques

Crete, Director for West Africa, Mr. Andre Gagnon, the Trade Commissioner for Africa, and Mr. John Coffee, the desk officer for Sierra Leone. On my side of the table was Alan Bell.

The meeting went well and everyone agreed that this was a good project. However, the question was the cost. Over the five years, the program would cost roughly US$13 million. According to Mr. Crete, the Department just did not have that kind of money available without ministerial approval. We all made our polite noises and left it at that.

Later, I went to see David Pratt on the same matter. We met on Parliament Hill and the meeting went very well. Pratt was supportive and promised to bring up the proposal at the next meeting of the Contact Group in London.

The next step was Sierra Leone. It took me nearly three weeks to get there. First I had to go to London for a week and meet with Control Risks and DSL to do some book research. Then it was South Africa for more of the same. Later, it was on to the Côte d'Ivoire and Guinea. Because there was still a state of war in Sierra Leone, no regular airline would fly there. When I arrived in the city of Conakry, in neighboring Guinea, I had no idea how I was going to get to Freetown. I had just planned to use my wits when I arrived.

To tell the truth, I wasn't impressed much by Conakry. I flew in at dusk on Air Afrique from Abidjan and had no idea what to expect. As the plane pulled to a stop on the tarmac and the ramp was pushed into place, I got my first look at the country. It was hot. Hot and windy. The airport terminal before me was illuminated in the fast-darkening evening by huge floodlamps. The brilliant sunset lit up the western sky and it was tinted red from the dust. Apparently it hadn't rained for a while. As I entered the terminal I had to go through the same ritual you find in most West African countries. As one of the few whites on the plane, I was beset by "workers" hoping for a handout. Immediately, one character pushed his way to the front.

"Passport," he demanded.

I looked at him suspiciously. He had on a uniform and a name tag for Air Afrique. He was clean cut and well groomed. Yet, I knew he was a local con artist. In my horrible command of the French language I told him to go away. Undeterred, he took up a station at my side, shooing the other scam artists away. Once inside the terminal, he grabbed a customs declaration and began asking me the questions listed on the form. I grabbed the paper from him and began filling it out myself. Eventually, I managed to complete the form with a mixture of French and English and made my way to the soldier manning the customs checkpoint.

After I explained I was an author researching a book, I was stamped in and cleared through. Inside the baggage area, my young sidekick was chased off by a tall, respectable-looking gentleman who asked me if I needed a cab. Normally I wouldn't take a local cab because of the chance of a hi-jack and robbery, but the hotel I had reservations with didn't seem to have an airport taxi. So I agreed.

Once outside the terminal I could see the airport was virtually mobbed by local people. They didn't actually seem to be doing anything; it just appeared that the airport was some sort of magnet for the local city-dwellers to hang out. Most were young men who were lounging around the dilapidated buildings. Garbage lay in piles everywhere, and the whole place smelled of rotting refuse. My "cab" consisted of a beat-up, old, brown Ford Escort with outrageous orange fur seat coverings. Climbing into the back, I told the driver the name of my hotel and asked how much?

"Twenty dollars," was the reply. I nodded and off we went. Much like Abidjan, Conakry consisted of one- and two-story buildings of brick and mortar. The streets were wide and jammed with all manner of beat-up old cars and modern Land Rovers. The corners were uniformly home to a gang of men, young and old, who seemed to congregate there as a matter of social function. They had the look of a lazy and unproductive segment of the populace.

Fortunately, the Novotel Hotel in Conakry was an oasis in this depressing mess. After a thoroughly relaxing night with the ocean waves outside my window lulling me into a deep sleep, I woke determined to find a way into Sierra Leone. I walked out of the hotel and found a cab to take me to the Canadian embassy. Here, I met with a charming young lady who conjured up the name of a respectable travel agent in town who should be able to help me.

Back in my cab, which had been waiting outside, we went in search of Ms. Norma Kazeen. Her office was situated just off a bustling roundabout, and I jumped out, telling the cab to find parking spot to wait. The driver simply drove up onto the curb and stopped.

Inside, I found Ms. Kazeem to be a middle-aged Lebanese woman buried deep behind a cluttered desk. She motioned me to a chair while she spoke rapidly into a phone in a language I took to be her native tongue. When done, she hung up and turned an inquisitive face to me.

"How can I get to Freetown?" I asked, thinking this might be a rather unusual request.

"You can go any day of the week," she replied quite casually. "One flight in, one flight out. The next plane leaves tomorrow at 10 AM How long do you want to go for?"

"Ten days," I replied. "How much?"

"One hundred American dollars each way."

So, five minutes later and two hundred dollars poorer, I climbed back into my cab. I was pretty excited; I was finally on my way to Sierra Leone.

The next day I boarded a small, eighteen-seat, twin-prop plane flown by Russians. The plane was full of all sorts of characters and it smelled of oil and grease. I took a seat at the front next to the side hatch. I'd flown with Russians before and wasn't taking any chances.

Once we were airborne, we turned out over the clear blue waters of the Atlantic. The flight would last only twenty minutes, meaning I didn't have long to wait. In almost no time, the coast of Sierra Leone came into view. It was lush, green, and dotted with small plantations. The coastal plain quickly gave way to a small range of mountains, each home to widely spaced chateaus and white-walled compounds.

The first stop was Luingi, where I was passed through customs by some very friendly police officers and then whisked back onto the plane to make the hop across the Sierra Leone river to the Hastings field outside Freetown. Hastings turned out to be a burnt-out shell of a one-room terminal and a taxi area littered with wrecked aircraft.

I was greeted as I got off the plane by a young boy in a wheelchair. He asked me if I had any candy and was quite disappointed when I had

to say no. Surprisingly, there were no hawkers and con artists descend-
ing on me as I approached the gutted terminal. Inside, my bags were
checked by some Nigerian troops, and it turned out I had served in
Rwanda at the same time as one of the Nigerian sergeants. We had a
chat about the military situation in Sierra Leone, and he told me that
things had been tense around Christmas but were much better now.

After being frisked by two tough-looking cops, I was out on the side-
walk. All without one request for a "donation," the hallmark of West
African travel. Here I met Dawda. He was about twenty-three years
old and was a police officer in the Sierra Leonean police force. Dawda
was about six-foot-three and skinny as a rail. He wore black jeans and a
brightly colored shirt that appeared quite new. Topping off the ensemble
was the pair of dark sunglasses that are de rigueur anywhere in Africa.

Dawda was off duty and we began talking about the situation in
Freetown. After a short chat, he asked if I needed a ride somewhere.
When I told him I was heading to the Cape Sierra he called over a character named Nepor. This short, stocky Sierra Leonean was to become
my driver, advisor, and confidant throughout my visit. I will always
remember that, before I left, he asked me to bring him some shoes if I
ever returned. His were literally rotting off his feet.

Dawda, Nepor, and I headed off to Freetown in a beat-up, rusty
brown Mercedes that made horrible grinding noises in the area of the
rear axle. As we cleared the airport, we were given the once-over by a
Nigerian guard and then were on our way. As we drove eastward on
a well-paved, winding road I was treated to a running commentary
on the war, the situation, and the plight of the people by Dawda and
Nepor. I listened and asked a few questions now and again but was
mainly content to just absorb the talk and the scenery.

Unlike Abidjan or Conakry, Freetown is a beautiful little town set on
rolling hills along the ocean shore. The streets are winding and the buildings reflect every sort of architecture. I was most amazed to discover
long lines of children dressed in blue school uniforms on their way home
for lunch. Also unlike other West African cities, I could see no groups of
lazy males lolling about. Everywhere, people were busy. Women rushing
about with shopping baskets, men hawking their armloads of shoes or

food or clothing. I found the whole place refreshing and exciting.

In the middle of town was a traffic circle that surrounded the most enormous tree. It rose up nearly a hundred feet and was easily 120 feet across at the wide, leafy top. I had to restrain myself from gawking at it like an eager tourist. Actually, I had a hard time trying not to hurt my neck as I tried to absorb as much detail as I could from all directions as we moved. I can easily say that, compared with other African cities I have visited, Freetown was much more pleasant than I would have thought possible under the circumstances. I'm not suggesting that there wasn't war damage or dilapidated buildings, but the whole feel and atmosphere was just a complete change from the dreariness of Conakry or Abidjan.

The Cape Sierra Hotel turned out to be another fine spot as well. Situated on the very tip of the Freetown peninsula it was surrounded by rocky ocean shore and boasted a fine view of the white sand beaches running along the coast to the east. The hotel compound was divided into two sections, with the main hotel section curving gracefully along the coast. Nearby, a whole community of cottages was laid out in a small, well-maintained park area that also sat directly on the shoreline. These cottages were designed in a variety of sizes and were for rent to aid workers, journalists, and other foreigners who would be staying for any length of time.

I was shown to a well-appointed room facing the ocean in the most westerly section of the building. While the air conditioner worked fine, I preferred to just open my window and let the sea breeze flow through my room.

Apparently, much of the hotel was empty because the furniture had been looted during the coup period. I was in one of the rooms where the little furniture that remained had been organized.

Each morning I would head down to the hotel restaurant for a fine breakfast of coffee and toast while I waited for Nepor to come for me. Most mornings, he would be waiting out in the parking lot for me, laughing with his friends who were also drivers for various guests.

Nepor had been a truck driver before the war and was now living as a refugee at the stadium. His wife and children were living with Dawda because his home had been destroyed during the RUF offensive of

December 1999. Although it took me a few days to begin trusting Nepor, I soon warmed up to him. He shepherded me around the city and even arranged meetings with local business people through his contacts.

Over the next several days, I met with the superintendent of police, the secretary of police, and the police commissioner. I also met with the British deputy high commissioner and had a long chat with the British military attaché. In the bar at the Cape Sierra each night, I would share beers with the most unlikely assortment of characters. Catherine Bond from CNN was there and easily eight months pregnant. Mark Doyle from the BBC was also in residence. There was the complete staff of the British Army Training Team and three mercenaries working for the Sierra Leonean government. Into this mix went doctors from an aid group, U.N. workers, and assorted NGO staff. Regardless of backgrounds and current employment, everyone seemed to forget their worries each night and have a grand time at the bar.

One of the mercenaries kept pulling out a pistol and threatening to shoot the bartender. At first I was quite worried until I discovered this happened regularly. It was some sort of peculiar running joke between him and the bartender. By day, the mercenaries would suit up, grab an AK-47, and head off to work. I got to know some of them. One was a former member of the SAS and a friend of Alan Bell. When introduced, I mentioned Bell's name and immediately the mercenary said, "Oh, how is old Brian?" Naturally, I was being tested and vetted. I corrected the mercenary on Alan's name and then he broke into a great grin and bought me a beer.

I finished my time in Sierra Leone with a tour of the former police academy at Hastings. The former dean of the school walked me through the ruins of his now abandoned offices, classrooms, and libraries and the overgrown parade square. Everything was gone, including the kitchen sinks.

"They took everything," Assistant Superintendent Francis Bundor told me.

He was right. I could easily imagine hundreds of police recruits sitting in the classrooms studying; rooms that were now filled with feces and not much else. In the kitchen, I imagined I could hear the din of conversation where now lay only dust. Not a chair, a table or a piece of cutlery escaped the RUF's looting.

"I hope you can help us," Bundor said quietly. I told him that it all depended on whether or not I could find someone in the Canadian government who would back the project and take up the challenge.

My departure from Sierra Leone was notable in that I was rushed to plane by the only serviceable jeep in the Sierra Leonean police inventory. A beat-up German Ilitis, it was the same type of vehicle I had driven for years in the Canadian Forces. The driver and I had a chat about it as we raced through numerous checkpoints. Since it was the Superintendent of Police's personal vehicle, we were not troubled by either soldier or policeman.

Back in Canada after an equally tedious trip out through Conakry, Abidjan, and Lagos, I began to take stock of what I had found. The Sierra Leonean government had no money. A speech I had heard the minister of Finance make on the state television channel's nightly broadcast stated that the country had less than eight million dollars in its accounts and most of that was foreign aid money. They couldn't even pay their own ministers, staff, and workers. The minister spent much of his speech urging Sierra Leoneans to pay their taxes so the government could continue to function.

No international firms were rushing into Sierra Leone at the time. The situation was just too chaotic. All legal diamond mining was under a force majeure, and the RUF still held nearly a third of the country, including most of the diamond areas. The British Army team was having a hopeless time trying to build a decent army and the prospects looked grim. The only bright spot seemed to be the hope and determination of the Sierra Leonean people.

As much as I tried, I could not see any way of establishing a profitable business in Sierra Leone at the moment. There just wasn't any money, either in the country or expected to arrive anytime soon. My thinking was that, to help the people of Sierra Leone, foreign investment dollars were required. This investment wouldn't come until the situation was secure enough to make western businessmen feel comfortable. Therefore the pivotal factor was security.

I began working with Alan Bell to find out who had held interests in Sierra Leone before the war and find out if they were interested in going back. Together we contacted every company we could find that had ever done business there. It was a frustrating process because most had either given up on Sierra Leone all together or were going to wait a year or two to see how things developed.

While this was going on, John Coffee from Foreign Affairs asked me to write a report for his office on the current situation in Sierra Leone. I did this free of charge as an act of goodwill. Still, I found it a little funny the Canadian government needed to ask a private citizen for a report on the state of another nation. I wrote John an eight-page report and it was received with enthusiasm.

The calling eventually paid off. I was introduced to a gentleman by the name of Allan Dolan. Dolan was a young and aggressive Calgary lawyer who had bought up a giant exploration concession in Sierra Leone just before the last coup. He was quite interested in my description of the situation in the country and we arranged to meet.

Within three weeks, I was on a plane to Calgary and into a meeting with Dolan. He turned out to be a thirty-ish, slim man with bright eyes and that almost predatory lawyer look about him. In reality, he quickly set my mind at ease as we began to discuss his interest in the region.

After some small talk about our separate histories, Dolan got out a map of his concessions and, when I got my first look, I was astonished. Dolan had managed to buy the rights to nearly one-third of the country in terms of exploration licenses. From my knowledge of the geology of the country, he was sitting on what could be the world's most profitable diamond properties. His new minted mining company, African Diamond Holdings, had bought the rights from the now defunct White Swan Resources, another Canadian junior mining firm. All Dolan was looking for was an end to the war and the financing to get his project underway.

We discussed security and he agreed that it would be better for him to retain a Canadian company like Globe Risk rather than hiring the South Africans from Lifeguard. Dolan liked our idea of hiring and training locals rather than importing expensive hired foreigners; it was better for everybody both financially and politically.

After a very positive meeting, I flew home and quickly jumped in my car to race to Ottawa again. I had arranged through Mr. Conteh in the Sierra Leone embassy to meet with the Dr. Sama Banya, Sierra Leone's foreign minister, during his trip through Ottawa. Accompanying the minister was the Honourable John Leigh, High Commissioner for Sierra Leone to the Washington Embassy. After a couple of rushed cell phone calls to our federal office of protocol, I was directed to the governor-general's residence.

Alan Bell was away on a project at the time, so I took Brian Hay along to support me in this critical meeting. Brian is a tall and distinguished former major in the Forces and has been a trusted advisor of Bell's for some time. Brian has an unusual intelligence and a calm, business-like manner. I thought we would make a good team.

We arrived in Ottawa just in time for the meeting and pulled up before the guest house in the governor-general's compound. Ushered inside by the staff, we were shown to a well-appointed waiting room by the meticulously turned out staff.

Banya and Leigh arrived a few moments later and we sat down to talk. Conteh had faxed Leigh a copy of our police proposal, and that gave us some ground to start with.

"High Commissioner," I began, "one of the main problems in Sierra Leone is that the balance of security power in the country is skewed. The army is on top and the police are below them in terms of authority and duties. As you well know, in a democracy, the police should be responsible for internal security while the army stays in its barracks and training areas until called for."

Brian listened carefully while I continued to lecture this elderly and wise old statesman.

"Sir, in addition to this problem we both know that the answer to Sierra Leone's problems in the long run is not handouts, it is investment from the private sector. To get that investment, however, you need security to make western investors feel safe. At the moment the army is a minimum of two years away from being ready to go, the police force is in tatters, and the human security factor is terrible.

"Here is what we are proposing: We will come in and, first, train a proper presidential security unit. The last coup was conducted by no more than twenty malcontent soldiers. They never should have made it past the front doors, and if they did, plans should have been in place to make sure they didn't get control of the country.

"Second, we would like to undertake this project to rebuild the police academy. It is my feeling that the focus for security should be on the police, not the army now that the war is over. For one thing, police forces don't normally overthrow governments, which your army has been prone to do.

"Finally, we want to set up a security company that can support you in securing the airport, port, and major infrastructure. The guards will all be Sierra Leonean, and we will make sure things run smoothly until the police and military systems are rebuilt."

Dr. Banya, after listening to my pitch, smiled and asked how much it would cost.

"Well, our offer is to provide the presidential security unit training at our own cost," I replied. "That is the key to everything, including Globe Risk's business plans. If the seat of the government isn't secure, the rest doesn't matter much. The police academy project will need financing from an outside source. We have already approached the Canadian government, but without a formal request in this regard from your government, I am not too optimistic. The security company would be at our own cost of course."

Banya seemed quite skeptical and asked some pointed questions, but Leigh could see where I was going. He had been living in the United States for years and saw that a Sierra Leone version of the secret service could protect the president and his cabinet and in doing so protect the true government from the next inevitable coup attempt.

In actual fact, I was only offering the same service David Stirling had offered African leaders thirty years before. The meeting went on, and it began to shift quickly to other subjects. Leigh suggested that we might be interested in getting involved with a plan to train a government mine security task force that would replace the private companies doing mine security. I responded that it would be worth looking at and agreed to follow up.

By the end of the meeting, I am sure that my enthusiasm for these projects must have had my hosts stumped. Why would a Canadian be so involved in their troubled little nation?

"Sir, look at your country from our view. First, it is quite small, that means any problems are manageable. It has the best deep water port in West Africa, and that makes it strategic. It is a member state of the Commonwealth, and that opens up political and economic opportunities. It has rich natural resources and used to have one of the highest standards of living in Africa. That gives us hope. The literacy level is pretty good and, although the infrastructure has been damaged, because of the small scale it is rebuildable. With some really hard work and cooperation, Sierra Leone could become the Switzerland of Africa."

The meeting ended with Dr. Banya and High Commissioner Leigh asking for a proposal for them to consider. They promised to bring up the topic in their meeting with our Canadian foreign minister, Lloyd Axworthy, the next day.

Soon afterwards, Allan Dolan flew down to Toronto, and we sat down to review where we were.

"Here is the situation," I said. "The war is over and the Lome Peace Accord has been signed. I don't like the details much, but at least it is something to work with. Aid money is beginning to flow, and the United Nations peacekeepers should be deploying soon. The problem now is the economy and the mines.

"The biggest problem is that we can't get to your diamond concessions until the RUF are disarmed, and that could take a while. Meanwhile, most of the diamonds being mined are being smuggled out through Liberia. That means no tax revenue for the Sierra Leonean government. The key here, I think, is to find a way to turn that diamond flow around and head it to Freetown instead of Monrovia."

"Jim," Dolan interjected, "I've already had the same thought. My motto is that we should do good, not just do good business. If we can help kickstart the local economy and strengthen the government's position, that will help the whole peace process, which will ultimately get us mining diamonds sooner rather than later."

Sitting around a large table in the offices of the prestigious Canadian mining consulting firm Watts, Griffis & McOuat, Dolan and I began tossing out ideas on how we could proceed. The facts were that people in the rebel areas had diamonds and no legal way to sell them. Because most diamonds in Sierra Leone are alluvial, which means they sit in the top ten feet of soil, anyone with a bucket and shovel can mine them. At the moment, most were being bought by the RUF, who were using them to finance their organization. We had to find a way to convince the locals in these areas to come to us to sell their stones. Then we could market them legally through Freetown, giving the government its slice and keeping the money out of the RUF's pockets. The sooner we could undermine their hold on the diamond regions, the sooner we would be in business.

Suddenly, I hit upon an idea.

"How about we set up a Hudson's Bay Company in Sierra Leone? Think about it. A couple of hundred years ago, these guys set up base camps in the forts near the shipping routes back to Europe. From there, one-man outfits headed out into Indian country to trade for furs with the Native Canadians. Let's transplant that idea to Sierra Leone. We set up a base in Freetown and send out traders by helicopter to set down near rebel areas to trade for diamonds. We bring in cash, food, medicine, and any special requests like building material or tools. In return, we trade for diamonds.

"If we move to the same general area over a period of weeks and build up a little trust, we can probably set up a semi-permanent post within a month. Then we hire the locals to become our security and we bring in all the necessities of life in return. All the diamonds are brought back and sold through the government evaluators at market prices. Hell, we can even buy weapons and turn them over to the U.N.!"

The concept would have the added benefit that, when the rebels did eventually give up the diamond areas, we would have already established good relations with the local populace. We would have shown ourselves to be strong supporters of the government in the tough times and could hope to count on a reward in the months ahead.

However, we didn't stop there. Dolan suggested setting up the "Friends of Sierra Leone." This would be a registered non-profit organization that consisted of various prestigious British and Canadian firms who were experts in their fields. This group would include macroeconomic consulting firms, engineering companies, geological policy and project development firms. There would be experts in law reform as well as technical and service companies. We would also include representatives from aid organizations and religious groups to keep the businessmen honest. The plan was to then lead this team to Sierra Leone and work together to develop a coordinated strategy to implement some change.

Dolan and I took our proposal to Canada's Department of Foreign Affairs in February 2000. In a large boardroom in the Team Canada Centre, we sat down on one side of a long conference table and faced off against representatives from the policy side, the trade side and even the military side of our federal government. For the next three hours, the government grilled us on our plan.

The military representative, Lieutenant Colonel Stephen Moffat, was particularly impressed with our security plan.

"How are you going to protect the trading posts?" he asked with a penetrating stare.

"Well," I replied confidently, "we're going to use the Malaysian model." All the non-soldiers in the room furrowed their brows at the reference but I did see Colonel Moffat suddenly smile a little smile.

"After we establish some trust with the local rebels and co-opt them, we are going to bring in aid groups to set up a hospital, a food distribution center, and supplies for building homes. Working with the locals, we will build a protected village. Eventually, we will ask for a platoon of U.N. troops or Sierra Leonean army when they come on line to handle security. Essentially, we are going to build a wilderness fort deep inside rebel territory.

"From there, we will encourage the locals to set up shops and will sponsor entrepreneurial activity. We will give everyone who comes in a reason and the means to resist the rebels. The government can send in a representative to set up an administration and eventually, we have a thriving little town, safe from rebel predation. The trading company runs it like a company town and everyone is happy. If it all works we set up another, and then another, until such time as the situation is resolved."

The excitement that the whole proposition generated was electric. Every one of our interviewers stayed well past their next appointment. Eventually, we came to the group conclusion that the next step was to get the Sierra Leonean government on side. As Dolan and I left Ottawa, we had a good feeling for the future. Rather than shooting us down, the government representatives we had met felt the idea had merit.

We next went to see one of the men who had just completed a damning report on the global diamond industry and how it fueled wars in Africa. Ian Smillie was one of the key members in Partnership Africa Canada (PAC), a think tank on international issues. Their recent report had caused a furor by laying out the facts that there has been an official policy of buying diamonds from rebels or their middlemen on the part of the world's biggest diamond distributors. These policies had fueled the wars in Sierra Leone and Angola for decades.

Dolan and I believed that this collaboration between an international security company and a diamond company interested in Sierra Leone would never survive public scrutiny unless we could convince men like Smillie our intentions were sound.

We met at Smillie's home, and he turned out to be as suspicious as we suspected. He was a tall man in his mid-forties with a laconic manner and a well-thought-out propensity for listening more than talking. With Smillie was another member of PAC who said even less and appeared to be a grad student or prodigy of Smillie. Together, they listened intently to our pitch.

The mood was somber until we began describing the Friends of Sierra Leone concept. Dolan explained that in Sierra Leone you have aid groups doing one thing, various government or U.N. representatives pursuing their particular mandates, the World Bank funding various little well-drilling programs, and entrepreneurs looking to take advantage somewhere. But no one seemed to be coordinating these efforts. Dolan's pitch was that this group would bring together all of these elements and give them a format to coordinate efforts, focus resources, and effect real change rather than more talk.

Smillie quickly warmed to the subject.

"I have always thought that you have to have some cooperation with the private sector. That is where the money is," he commented.

By the end of our meeting, Smillie was suggesting which aid agencies might be open to joining such a project and suggested we might want to speak at several conferences going on in the near future. He even hinted that he might be interested in chairing the Friends of Sierra Leone group.

On March 5, 2000, Allan Dolan boarded a plane for New York. He was beginning a trip that would take him to London, Johannesburg, Tel Aviv, Antwerp, and finally Freetown. Once there, he was going to meet with President Kabbah and lay out our plans. His advance team was a group of Sierra Leonean entrepreneurs who had been Dolan's partners for years. These men had begun the process of winning over various business leaders and government ministers. It was going to be an ambitious effort that touched ever facet of life in Sierra Leone. With any luck....

I stayed home this time. Dolan and I believed that an international security consultant for a security services company travelling to Africa hand-in-hand with a diamond company gave the wrong impression. As the author of this book, I knew quite well the unpopular precedents that had been set in this regard. Though I have never touched a weapon since I left the Forces, I am still a bloodthirsty, diamond-hungry mercenary in many people's eyes. While Globe Risk's part in this whole process is critical, we might not be welcome at the table of any politician who wants to avoid the condemnation of men like Special Rapporteur Ballesteros.

Dolan's meeting with President Kabbah went quite well. The president suggested that we should put the Friends of Sierra Leone concept on the shelf for now and concentrate on the trading company. That was where the real need was. Kabbah could easily see that our plan of stimulating the micro-economy of his nation would be a crucial step in the process of broad economic reform. He stated that he would fully endorse our plan and would be prepared to draft a letter for our use.

On his return, Dolan began looking for the investors, equipment, and the expertise he would need to get the Sierra Leone Trading Company up and running. In April, a young geologist by the name of Jason DeCarlo and I were reviewing trucks for purchase, and initial feelers were sent out to find a source for various commodities that would be traded.

However, nothing in Sierra Leone is ever that easy. Almost three years to the day of the 1997 coup, disaster struck once again. In the opening days of May 2000, hundreds of peacekeepers began going missing. RUF rebels began attacking U.N. outposts and disarming the hapless U.N. soldiers. Chaos rained throughout the nation.

May 7 found Allan Dolan and I in Washington meeting with U.S. State Department officials concerning our project in Sierra Leone. We had hoped that our trip would help us raise the international support we would need to get our business underway. Unfortunately, the latest crisis in Freetown made all of our efforts seem wasted.

On Wednesday, May 10, we were on the phone to our local partners in Freetown. They told us that Foday Sankoh had planned another coup d'état for the night of Monday, May 8. Large numbers of rebel fighters had been moved to within striking distance of the Freetown peninsula. Other RUF units had seized the main road access routes out of the country. At Kambia, on the road to Guinea, the RUF had captured and disarmed a hundred Nigerian peacekeepers and sent them running down the roads. The strategic towns of Makeni and Magburaka in the central region had also fallen to the RUF. The U.N. forces were in shambles and everywhere there was a sense of doom.

The RUF knew that the United Nations had no stomach for fighting and if they attacked enough peacekeepers, the U.N. would run with their tails between their legs. So in the days prior to the coup, rebel fighters attacked, killed, and captured hundreds of peacekeepers to render the U.N. completely ineffective.

The stage was set.

The only event that prevented the coup from taking place occurred when Sankoh's former ally, Johnny Paul Koroma (the leader of the army's 1997 coup), turned on him and informed President Kabbah on Sunday evening. As news of the intended coup raced through the streets the next day, a mob of more than five thousand Sierra Leoneans descended on Sankoh's luxurious government-appointed residence. After Sankoh's bodyguards had opened fire on the crowd, in full view of the hapless U.N. peacekeepers stationed there, the collective anger of the populace turned on the rebels, and they were quickly overrun. Sankoh disappeared while the mob cut down the bodyguards and ransacked Sankoh's residence.

As I sat with Dolan on the train from Washington to New York, I tried to make sense of the whole mess. In 1997, I had studied this country and knew what was coming. This time, all the signs were there again, but even I had believed that with eight thousand peacekeepers deployed, the RUF could be contained. Now, it was all coming apart again.

Before me was a collection of news clippings from around the world concerning the situation in Sierra Leone. There were comments from U.S. diplomat Richard Holbrooke, U.N. Secretary-General Kofi Annan, and British Prime Minister Tony Blair condemning the RUF's actions. The page that I kept coming back to, however, was an article written by Lans Gberie for the Sierra Leonean newspaper, *The Concord Times*. Gberie was a partner of Ian Smillie, who had contributed to Partnership Africa Canada's damning report on the diamond trade.

In his article, one passage stood out:

Foday Sankoh and his RUF can understand only the language of force, nothing more, nothing less. To reason with them, to pretend that reason can conquer them, is to ignore some very basic home-truths: the RUF is the product of a scum culture, its guiding principle remains the politics of the fastest gun (or the sharpest machete), it is a wholly predatory group out for loot.... there is no other way: to vanquish the RUF, Foday Sankoh has to be taken out."

While I agreed completely with Gberie's opinions, I was a little surprised that such a tirade should come from a major partner in a prestigious NGO. "Foday Sankoh has to be taken out"– the intent of that sentence is pretty clear.

Other articles commented on how the U.N.'s largest peacekeeping force fell apart in the face of a rebel army made up largely of thugs, drug addicts, and children. *The Washington Post* suggested that the attacks on peacekeepers were "the worst the United Nation's peacekeepers had suffered since ten Belgians were killed in Rwanda in 1994."

As the train raced northward for more meetings, I suddenly felt very tired. I was also growing increasingly angry. How much horror could Sierra Leone endure at the hands of the world body? While some may blame Foday Sankoh and the RUF, I do not. Sankoh is a psychotic megalomaniac. The RUF are criminals, murderers, rapists, and bandits. As such, they should be dealt with accordingly. However, the only reason they have never been properly dealt with can be laid directly at the feet of the international community.

In 1994, Valentine Strasser asked the British government to help him defeat the RUF. The British refused. In 1995, Strasser hired Executive Outcomes and the RUF were smashed and peace restored. However, the world couldn't leave well enough alone. In 1996, the United Nations, the World Bank, the United States, and the British government, along with scores of media pundits, political think tanks, and other luminaries, forced the newly elected President Kabbah to send his mercenaries home. The RUF resurfaced from protected camps in Liberia to seize the government in a coup only a few months later.

For over a year, the world sat by without lifting a finger while the RUF looted, pillaged, raped, and tortured its way across Sierra Leone. Only the brave but ineffective Nigerians made any significant commitment to ending the horror. Yet, the world didn't show them much support either.

Finally, when the RUF had their fill and returned to camp upon the diamond mines, President Kabbah was allowed to return to his capital and his people. In the days to come, however, he was forced by the world at large to sign the Lome Peace Accord, which gave the RUF a major share in government and exonerated them from any wrongdoing. Kabbah was forced to sign this deal with the devil because the World Bank's sword of Damocles had been held threateningly above his head.

Such luminaries as President Bill Clinton's special envoy for democracy in Africa, the Reverend Jesse Jackson, were key negotiators in this process, declaring the RUF a legitimate political force with a platform for social change.

In 1999, President Kabbah entrusted the security of his country to the United Nations and allowed a collection of Third World peacekeepers to take over the reigns of security. This move, in essence, took control of his nation's destiny out of his hands. His nation's fate then rested with whatever U.N. Secretary-General Kofi Annan could pry out of the Security Council. Which, we now know, was nothing particularly useful or reliable.

As a former peacekeeper who has been surrounded by overwhelming forces in Sarajevo while leading a small patrol, I can speak with authority. My patrol was ordered to disarm and we refused. The Bosnian Muslims threatened repeatedly to shoot us down, but we held. We kept up a Mexican standoff until the situation was resolved. When hundreds of peacekeepers backed up by armored vehicles drop their weapons in the face of a motley collection of bandits, I have little sympathy or understanding.

In 1995, two hundred mercenaries drove the RUF out of the entire country. Now eight thousand peacekeepers ran in the face of the same enemy. Not only was it another total failure for U.N. peacekeeping, but it was a slap in the face for President Kabbah and his people, who had placed their trust in this institution.

As we bumped along on our train, British Paratroopers were landing in Sierra Leone. Sankoh had gone missing and the RUF plans seemed thrown into disarray. I couldn't help but laugh at the thought of several hundred tough Brit paras coming to rescue thousands of peacekeepers and restore order when the entire United Nations had failed.

We knew from our local partners that Kabbah had flown into a rage over the U.N.'s failure and had ordered his own meager army out of their barracks and onto the offensive. We also had heard that, as far as Kabbah was concerned, the Lome Peace Accord was dead, and that there would be no more negotiations with the RUF. While I would like to believe that, I have my doubts. In the days ahead,

Liberia's Charles Taylor, Libya's Mohammar Ghadafi, and the United States' envoy Reverend Jesse Jackson each stated that the government must reconcile and negotiate with the RUF. That taking action against them would only worsen the situation.

After thinking over this issue, twisting it and turning it in my mind, I could come to only one conclusion. Sierra Leone must take responsibility for its own destiny. It has relied on others for too long. In 1993, it turned to the Nigerians for help. In 1994, it begged for British support. In 1995, it hired South African mercenaries but was forced to send them home by a cabal within the international community. In 1999, Kabbah handed over control to the United Nations. Now, he was depending on a few hundred British paratroopers.

When these groups tired of the challenge and went home, what would be left? No, I was convinced that the only hope for long-term peace and security must come from within Sierra Leone. The only question that remained was how?

I pulled out my laptop computer and began to write a proposal to President Kabbah. I took all of my knowledge of international security and conflict resolution and balanced it with historical precedent and modern examples to produce a plan that could finally resolve that nation's conflict.

Sierra Leone is surrounded by very dubious allies. Liberia makes much of its money from illegally importing Sierra Leonean diamonds. President Charles Taylor publicly admits he is a personal friend of Foday Sankoh. He also harbored RUF fighters whenever they needed rest and refit during the nine years of war. Burkina Faso to the north beyond Liberia is suspected of not only buying diamonds but also supplying arms to the RUF during the war.

Within the country, the democratically elected government is opposed by several thousand criminals and thugs who work for a despotic warlord and have no support from the people. There can be no legal complaint by the world at large if these rebels are hunted down and defeated.

However, once that task is accomplished, the nation will need to be defended against further criminal gangs supported by neighbor states. If this can be achieved, the nation has the education, the resources, and, I believe, the national will to rebuild the country into a successful state.

As we have witnessed over the last nine years, the Sierra Leonean army is not up to the task. African soldiers in general are simply not well enough trained, nor personally inclined to fight professionally at a western standard. We saw this demonstrated quite clearly with the U.N. peacekeepers stationed there.

The only successes that have been scored, whether it is politically correct or not, occurred when either two hundred South African mercenaries or a battalion of British paratroopers became involved. The only conclusion that can be drawn, then, is that Sierra Leone needs a western-quality military capability that will never be available locally. Not in the next decade or so anyway.

However, there are no reliable mercenary companies in existence at the moment to fill this need. Even if there were, I wouldn't recommend them. Mercenaries work for themselves and do not owe their long-term loyalty to their clients. If the solution is to be found within Sierra Leone, a private military company is not the answer.

So what is?

The solution lies with two current members of the United Nations Security Council. In France, since the mid-1800s, the most professional force at their disposal has been the French Foreign Legion. I served alongside them in Bosnia and Rwanda. They also represented France in the Gulf War and in numerous other small conflicts. The Legion is France's cutting edge formation, and it is made up of mercenary volunteers organized into a regular foreign unit.

Each year the Legion attracts so many potential recruits, there is often a surplus of up to six or seven thousand applications. More importantly, it maintains these numbers without offering high pay rates, luxurious accommodations, or perks of any kind. What it does offer is adventure, discipline, and military professionalism.

Britain, as we well know, employs the Gurkhas and regularly sends its officers off to serve with foreign armies such as the Sultanates of Oman and Brunei. Critical here is that the British army also recruits across the Commonwealth. Within the ranks of the Paras who landed in Sierra Leone will be Australians, Canadians, New Zealanders, and Fijians. The SAS, which is also rumored to be involved and I will say no more on that subject, is a virtual foreign legion in this regard.

Using these precedents from within the walls of the U.N. Security Council, my proposal to President Kabbah was to use this model to take control of his nation. In the document I suggested that the ranks of the Sierra Leonean army should be opened to volunteers from other Commonwealth countries. These volunteers could be screened and then subjected to a rigorous selection process to ensure they are fit, well trained, and prepared for their duties. They can then be formed into two categories of units.

The first unit will be along the lines of France's Foreign Legion and will consist exclusively of foreigners. It could be led by officers seconded from the British army or another reputable Commonwealth state to ensure both loyalty and discipline. This force, probably battalion in size, would then become the sharp edge of the Sierra Leonean armed forces.

The second group of volunteers would be incorporated directly into the ranks of the regular army. While select individuals could take over leadership roles, the majority would simply become enlisted soldiers within the ranks. This then would produce a force that is reliable at all levels.

The cost of such an initiative would be high, but not impossible. Unlike mercenaries, volunteers for regular foreign units do not receive high pay rates. In fact, often the pay is rather poor. Equipping the force should not be difficult, considering the amount of equipment that already exists in country. Supplying the force would present the greatest challenge, but I think that if Sierra Leone finally agreed to take responsibility for its own security, a few nations might volunteer to lend some logistic support.

To further offset the costs, the government could agree to pay all volunteers a low wage during their contracts with a large bonus coming at the end. If five years' good service are achieved, volunteers can be awarded citizenship (a French practice) and given land grants in diamond production areas. This could also be done with Sierra Leonean recruits to increase both the quality of volunteers and their level of dedication.

I have no doubt that such a combined force would end the RUF's reign of terror in a matter of months and forever put an end to any revival of their organization. It would also be a professional enough force to discourage neighboring states from ever interfering in Sierra Leone's affairs again.

Finally, such a force could be a source of revenue for the Sierra Leone government in the long term. It could achieve this in two ways. First, the very presence of such a military capability will reassure foreign investors that the nation is a good investment for the long term. Second, Africa is in desperate need of high-quality peacekeeping troops. Since the U.N. pays a bounty for each volunteer on a mission, the nation could earn hard currency on deployments while keeping their forces constantly busy and upgrading their skills.

The final benefit would come from the political stability involved in such a force. If the army was commanded by a seconded British officer or other similar leader, the chance of a coup d'état is almost completely removed. Since historically the Sierra Leonean army is a political force in addition to an element for national security, such an arrangement would remove this threat from the deck. The odds that the foreign volunteers would revolt en masse is miniscule as well if discipline, esprit de corps, and good leadership are maintained.

Finally, such a force could be the critical element in setting Sierra Leone back on the path to peace and prosperity. As David Pratt stated in his report, until you have human, national, and regional security, there can be no progress. With peace would come investment, rebuilding, and a return to a time when Sierra Leone was the most prosperous nation in central Africa.

That the answer to this nation's crisis could come from hired foreign soldiers should come as no surprise. That has been the way of the world for the last three thousand years. Who are we to begrudge Sierra Leoneans the same tools that built every great nation on this planet?

My proposal was delivered to President Kabbah, through our local partners, in late May 2000. I only hope that the president has the strength, wisdom, and moral courage to finally take responsibility for the salvation of his people, whether it be through my proposal or some other initiative. If he chose my concept, I might even volunteer for such a force. To fight for a country in a good cause against an enemy that is undeniably evil ... that is the stuff that legends are made from. I could finally cross the line and do what I do best once again: soldiering.

Index